JEWS, RACE, AND THE POLITICS OF
DIFFERENCE

JEWS IN EASTERN EUROPE
Jeffrey Veidlinger, Mikhail Krutikov, Geneviève Zubrzycki, Editors

JEWS, RACE, AND THE POLITICS OF DIFFERENCE

The Case of Vladimir Jabotinsky against the Russian Empire

Marina B. Mogilner

INDIANA UNIVERSITY PRESS

This book is a publication of

Indiana University Press
Office of Scholarly Publishing
Herman B Wells Library 350
1320 East 10th Street
Bloomington, Indiana 47405 USA

iupress.org

© 2023 by Marina Mogilner

All rights reserved
No part of this book may be reproduced or utilized in any form or by any means, electronic or mechanical, including photocopying and recording, or by any information storage and retrieval system, without permission in writing from the publisher. The paper used in this publication meets the minimum requirements of the American National Standard for Information Sciences—Permanence of Paper for Printed Library Materials, ANSI Z39.48–1992.

Manufactured in the United States of America

First Printing 2023

Library of Congress Cataloging-in-Publication Data

Names: Mogilner, Marina, author.
Title: Jews, race, and the politics of difference : the case of Vladimir Jabotinsky against the Russian Empire / Marina B. Mogilner.
Other titles: Case of Vladimir Jabotinsky against the Russian Empire
Identifiers: LCCN 2022052073 (print) | LCCN 2022052074 (ebook) | ISBN 9780253066121 (hardback) | ISBN 9780253066138 (paperback) | ISBN 9780253066145 (ebook)
Subjects: LCSH: Jabotinsky, Vladimir, 1880-1940. | Zionism—Russia—History—20th century. | Jews—Russia—Politics and government—20th century. | Jews—Russia—Identity—History—20th century. | Jews—Russia—Intellectual life—20th century. | Intellectuals—Russia—History—20th century. | Russia—Politics and government—1894-1917.
Classification: LCC DS151.Z5 M64 2023 (print) | LCC DS151.Z5 (ebook) | DDC 305.892/40470904—dc23/eng/20230405
LC record available at https://lccn.loc.gov/2022052073
LC ebook record available at https://lccn.loc.gov/2022052074

To my mother, Raisa Mogilner

CONTENTS

Acknowledgments   ix

Notes on Transliterations, Translations, and Names   xiii

Introduction: When Race Is a Language and Empire Is a Context   *1*
1. Race, Zionism, and the Quest for Jewish Authenticity   *26*
2. Mediterranean as New European: Race and Europeanness in Zionism and Other New Nationalisms   *48*
3. Racial Purity versus Imperial Hybridity: Vladimir Jabotinsky against the Russian Empire   *74*
4. Jewish Race versus Russian Race   *107*
5. Nationalizing Politics in the Empire   *126*
   Conclusion   *150*

Notes   159

Bibliography   185

Index   209

ACKNOWLEDGMENTS

JEWS, RACE, AND THE POLITICS OF DIFFERENCE: *The Case of Vladimir Jabotinsky against the Russian Empire* develops themes and approaches introduced in my previous book, *A Race for the Future: Scientific Visions of Modern Russian Jewishness, 1860s–1930s* (Harvard University Press, 2022), but from a new perspective. Whereas *A Race for the Future* investigated Russian Jewish race science and biopolitical movements, this book explores ways of understanding the Jewish politics of race in the late imperial context. It was only in the last years of working on this project that I began to think of it as having three distinct dimensions: science, biopolitics, and politics. In the process, the political part grew into a separate book project. I am deeply grateful to the editors of the Indiana University Press series Jews in Eastern Europe, Jeffrey Veidlinger, Mikhail Krutikov, and Geneviève Zubrzycki, for seeing it as such. My understanding of Jewish political and cultural modernism was formed under the influence of works by these wonderful scholars, and I felt truly inspired by their endorsement of my version of Russian Jewish imperial modernity as framed by the themes of race, empire, and anti-imperial nationalisms. The anonymous reviewers' critical comments and suggestions helped improve the manuscript.

At its different stages, the project was financially supported by the following foundations and organizations: Gerda Henkel Stiftung (Germany, 2002–2004); International Center for Russian and East European Jewish Studies (Russian Federation, 2003–2004); Volkswagen Stiftung (Germany, 2006–2008); and the American Council of Learned Societies (2009). I was privileged to be a visiting fellow at Centre d'études des mondes Russe, Caucasien et Centre-Européen, CNRS-EHESS (France, 2010); National Research University Higher School of Economics (Moscow, Russia, 2016, 2017); University of Illinois at Chicago (UIC) Institute for the Humanities (United States, 2017–2018); and Ludwig-Maximilians-Universität, Graduate School for East and Southeast European Studies (Munich, summer 2018). I am grateful to colleagues at all the foundations and institutions listed here as well as to participants of multiple workshops and conference panels where I presented early versions of the future chapters of this book, for their critical comments, good questions, and shared knowledge.

At my academic home, the University of Illinois at Chicago, I was fortunate to spend a year at the UIC Institute for the Humanities, writing about Jews and race and trying to narrate the three different stories: that of Jewish race science (intellectual history); Jewish biopolitics (social history); and Jewish racialized political visions, language, and acts. While discussing selected chapters with my cohort of fellows at the institute—the most attentive and helpful readers and interlocutors—and later, with my colleagues in the UIC Department of History, I came to the realization that the political part, as I had imagined it, differed from the much more systematic, archive-oriented approach, which considers all aspects of a problem, in the other two parts of the project. I am grateful to my UIC colleagues for their constant interest in my research, for their very helpful suggestions, for letting me learn from them and their scholarship, and for emboldening me to implement my vision of the "politics of race" in a separate book. The two UIC colleagues to whom I (and this book) owe probably more than they know are Keely Stauter-Halsted and Julia Vaingurt. Our many exchanges in formal academic settings or over coffee in my office greatly influenced my thinking about politics, modern culture, language, and social imagination.

The list of people outside of UIC, who have helped me throughout all these years of work on the project, includes Eugene Avrutin, Jane Burbank, Frederick Cooper, Bruce Grant, Sergei Kan, Louise McReynolds, Harriet Murav, Svetlana Natkovich, Riccardo Nicolosi, Brigid O'Keefe, Dmitry Shumsky, Charles Steinwedel and Francesca Morgan, Darius Staliūnas, Vera Tolz, and many others. Therese Malhame greatly helped me with finding my own voice through my imperfect English. I am grateful to Anna Francis and Nancy Lightfoot, my editors at Indiana University Press, who shepherded this manuscript through all its stages. My gratitude goes to Elmira Amirkhanova, the chief librarian of the Kazan University Library's Manuscript and Rare Books Division, who helped procure images for this book during the COVID-19 pandemic.

Finally, as I do in all my books, I want to acknowledge a small group of my longtime colleagues and friends who are involved in all my projects and are always there for me when I need help, intellectual support, or fair criticism. With this small group, I share the long and challenging history of founding and coediting the *Ab Imperio Quarterly*. They are the source of the interpretations of empire as an analytical category and a context that inform my analysis in this book. Alexander Semyonov of the Higher School of Economics in St. Petersburg (currently a refugee scholar and John J. McCloy '22 Visiting Professor of History at Amherst College), Sergei Glebov of Smith and Amherst Colleges in Massachusetts, and Ilya Gerasimov, the executive editor of *Ab Imperio* and my most dedicated reader and partner in life, have been involved in this project at every stage. I only hope I can return the favor by being as good a colleague and friend to them as they are to me.

An article version of chapter 2, "Mediterranean as New European: Race and Europeanness in Zionism and Other New Nationalisms," was published as: "Mediterraneanizing Europe: The Project of Subaltern Race and the Postimperial Search for Hybridity," *ISIS, A Journal of the History of Science Society* 112, no. 4 (2021): 670–93.

NOTES ON TRANSLITERATIONS, TRANSLATIONS, AND NAMES

ALL TRANSLATIONS IN THIS BOOK are mine unless otherwise specified. For Russian transliterations, I have used the Library of Congress system. For the transliteration of the broadly known names, I have opted to use the most common form (for example, Jabotinsky instead of Zhabotinskii; Sikorsky instead of Sikorskii).

JEWS, RACE, AND THE POLITICS OF
DIFFERENCE

INTRODUCTION
When Race Is a Language and Empire Is a Context

THIS CONCISE BOOK ASPIRES TO tell a complex story of race as an important concept structuring the Russian Jewish political imagination during the epoch of mass politics and revolutionary upheavals of the early twentieth century. It brings race and Jews, as well as imperial nationalization and modernization, together in a framework that is more multifaceted and controversial than that implied by the usual narratives of racial antisemitism. The book explores Russian Jews' self-racializing as a response to the challenges of their evolving imperial situation in the modernizing and nationalizing Russian Empire.

The life, politics, and writings of Vladimir (Zeev) Jabotinsky (1880–1940)—one of the best-known Russian Zionists who greatly contributed to racializing the discourse of Russian Zionism—provide structure and coherence to this complex and controversial story. As a prolific writer, Jabotinsky left quite a trail of narratives that help explicate the evolving semantics and contextual usages of *race* in Russian Jewish politics. As an imperial intellectual who had very consciously nationalized himself, and whose carefully constructed Jewish identification was founded on the learned "objective" and "scientific" notion of Jewish race, Jabotinsky represents a paradigmatic case of modern Jewish self-racializing. In many respects, his experience as a secularized, urban imperial Jewish subject, a native of Odessa, acculturated and integrated into Russian imperial culture, was quite typical of his generation and social cohort. But his case can be called paradigmatic for yet another reason. Jabotinsky's deployment of race in personal, artistic, and political texts and praxis illustrates, with remarkable clarity, the essential connection between the modern individual Jewish self—the sense of personal Jewish body and personal national Jewishness—and the collective body of the nation as imagined by modern intellectuals such as Jabotinsky. The supposedly preexisting and objective connection between the two—the Self and the Nation entitled to a legitimate post-imperial political future—resolved the most troubling problems for hybrid imperial subjects who, like Jabotinsky, were alienated from the routine and everyday patterns of traditional Jewishness.

In addition, Jabotinsky—a Jewish politician and public intellectual whose career coincided with the epoch of rising mass politics in the empire in the early twentieth century—provides a unique perspective on the moment when the construct of race emerged as a broad discourse of anti-imperial mobilization, of collective (self)-disentanglement from the imperial mix, and a new category in political debates. Jabotinsky was among those imperial politicians who actively promoted a racialized language in the broadened and democratized post-1905 public arena. He thus embodied or even led a characteristic trend in imperial politics in general. That Jabotinsky was a political Zionist both explains his familiarity with race and complicates the assessment of his case as paradigmatic. We still know very little about race, racialized politics, discourses, and racism in Russian history. Against this empty backdrop, Jabotinsky may seem an extravagant political creature to historians of late imperial Russia. On the other hand, from the history of Zionism perspective, there is nothing unexpected about his deployment of racial statistics and "blood and soil" rhetoric. As I show in this book, both interpretations can be equally misleading. The case of Vladimir Jabotinsky deviates from patterns familiar to historians of Western Zionism in some important ways, and these deviations are particularly interesting and significant for historians of Russian Zionism and the Russian imperial formation. They help us grasp the apparent paradox of race functioning as an anticolonial discourse, a weapon of subaltern politics of the weak in the imperial situation.

I hope, by this point it has become clear that the reader should not expect this book to be yet another political biography of Jabotinsky. For this, I am fortunate to rely on excellent studies by other historians.[1] My book is an attempt to approach the life story of Jabotinsky as an imperial biography, selectively emphasizing those—often mutually exclusive, as in every imperial biography—aspects and contexts that make it so. Whereas Jabotinsky's imperial biography frames my narrative of race and the politics of difference in the Russian Empire, "race" as a concept provides a new perspective on Jabotinsky's own imperial condition, his and his fellow Jewish activists' anti-imperial nationalism and political choices.

This book is not a biography of Jabotinsky in one more sense—it does not follow his life to the end. Instead, it concludes with the collapse of the Russian Empire and considers only narratives that originated in the imperial period, even if some of them were finalized and (re)published in the 1920s or even 1930s. I consciously avoid the temptation to draw a linear genealogy of Jabotinsky's rightist political turn in the interwar years, when, as a founder of revisionist Zionism, he openly flirted with protofascist and fascist regimes and supported the Jewish right-wing youth movement, Betar.[2] The short "imperial" chronology of this study is based on carefully thought-out methodological considerations. Here, as in my scholarship in general, I treat *race* as a language that can convey different semantics depending on the situation. It was the Russian imperial situation and imperial contexts that made Jabotinsky's racializing an example of subaltern politics. His structural situation changes with the disappearance of the Russian Empire (as well as the Habsburg and Ottoman Empires) and the rise of the post-Wilsonian orientation toward the nation-state as a normative political ideal. This is not to say that the "Russian case" of Vladimir Jabotinsky is not relevant for understanding his later, postimperial politics of race. If anything, Jabotinsky was well prepared to apply race in subsequent political struggles, but in the new postimperial reality the language of race, as he deployed it, lost its former ambiguity and hence its potential to hybridize hegemonic imperial hierarchies.

—⚜—

Russian Jewish intellectuals discovered the construct of race as a discourse of modern natural sciences and social analysis in the wake of the Great Reforms of the 1860s–1870s that had boosted the empire's modernization and nationalization.[3] This transformative historical moment favored the spread of interest in race as a scientific and universally applicable concept. The mid-nineteenth century's scholarly and socially most progressive science of biology historicized the observable natural diversity as resulting from the inheritance of acquired physical characteristics (Lamarckism) and natural selection of these characteristics over longer periods of time (Darwinism). From its inception, Darwinism was never a pure natural science theory. It emerged "as a theoretical orientation firmly rooted in philosophy and history, philology and jurisprudence, ethics and aesthetics, psychology and sociology, anthropology and political science, comparative anatomy and ethology."[4] The historicization of biology as a natural history of humanity, accomplished within Darwinism, enabled the reverse process of the biologization of social sciences and social thinking in general, with diverse implications. These intellectual transformations turned race, a biosocial concept by definition, into an intersectional, to use our contemporary language, discourse capable of activating the paradigm of natural progressive development, on the one hand, and nourishing developmental inequalities together with the demands for science-based politics (progressive or conservative), on the other. Many advocates of the latter approach connected the desired transformation of politics to its nationalization, seeing in nation a natural and scientifically objectifiable form of groupness. In 1883, the publisher of the Russian Jewish weekly, *Russkii Evrei* (the Russian Jew) even imagined the political science of the future as a "comparative biology of nations": "Such a science would call to life other related sciences such as the embryology of nations, psychology of nations, psychiatry of nations, anatomy of nations, hygiene of nations, pathology of nations, and so on. The results produced by these scientific disciplines could lay the foundations for a purely practical science— anthropo-valentology—that is, a theory of exact estimation of the value and merits of human individuals and nations."[5]

In real life, this was race science—physical anthropology— which supplied "scientific" measures of individual and national merits. That Jews were a popular if not the favorite objects of physical anthropology is widely known.[6] Their role as race scientists, themselves studying Jews as a race, especially outside of what is usually identified as the West, still remains quite obscure.[7] Retrospectively, from the perspective sealed by the Holocaust, it is hard to ponder that Russian Jewish race science was a noticeable phenomenon in the empire, but that was indeed the case. Suffice it to mention that one of the most widely acclaimed anthropological dissertations in Russia was written on a Jewish theme ("The Jews: A Comparative Anthropological Study based Primarily on Observations of Polish Jews"), by a Jewish scientist, Aron Girsh Donov (Arkadii Danilovich in the Russified version) El'kind (1868–1921).[8] An acculturated Jew living in Moscow, a graduate of the Department of Medicine of Moscow University, and a member of the Moscow liberal anthropological network, El'kind selected as his object of study the "most Western" and modern category of Russian

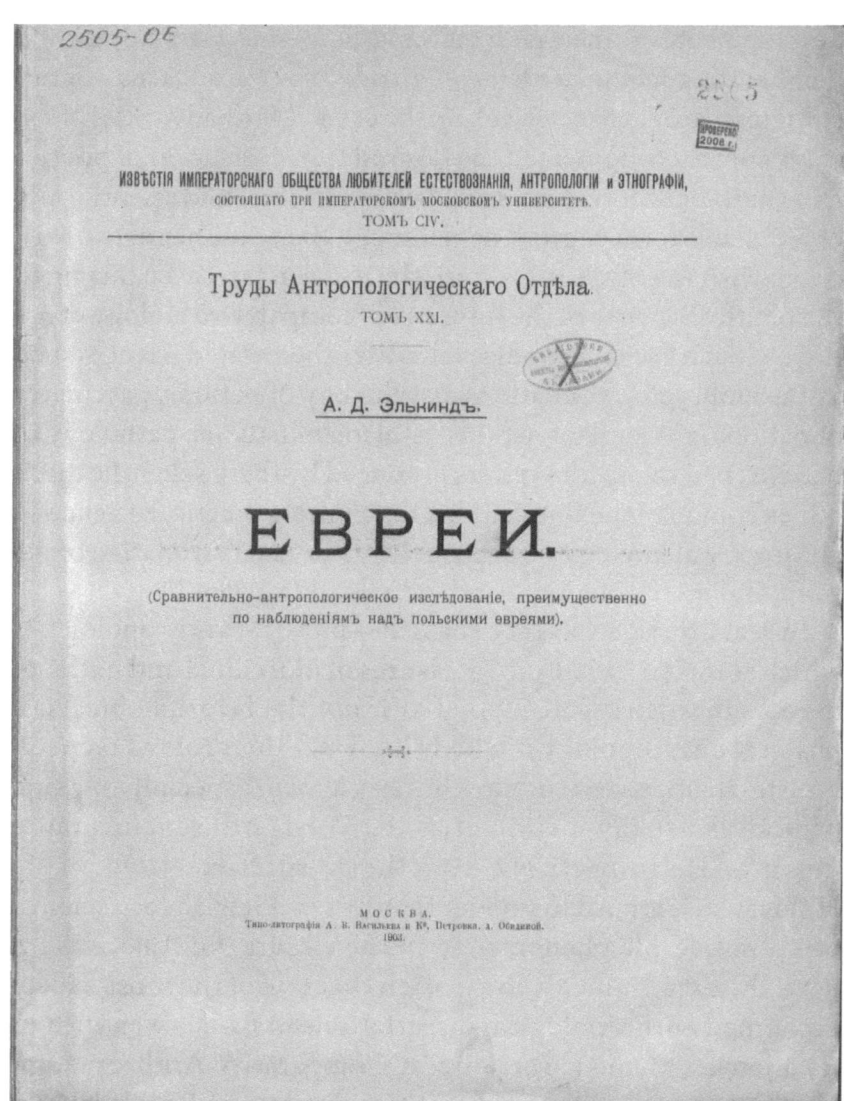

Fig. 0.1 Cover page of A.D. El'kind's *Evrei* (The Jews), a separate edition of the main research part of his dissertation in *TRUDY* [Proceedings] *of the Anthropological Division of OLEAE* [Society of Lovers of Natural Sciences, Anthropology, and Ethnography] (Moscow, 1903).

Jews—industrial workers at a Warsaw factory. His race science, which was otherwise impeccable for his time, pursued an undercover agenda of proving the possibility of Jews assimilating directly into Western modernity without losing their national Jewishness. El'kind distilled this assumed eternal and objective Jewishness in the anthropologically distinct and universally recognizable "Jewish physiognomy," which, he presumed, made the otherwise indistinct, modern, and urban bodies nationally Jewish and thus legible for the future nationalized modernity.[9] In the informal hierarchy of Russian liberal anthropology, El'kind reached the highest possible recognition when, in 1914, he became secretary of the Moscow Anthropological Division of the Society of Lovers of Natural Sciences, Anthropology and Ethnography and the editor of the *Russkii Antropologicheskii Zhurnal* (Russian anthropological journal). The all-Russian network of liberal anthropology offered this physician "of the Judaic faith" opportunities for a surrogate academic career, which he was otherwise denied by Russian imperial law. The society even awarded El'kind its most prestigious prize instituted by and named after the notorious antisemite Grand Duke Sergei Aleksandrovich.[10] Moreover, another leading Russian Jewish race scientist, Samuel Weissenberg (1867–1928), a proponent of the autonomist political solution for the Jews and the author of the original anthropological theory of Jewish "Caucasians," was also honored with this same prize by his Russian colleagues. Clearly, this was a gesture aimed at normalizing Jewish race science within the common imperial anthropological project.

A graduate of a German university, member of many Russian and European academic societies, and contributor to major Russian and German anthropological periodicals, Weissenberg could not legally reside in imperial capitals or university cities, and he never attempted to permanently leave his native Elisavetgrad in the Jewish Pale of Settlement. He was the first non-Western Jewish

— 139 —

были родомъ изъ Кубы или Кутаиса, я позволилъ себѣ всѣхъ измѣренныхъ соединить въ двѣ общія группы: горскихъ и кутаисскихъ евреевъ, на что я имѣлъ тѣмъ большее право, что даже обѣ эти группы, какъ видно будетъ изъ дальнѣйшаго, составляютъ только вѣтви одного цѣлаго и могутъ быть разсматриваемы, какъ единая, дифференцировавшаяся только этнографически, народность.

Всѣ измѣренные мною были взрослые люди, въ возрастѣ не ниже 18 лѣтъ, при чемъ въ возрастѣ отъ 18 до 20 находились только единичныя личности. Одному горскому еврею, измѣренному въ аулѣ Тарки, было, по словамъ окружающихъ, 110 лѣтъ. Это былъ совсѣмъ еще бодрый, ровно держащійся старикъ.

Въ нижеслѣдующихъ таблицахъ я счелъ лишнимъ вычислять процентныя отношенія для отдѣльныхъ варіацій, такъ какъ тамъ, гдѣ число случаевъ 100,

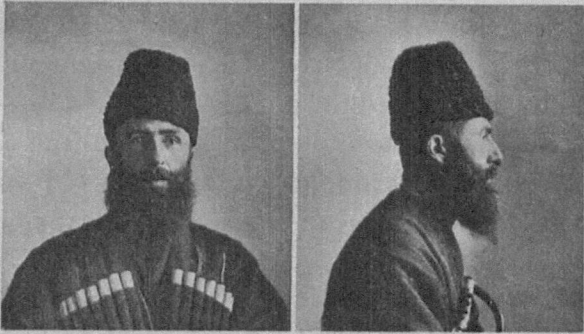

Рис. 1. Грузинскій еврей.

эти отношенія очевидны, тамъ же, гдѣ ихъ 50, соотвѣтствующую цифру слѣдуетъ только помножить на 2, чтобы получить требуемое число.

По таблицѣ I р о с т ъ изслѣдуемыхъ нами группъ, составляя въ среднемъ для грузинскихъ евреевъ 1637 и для горскихъ 1642, разнится только на 5 mm. при почти одинаковыхъ минимальныхъ и максимальныхъ величинахъ. Обѣ группы, такимъ образомъ, ниже средняго роста, приближаясь, однако, къ средней его нормѣ, при чемъ слѣдуетъ замѣтить, что болѣе 60% измѣренныхъ падаетъ по своему росту на среднерослыхъ, обнимающихъ колебанія отъ 1601 до 1700, давая съ другой стороны значительный процентъ для низко- и малый—для высокорослыхъ.

Fig. 0.2 Georgian Jew, an anthropological photo from Samuel Weissenberg's article on Caucasian Jews in *Russian Anthropological Journal*. "Kavkazskie evrei v antropologicheskom otnoshenii," *Russkii Antropologicheskii Zhurnal*, no. 2–3 (1912): 139.

— 145 —

Табл. IX. Носовой показатель.

Колебанія.	Грузинскіе евреи.	Горскіе евреи.
40,1 — 50,0	1	2
60,0	28	23
70	19	24
80	2	1
Minimum	50,0	50,0
Maximum	79,6	73,1
Средняя	59,6	59,6

Переходя къ цвѣтовому типу, остановимся сначала на **цвѣтѣ глазъ**, имѣвшихъ слѣдующіе оттѣнки:

	Грузинскіе евреи.	Горскіе евреи.
Свѣтлокарій	18	36
Карій	18	26
Темнокарій	53	28
Сѣрый	10	10
Голубой	1	—

Рис. 2. Грузинскіе евреи (Кутаисъ).

Fig. 0.3 Georgian Jews (Kutais), an anthropological photo from: Samuel Weissenberg, "Kavkazskie evrei v antropologicheskom otnoshenii," *Russkii Antropologicheskii Zhurnal*, no. 2–3 (1912): 145.

anthropologist to collect anthropometric data on non-European Jews, including Jews of southern Russia, the Caucasus, Turkestan, and Crimea (Karaims), as well as Jews of Palestine, Syria, and Egypt. Weissenberg's ethnographic self-fashioning was extremely complex and controversial. In the language of racial anthropology, he spoke from the midst and on behalf of Jewish groups that were the objects of orientalizing, romantic, and even explicitly degrading discourses. While building a name for himself in Western science, especially in the German-language academic world, he remained equally active in both Russian imperial and specifically Jewish scientific circles. Weissenberg's Western race science decentered the West by locating the origin of the European Jewish mixed type within the Russian imperial borders, in the Caucasus, and by connecting hopes for the revival of Jewish national life with non-Western Jewry and their "natural" Eastern European environment.[11]

The professional recognition that Weissenberg, El'kind, and other Russian Jewish race scientists enjoyed in Russia did not prevent them and their fellow Russian anthropologists from categorizing the Russian Jews as the only race set apart from the imperial family of "racial relatives," the only pure race that did not mix with the surrounding populations. Jews were included in the racial classification of peoples of the Russian Empire, built on the calculation of degrees of racial kinship as elaborated within the Moscow school but demonstrated zero degrees of kinship.[12] The seemingly scientifically apparent racial otherness of Jews justified Jewish racial anthropologists' specialization exclusively on Jews, while all other members of the Moscow liberal anthropological network followed the unwritten rule of studying not peoples but territories and the regional distribution of racial types. This epistemological singling out of the Jews as an object of study narrowed the range of political choices for the advocates of a scientific politics of Jewishness. It is not so difficult to see why, despite the absence of discrimination within Russia's leading, generally philosemitic and multiethnic, liberal anthropological network, Jewish scientists were turning into Jewish activists.

—⁂—

Russia's intellectual class in general, regardless of nationality, could lack political power and influence, but it retained discursive authority that the state, in turn, lacked. With regard to scientific politics and race as one of its pillars, this imbalance between the official imperial regime and intellectual elites within the empire manifested itself with particular clarity: whereas the regime was weakly motivated and poorly equipped to deploy a scientific racialized politics of difference in any sustained manner, the imperial subalterns turned out to be better prepared and keenly interested in advancing a racialized critique of Russia's "unnatural" imperial formation.[13] They deployed race as an authoritative and empowering political language of subaltern groupness. Moreover, as I argue in this book, a racialized politics of subalternity equally characterized modern Jewish and modern Russian nationalisms, both struggling to purge their respective imagined national bodies from the debris of imperial hybridity and establish clear external boundaries and internal cohesion of the newly construed horizonal communities of political action.

The Great Reforms of the late nineteenth century unleashed these developments by broadening the sphere of discursive and political participation. Even more importantly, the Emancipation Reform of 1861 had turned former personally unfree and disenfranchised serfs, the majority of whom were Orthodox Christians and Slavs, into free peasants—the potential basis for a modern Russian nation, itself seen as a victim of the imperial regime.[14] In the postreform decades, the romantic dream about the awakening of the spiritual but sleeping *narod*, the people, to national life gave way to the positivistic statistical, sociological, anthropological, and economic exploration of the imperial population, to the intelligentsia's "going to the people" with the goal of mobilizing peasants for immediate political action, and to multiple versions and practices of nationalism generated from below and from above. The last two monarchs of the Romanov dynasty embraced explicitly Russian nationalist scenarios of power, thus contributing as no one else to their empire's ceasing function as a space of hierarchical integration and management of diversity.[15] Instead, the monarchy itself reinforced modern divisions and identifications and deepened the crisis of the old imperial order that used to embrace multiple coexisting logics of organization of difference (by religion, social estate, economic status, ethnicity, civilizational level, and so on).[16]

As in other empires, the official hierarchies and categories of Russian imperial rule were exploitative, exclusive, and manifestly unequal, but until the turn of the century they did not neatly coincide with any particular national groupness. Nationalism was not an alien idea for the imperial elites, but particularistic politics of empire could best be characterized as anational, splitting and hence demobilizing potential national communities along class (social estate), regional, or religious lines. The only exclusion from this rule was the empire's treatment of Poles, and only after the uprising of 1863.[17] However, by the turn of the century the situation had changed: while the actual diversity of imperial society remained contextual and fluid, nationalism started to play a significantly larger role in administrative and political discourses. In this transitional context the problem of Jewish nationhood, or rather national insufficiency, had emerged as a problem of modern science and politics. Jews as a modern group that did not fully coincide with a confessional community or a social estate could not present the required attributes of a nation: the communality of language, culture, and traditions. Neither did Jews have an ancestral "national" territory within the nationalizing Russian and Habsburg domains. For the modern, and also the modern Jewish, political imagination that associated biopolitical and sociological fitness with citizenship, these defects seemed detrimental. As many advocates of Jewish self-racializing believed, antisemitism was destined to disappear in the postimperial and democratic new world of the future. Jewish biopolitical otherness, however, was to stay unless Jews themselves redefined their nationhood and took responsibility for preparing for modernity.

—⚉—

A vocal proponent of this idea was, for example, Lev Shternberg (1861–1927), a leading Russian Jewish race scientist, imperial ethnographer, and activist, first of Russian populist and then of Jewish liberal politics, in which he was a political opponent of Jabotinsky. He demanded that Jewish science prioritize self-exploration: "Under the sign of militant nationalism [*pod znakom boevogo natsionalizma*], . . . it seems that there is no Jewish group for which the problem of nationalism would not be at the forefront."[18] In his 1911 polemics with Israel Zangwill, then the president of the International Jewish Territorial Organization and the spokesman regarding the "Jewish problem" at the Universal Races Congress in London (July 1911), Shternberg criticized Zangwill's inclination to exaggerate the role of racial antisemitism and downplay the role of race in enforcing the sense of Jewishness among Jews in modern societies. Racism and racial inequality—these shameful results of ignorance and colonialism—were destined to disappear with the advancement of science and progressive forms of political life, Shternberg argued. But Jewish uniqueness or even otherness did not directly depend on this change of external environment and had to be reinforced and retained by means of informed choices by Jews themselves.[19] For Zangwill, self-withdrawal was the only such choice. In his paper for the Universal Races Congress, Zangwill distinguished between the two "Jewish problems." The first one was the general "Jewish problem" of persecutions, which could be resolved through civic and political emancipation. The other was the "Jewish 'Jewish problem'" derived from the same political emancipation: "Social intercourse would lead to intermarriage" and the disappearance of the structural ghetto would lead to Jewish cultural assimilation. There was no way for Jews to remain (or become) a nation under the conditions of inclusivity, for any form of cultural, religious, or political Jewishness/national separateness would galvanize antisemitism. This, in turn, would be an entirely natural reaction, a manifestation of the Darwinian general "law of dislike for the unlike."[20] Zangwill's contraposition between all Jews as being collectively "unlike" and all gentiles united by likeness was deeply racializing, and his resort to Darwinian language was an important claim for a natural-scientific legitimization of his cultural and political arguments. Shternberg, however, remained unconvinced. He ridiculed Zangwill's misuse of Darwinian concepts, on the one hand, and his culturalist analysis, on the other. He considered what force could keep Jews together in places like New York, where they were free to integrate and intermarry. The only plausible explanation for Shternberg was race, the fundamental biological unity that prompted Jews to exercise communal endogamy, especially under the welcoming conditions of the United States. A few months before the Universal Races Congress, Shternberg wrote: "Out of all these attributes [race, national territory, language, religion—as listed in the paragraph directly preceding the quotation] only one stands for Jews without any doubt—the anthropological, racial attribute. From the point of view of this attribute, Jews, thanks to the purity of their blood, are of course a nation par excellence; they are unrivaled. It is remarkable, however, how nationalists completely ignore this most obvious and exceptional attribute when they discuss our nationality."[21]

Many Russian Jewish nationalists supported this view of the Jewish "nation par excellence," or at least incorporated a muted racialized conception of Jewishness into projects that prioritized other aspects of Jewish nation-building, such as language policy or territorial struggle. Even when class provided the main framework for Jewish political self-organization, the perception of Jewishness as something objectively existing and rooted in

Fig. 0.4 Israel Zangwill. Portrait published in the Russian Zionist magazine, *Evreiskaia Zhizn'* (Jewish life) 1904, no. 4 (April): 17.

a shared nature, in addition to shared experiences and double exploitation, informed Russian Jewish "prophesy and politics."[22] Exceptions only proved the rule: a disregard for the biosocial commonality of Jews often led to the admission that Jews did not constitute a nation, which in early twentieth-century terms meant their delegitimization as independent participants in the future postimperial modernity. Thus, another famous Russian Jewish political activist and Jabotinsky's older contemporary, the creator of Esperanto and founder of the global Esperantist movement, Lazar' Markovich Zamenhof (1859–1917), did not believe in race and saw in Jews "an abnormal nation," one that did not share a single language, territory, and polity. All they had in common was Judaism, but even its significance was diminishing as more and more contemporary Jews became irreligious.[23] As Brigid O'Keeffe has convincingly shown in her innovative study of Esperanto and Russian Esperantists, Zamenhof's international "auxiliary language" and the associated philosophy of Hillelism as a secularized ethical Judaism were intended to disjoin territory, language, and traditions and hence undo nationality as the main framework for social imagination and political recognition. "The Jewish pioneers of the future," O'Keeffe writes, equipped with Esperanto and Hillelism and free from the illusion of nationality, "would, Zamenhof argued, feel welcome in this homeland and among their fellow human beings, no matter their origins and ethnicities. The Hillelists' homeland would ultimately be the world."[24]

Race—the collective physical body of the nation—seemed to offer a viable alternative to this utopian cosmopolitanism. It served as a substitute for all the absences from Zamenhof's or Shternberg's lists, for all the insufficiencies generally attributed to a subaltern, who, in the words of Dipesh Chakrabarty, is always defined "in terms of lack, of absence, or an incompleteness that translates into 'inadequacy.'"[25] As I show in this book, in an explicitly interiorized subaltern perspective, race functioned as a shared language (of self), a common culture and tradition (of national biopolitics), and a territory always inhabited by Jews. In other words, reliance on the race argument made Jews, at least theoretically and potentially, equal participants in the modern imperial political sphere.[26]

―☸―

This interpretation of the connection between Jews, race, and the politics of difference was long in the making, but it had crystallized as a coherent narrative in the course of the First Russian Revolution of 1905–1907. Again, as we are going to see, Jabotinsky epitomizes this development particularly well. But he was not alone. In 1905, the previously mentioned Lev Shternberg became a Jewish scientist and a Jewish politician, simultaneously and quite suddenly, when his powerful pamphlet "The Tragedy of the Six Million People" announced his decisive turn from general imperial scholarly and political pursuits to Jewish politics and science.[27] Soon Shternberg became a founding member of the Jewish People's Group (Evreiskaia narodnaia gruppa, ENG), an expert club for the parliamentary caucus of the liberal party of Constitutional Democrats (ENG was officially registered in January 1907). Amid the political turmoil of the unfolding revolution, the ENG activists in their foundational collection *On the Eve of Awakening* (Nakanune probuzhdeniia, 1906) reminded their followers that Jews represented "one of the most characteristic and distinct anthropological types that has preserved its particularity for centuries despite differing geographic and other conditions." According to Shternberg and the ENG, the "contemporary formulation of the Jewish question" rested on a number of basic scientific facts: Jews belonged to the Semitic race; the Jewish racial type had been formed in antiquity and today could be seen in the "images of Jews on Egyptian and Assyrian monuments, where they are easily distinguishable from the images of other Asiatic and African tribes"; the stability of the Jewish type was reinforced by isolation, endogamy, and a weakly developed spirit of proselytism; and the distinct Jewish psychological personality matured on this biological and social basis.²⁸ Nationality was, therefore, a higher cultural formation developing on racial foundations. For the ENG theoreticians this conclusion signified "the alpha and omega of normal human existence." It served as an objective proof that the postrevolutionary progressive empire of knowledge would inevitably embrace the principle of nationality grounded in race, which would include the Jewish nation. Then "the common motherland of all these nationalities will impress the world with the richness of its spiritual content and with the splendid blossoming of its spiritual culture."²⁹ The embrace of the racialized principle of nationality would produce the effect of the empire's real democratization and modernization.

The latter term, *modernization* (or *modernity*), was another key word in the collective narrative of *On the Eve of Awakening*, in addition to and in combination with *race*. In the next chapters, we encounter this combination multiple times in texts by Jabotinsky as well as his supporters and opponents. One of the challengers, a Marxist turned leading Russian liberal politician and a proponent of Russian nationalism after the 1905 revolution, Peter Struve, "officially" introduced the concept of modernity into the Russian political language in January 1907: "The Russian Revolution, as I have noted elsewhere, represents a phenomenon . . . that can be called 'contemporaneity.' . . . I use the word 'contemporaneity' for the lack in the Russian language of an expression equivalent to the West European 'modern.' The Russian Revolution is very 'modern.'"³⁰ Struve's contribution to the new post-1905 political language of empire was not limited to modernity, and it was not a coincidence that his main sparring partner in this rhetorical experimentation was Vladimir Jabotinsky. Both felt the inadequacy of the existing rhetorical repertoire for reflecting a new, nationalized, and "very 'modern'" vision of the imperial political scene, and both introduced racialized tropes into the postrevolutionary public political debates. After 1905, Struve, Jabotinsky, and many of the other participants in literary and political discussions considered in these pages had succeeded in firmly establishing race, along with capitalism, industrialization, parliamentary democracy, scientific governance, basic civility, individualism, the advancement of women's rights, emancipated sexuality, and triumphant nationalism, as a constituent element of modernity. With this transformation of the popular social imagination, the proper Jewish connotations of modernity that included Haskalah, immigration, assimilation, the language debate, and the decline of the shtetl had been modified and diversified through imperial comparisons, especially with other anti-imperial national projects. The very possibility of their dialogue greatly intensified during and after the First Russian Revolution of 1905–1907, and it is then that race assumed a prominent place in the political language of anti-imperial advocates of nationalism and modernity.

—⁂—

"I do not know how others number the years. But I count them from 1905."[31] Mikhail Krutikov uses this line by the Yiddish poet David Einhorn to open the discussion of the pivotal role of the revolution of 1905–1907—a moment of unprecedented mass political mobilization and participation—in the chronotope of Russian Jewish modernity and perceived crisis of Jewish national authenticity.[32] With the similar goal of conveying the role of the revolution in the chronotope of modern Jewish political subjectivity, Scott Uri quotes one of the founding members of the Poale Zion group in Warsaw, Yitzhak Tabenkin: "This is one of those periods in history designated as turning points, a *special* period in the life of the people—not just in the social perspective but also in all the transformations in the spiritual and cultural domain."[33] Uri translates Tabenkin's words into a research question: What exactly "happened in and around the Revolution of 1905 that irrevocably altered reigning conceptions and practices of community and self?"[34] Jeffrey Veidlinger's analysis of Russian Jewish public culture as a modern national space similarly accepts the centrality of the revolution of 1905 and recognizes the "tendency among

Jewish intellectuals to heap scorn on their own community for its perceived failure to modernize," and the sense of "exasperation and shame" due to this.[35] The post-1905 rise in the popularity of race as a political concept pioneered by Jewish politicians, Zionists in the first place, should be understood in this context. It reflected the same tendency that Veidlinger registered in Jewish public life, that Uri ascribed to modern Jewish politics, and that Krutikov diagnosed in pre-1914 Yiddish literature: the "strong yearning for 'normalization' of Jewish life, ... a potentially open perspective, capable of incorporating different visions of the future."[36] As I argue in this book, one needs to take seriously the desire to embrace a modern political subjectivity and the subaltern self-identification of the enthusiasts of self-racializing to understand why and how race for them came to signify progress, development, and open-ended national modernity.

—⁂—

Thus, my interpretation of the connection between Jews, race, empire, and modernity is centered on subalternity as a prime condition for self-racializing. It clearly collides with the popular branding of Jews as archetypal Mercurial moderns and of the twentieth century as "the Jewish century," offered by Yuri Slezkine in his influential book *The Jewish Century*. Slezkine's modernity is "about everyone becoming urban, mobile, literate, articulate, intellectually intricate, physically fastidious, and occupationally flexible.... Modernization, in other words, is about everyone becoming Jewish."[37] Not only does this provocative thesis downplay the story of the Jews' own modernization and of those Jews who were illiterate in "modern" languages, occupationally inflexible, and provincial, it also makes us forget that "everyone" was becoming modern in the former world of the Russian and Habsburg Empires in the framework of the postimperial nation-states (or national Soviet republics), an organizational structure which did not exist for Jews until the second half of the twentieth century.[38] As some of the examples discussed in this introduction suggest, Russian Jewish adepts of scientific race, themselves very modern individuals, were deeply troubled by the outcome of Jews becoming the assimilated "everyone"—urban, mobile, and modern—especially in the imperial situation. They thought about Jews in terms of perceived lacks rather than their archetypal modernity and searched for ways to turn this everyone's modernity into a Jewish national project. Moreover, they worked to denaturalize imperial hybridity in order to nationalize imperial politics on the grounds of what race theorists defined as natural authentic groupness and downplay the assumed connection between modernity and nation-state so central to the twentieth century's history. Taking their concerns and their own language of modernity seriously and placing these in the historical context of the turn-of-the-century Russian Empire yields a narrative of subaltern self-racializing rather than modern universalism. If Jewish experience in the twentieth century can be considered paradigmatic for modernity, it is rather in the following sense: as capable of exposing imperial situations within both imperial and national, dubbed as Western and non-Western political formations, and of confirming the power of the "realism of the group" in modern politics.[39] This is how the case of Vladimir Jabotinsky is used in this book—as a model case of the Russian Jewish subaltern imperial modernity and a racialized anti-imperial nationalism.

But if these were indeed real phenomena, and if the case of Vladimir Jabotinsky is paradigmatic of not only Jewish but also other modern anti-imperial subaltern nationalisms, why do we have so few studies of race in imperial and anti-imperial politics? Why is it still necessary in such studies to argue at length that race should have a place in the historiography of Eurasian imperial formations? How do we explain that the first truly significant interdisciplinary conversation about the place of race in Russian/Eurasian studies in the flagship journal of this field,

Slavic Review, had to wait until 2021?[40] Compared to other imperial historiographies, the historiography of the Russian Empire remains remarkably race-free and aloof from theoretical debates about the intersectional nature of race and, especially, the ability of the racializing episteme and politics to perform through cultural idioms. While working on this book, I could not but reflect on the structural conditions that made learned ignorance on race the most stable feature of the old *Sonderweg* narrative of Russian/Eurasian history. In sharing some of my conclusions here, I hope to productively challenge the race skeptics in my field and, possibly, influence the way this book is read.

In the 1990s, before I had even contemplated this project, the field of Russian studies pursued two main directions of conceptual innovation: through critical and creative adaptation of the Foucauldian modernity paradigm and through the deconstruction of Russia as an imperial formation. Laura Engelstein's daring *Keys to Happiness* launched the debate about Russia's "combined underdevelopment" and politics of expert modernity.[41] A path-breaking contribution to the field, the book did not mention race at all. Most importantly, it was characteristically blind toward empire as a formative context for "underdeveloped" Russian modernity. To take just one example, Engelstein's innovative gender-centered discussion of the physician Praskovia Nikolaevna Tarnovskaia's anthropological study of Russian female murderers and prostitutes (a "Russian" contribution to the European canon of criminal anthropology) entirely overlooked Tarnovskaia's obsessive concern with race. Tarnovskaia's struggle to ensure the homogeneity of her Russian "material in terms of race" remained unnoticed and hence irrelevant for this influential book's argument.[42]

Since then, empire blindness has never been truly overcome or reflected on by representatives of the "modernity school."[43] A more recent revision of Engelstein's original argument, by Daniel Beer in *Renovating Russia*, is emblematic of such a selective vision.[44] In his rich and important book, Beer issues a call to fully appreciate the disciplinary power of late imperial biomedical discourses and experts and their influence on the Bolshevik version of modernity. However, he never questions the imperial/colonial/subaltern positionality of these experts and the objects of their biopolitics. For example, one of Beer's protagonists is the Kyiv University neurology professor Ivan Sikorsky, who also appears in this book as one of Jabotinsky's interlocutors. As an advocate of modern population politics and a Foucauldian-type expert, Sikorsky was concerned with uplifting the peasant population through sanitizing measures and psychiatric control, and this is how he is treated in Beer's book. Beer pays much less attention to Sikorsky as a leading representative of modern Russian racial nationalism, who advocated transformation of the old empire into a nation-state surrounded by inferior colonial peripheries, and who, as we will see, racialized both Russians and Jews, as well as other imperial subjects, but in profoundly different ways. Beer, however, identifies in Sikorsky's studies a typical liberal trope of peasant backwardness and misses the imperial psychiatrist's obsession with establishing and protecting a Russian racial/national norm.

The tenacious empire-blindness of the modernity paradigm is hardly accidental and exposes its roots in the Foucauldian concept of modernity. Its subsequent "rerouting" by Ann Laura Stoler "through the history of empire" that allowed race to be reincorporated into the original Foucauldian design passed over the modernity school in Russian/Eurasian field.[45] Similarly, the modernity school never seriously engaged with the imperial "strategic relativism" thesis that problematizes monological explanatory narratives in the imperial situation.[46] James Clifford's exposure of Foucault's "scrupulous ethnocentrism" and Stoler's critique of the "metropolitan" view of modernity by locating its shaping "outside those forced fields in which imperial knowledge was promoted and desiring subjects were made" contributed to the imperial turn in Eurasian studies and their direct engagement with postcolonial critique but not to the modernity school itself.⁴⁷ Therefore, it comes as no surprise that the new take on empire as an idiom of irregular diversity was missed by a field still largely defined by the "strategic essentialism" of the modernity paradigm. Hence, today Vera Tolz's or my own work on race as an important imperial semantic field in need of thorough contextualization coexists with the Sonderweg approach to race, so consonant with the empire-blindness of the modernity school. Regardless of the accumulated body of historical scholarship on race and the general consensus in contemporary humanities and critical theory,⁴⁸ the conversation in our field is still often structured by the artificial segregation of cultural and biological categories of groupness, and the Russian and Soviet modernities are still often interpreted as race-free (an "archaic" empire and a regime operating through social idioms).⁴⁹ The way out of this narrow Sonderweg vision seems obvious to me—it requires an analytical reincorporation of empire as a context-setting category in studies of *imperial* modernity. This has been the principal methodological premise of this project. Regardless of whether one agrees or disagrees with my interpretation of the role of race and self-racializing in modern Russian Jewish politics, I invite readers of this book to appreciate the new perspective it offers on the complex dynamics of the Russian imperial formation engaged in self-modernization from above and from below.

—⁂—

In the most succinct formulation, this book explores Jewish political doctrines of the early twentieth century that legitimized themselves through references to modern science and used race as a valid concept in imperial politics. Since Zionism was one Jewish national ideology that most consistently embraced a normative scientific view of the nation and relied with equal enthusiasm on the language of race and blood, Russian Zionism is central to my discussion. The chapters contextualize racialized Zionism as an anti-imperial ideology and a postcolonial political strategy.

Chapter 1 places the Russian Empire on the map of scientific Zionism that hitherto has been limited to western European countries. Most important, it shows that after the First Russian Revolution of 1905–1907, Jewish nationalists proved to be better prepared to engage in the politics of race and nationalism than were other actors of mass politics in the empire. One of the brightest and most controversial leaders of racialization of Jewish and imperial politics, Vladimir Jabotinsky, is the focus of chapters 3, 4, and 5. Jabotinsky's political deployment of the race argument, his provocative language policy, criticism of biological and cultural hybridity, search for new political idioms of organic nationhood, and political alliances with other anti-imperial nationalisms are classical examples of anticolonial politics as we know it from studies of anti-British or anti-French colonial resistance. While exploring specific examples of racialized Jewish politics, the book shows that in most such cases race was deployed contextually and rarely for racist purposes. Thus, whereas in Zionism race helped express and safeguard national authenticity and purity, and disentangle Jewishness from the imperial mix, in a broader transnational context it could serve the goal of claiming a European status for the Jews and could even redraw the imagined European geography (the topic of chapter 2). Unlike racist politics of imperial and national regimes aimed at delineating lines of social, economic, and political exclusion, subaltern self-racializing in the imperial situation served the goal of justifying the political inclusion of an oppressed minority. Instead of sealing the future by means of retroactive genealogies of race and hence social privileges and rights, subaltern self-racializing in the imperial situation ensured that the future remained open. The story of Russian Jewish political self-racializing thus invites a more general historical revision of race as a language of difference and sameness, for as Ann Laura Stoler reminds us in *Duress*, "that race is invoked by, and coexists with, a range of political agendas is not a contradiction but a fundamental historical feature of its multiplex political genealogies."[50]

ONE

RACE, ZIONISM, AND THE QUEST FOR JEWISH AUTHENTICITY

> I dream of how great it would be to compose a book that would offer a firm substantiation of Zionism from the point of view of the most contemporary science.
>
> Vladimir Jabotinsky, "Gertsl'. Idealy, taktika, lichnost'," 1904

"WHAT BROUGHT HIM TO ZIONISM ... was a quest for authentic identities, grounded in the historical realities of that place, time, and milieu. It was a generational sensibility; he and his friends had grown increasingly skeptical of their parents' Jewishness. For the young, authentic identity seemed to be grounded in nationhood ... as anchored in blood, soil, and a distinctive national culture," Adi Gordon wrote about the well-known Zionist Hans Kohn, a young intellectual of the Habsburg Empire, who later became the founder of academic nationalism studies and converted his experience as a politically disillusioned late imperial Zionist into an influential social theory.[1] Gordon's words can also be justifiably applied to Vladimir Jabotinsky, the author of this chapter's epigraph and today's best-remembered Russian Zionist. Kohn and Jabotinksy never met in real life, but they shared common generational experiences and advanced a new racialized politics of Jewish nationalism in particular circumstances of time and space—late imperial time and the imperial space. My analysis in this and the following chapters prioritizes late imperial political visions and language of people like Kohn and Jabotinsky over theirs and their peers' political actions because it was in the sphere of discourse and ideology that the new ideals of racial purity and biopolitics were originally articulated and tested.

Reflecting on Kohn's intellectual trajectory, Gordon advances his own theory of modern Jewish nationalism as a quest for a postimperial authenticity rooted in the specific circumstances of the dissolution of old empires and in a very conscious critical engagement with the normative scientific paradigms of modern groupness. I develop this approach by embracing empire as a context-setting category, a semantic field, and a political framework that informed and influenced the Russian Jewish politics of race and the search for true authenticity (which, depending on the narrative, was imagined as being completely obliterated, forgotten, or distorted due to colonial domination, assimilation, exploitation, diasporic existence, and the predicament of subalternity).

At the turn of the century, race and culture, materiality and spirituality, class and nation, and social and biological/natural did not constitute ultimate opposites in the universe of the modern Jewish political imagination. The language of "blood" and primordial unity featured prominently even in ideologies stressing cultural work and explicitly rejecting the notion of biological race. Gordon traces the same dialectic of race and culture in the case of Hans Kohn and members of his Prague circle of assimilated Jewish intellectuals. These young, educated Jewish nationalists "generally rejected both race theory and any notion of racial hierarchy," but often referred to the power of "blood" to express a sense of national belonging "beyond one's choice, control, or even comprehension."[2] This semantic slippage could assume very disturbing manifestations, as in the case of the venerated Jewish poet, Chaim Nachman Bialik, who in 1934, during a press conference at the Hebrew University, admitted: "I too, like Hitler, believe in the power of the blood idea."[3] The most charismatic member of Kohn's generation and the intellectual inspiration for the members of his Prague circle, the modernist philosopher and Zionist Martin Buber, dedicated many pages to the mystique of "blood." He obviously preferred this concept to the then scientific construct of "race," but as Raphael Falk has shown in his study of Zionist eugenics, the idiom of blood helped Buber "to establish the Jewish national identity in biological (though very much Lamarckian) terms." In support of his assertion, Falk quotes from Buber: "The innermost stratum of man's disposition, which yields his type, the basic structure of his personality, is that which I have called blood: that something which is implanted within us by the chain of fathers and mothers, by their nature and by their fate, by their deeds and by their sufferings."[4] For intellectuals like Bialik, Kohn, Buber, and many others, blood was a mysterious inward-looking prism that could echo some traditional—that is, "authentic"—sense of Jewish lineage and at the same time ally with modernist aesthetics. But in the epoch of mass politics, these modern intellectuals' subjective preference for "blood" over "race" held little weight, because both signified what was at the time considered to be the same primordial, biological, objectively existing unity and authenticity and were used as such in political debates among Jewish nationalists as well as between them and other nationalists or socialists.

References to blood and race were present in many Russian Jewish political ideologies of the turn of the century. This was certainly the case with the Diaspora autonomism of Simon Dubnov, the premier Jewish historian and cultural and political activist, or of Samuel Weissenberg. This was equally true of Lev Shternberg's Jewish liberalism, Arkadii El'kind's ideology of acculturation into Western modernity, and socialist versions of Jewish nationalism and ideologies of cultural and spiritual revival. But

Zionism was the Jewish national ideology that most consistently embraced a normative view of the nation as developed by social and political sciences since the second part of the nineteenth century and relied with equal enthusiasm on the language of race and blood. As Mitchell Hart has succinctly put it in speaking of Zionism, "racial ideas and images proved quite attractive to many Jewish nationalists, offering them a language with which to define Jewishness as an objective fact, a matter of biology and history as well as subjective will. Moreover, the fact that racial thinking was closely aligned with science, that it drew much of its content ... from the natural and social sciences, was also attractive to Zionism, a movement that portrayed itself as scientific."[5]

In his book on Zionist political imagination "beyond the nation-state," Dmitry Shumsky argues that the political ideal of the key founding fathers of Zionism was not a sovereign nation-state but a hierarchical statehood (within the reformed imperial formations) and that this view of the Jewish state did not disappear as the ideology penetrated the masses. Shumsky's close historical and contextual reading of the major texts of European and Russian Zionism reveals that it afforded enough space for theoretical separation between the state (the land) and the nation and inspired the cultivation of spiritual and biological expressions of nationality.[6] In turn, Taro Tsurumi, who tends to agree with this point, suggests that a racialized national self-perception "was less territorially based or statist than the one based on culture and community" and hence better suited those for whom "the multinational state—or the social order that was based on various historical collective entities—is axiomatic."[7] Tsurumi implies that the political mobilization of Jews in the Russian Empire revealed their predisposition toward racialized concepts of the nation that were predicated on their imperial condition.[8] Such historiographic insights set the scene for the further in-depth exploration of modern Jewish politics in the Russian Empire through the prism of race, especially in the case of Russian Zionism. Building on them, I also maintain that approaching Zionism through the prism of the imperial situation in which it operated helps us appreciate it as a form of postcolonial nationalism that, according to Derek Penslar, "was historically and conceptually situated between colonial, anticolonial, and postcolonial discourse and practice."[9] My analysis here is inevitably selective and does not nearly cover the entire spectrum of Zionist thought and politics in the Russian Empire,[10] but it situates Zionism historically so that Penslar's argument becomes apparent, and the role of Jewish intellectuals and political activists in defining the semantics of race in the early twentieth-century Russian Empire is treated in a contextualized and critical way.

JEWISH POLITICS AS MASS POLITICS

The element of sheer utopianism in Zionism was greater than in other modern nationalisms simply because the realization of its ideal depended on improbable international diplomatic solutions and on equally improbable internal conformity within the de facto diverse and transnational people called Jews. Students of Eastern European Zionism have shown that Zionist realpolitik counterbalanced its utopianism by emphasizing Jewish problems in the Diaspora, here and now.[11] In Russia, this became especially apparent after the revolution of 1905–1907, when the masses were drawn into political discourses and actions on a scale unseen in the past. Under mounting pressure from below, the regime introduced a parliament (the State Duma) and legalized many previously prohibited forms of political life. The Jewish public reacted to this change by assuming a more engaged position vis-à-vis national and local politics, from participating in the Duma elections to organizing self-protection during pogroms. The empire's political culture was changing and so were the hopes of those who fought for the civic and national rights of imperial subjects.

In 1905, the representatives of different Jewish political movements, including Zionists, joined forces in the Society for the Attainment of Full Civil Rights for the Jewish People in Russia, which worked to organize Jews for the State Duma elections. In March 1905, on behalf of the new society, the political Zionist Vladimir Jabotinsky addressed the leader of spiritual Zionism, Ahad Ha'am. Jabotinsky's letter to Ha'am expressed a sense of urgency ("not to miss the political moment and gain equal rights"; "it would be unfortunate to lose such a moment") and a profound interest in developing Jewish political life within the framework of liberal politics in the empire.[12] In urging Ha'am to join the society, Jabotinsky presented it as a sort of Jewish parliament, an "embryo of the common Jewish organization that would include all the parties and all the neutrals—a 'kahal,' in one word." Jabotinsky expected elective representatives of Jewish communities and professional unions in this "kahal" to launch a broad public campaign "with banquets, resolutions, telegrams, and so on," with the aim of influencing the legislative process and public opinion in the empire in favor of Jews. His ambitions extended well beyond general constitutionalism. Jabotinsky shared with Ha'am the vision of a "network of such organized communities across all of Russia, and in the future—even beyond Russia, with a common congress and one center."[13] This was the vision of a supranational, nonterritorial, organized and politically engaged Jewish nation in the Diaspora. At a superficial rhetorical level, Jabotinsky's political utopia vaguely alluded to the Va'ad Arba Aratzot, the Council of Four Lands—the national council or parliament that existed in the Polish-Lithuanian Commonwealth from the mid-sixteenth to the eighteenth century. But his most obvious and immediate inspirations were the Zemstvo activists' "banquet campaign" on the eve of the 1905 revolution ("with banquets, resolutions, telegrams, and so on") and the general political mobilization of the entire imperial political nation. The dream, however, had already faded away by 1906, as disagreements among different factions within the Jewish movement became apparent (the society was formally dissolved in 1907) and the revolution produced even deeper social differentiation. Nonetheless, by the end of the revolution, practically all Jewish parties, including Zionists, had adopted the demand for Jewish nonterritorial—that is, cultural and administrative—autonomy in their programs and were prepared to fight for it and invest in local and all-imperial Jewish politics.

The Helsingfors Program, promoted by Jabotinsky and passed by the Third Russian Zionist Conference in Helsingfors (Helsinki, Finland) in December 1906, advanced the concept of *Gegenwartsarbeit*—work in the present for the "recognition of Jewish nationality as a unified whole with the right to self-government in all the affairs of national life."[14] Jeffrey Veidlinger maintains that this political declaration was just one early manifestation in Russia of the general reorientation of various Jewish parties and movements toward legal, primarily cultural, work under national slogans in the Russian Empire.[15] Many nationally minded Jewish socialists shared this goal, whereas more radical Jewish nationalists such as, for example, Vladimir Jabotinsky, read the moment as their chance to nationalize not only Jewish politics but the entire political sphere in the empire. By virtue of this very moment marked by the rapid expansion of the political sphere, the mobilized Jewish public, regardless of one's specific ideological orientation, was contributing to the emerging new repertoire of political discourses and actions in the diverse and volatile imperial political field.[16]

The two main tendencies that defined the development of this field at the turn of the century were unification and systematization, on the one hand, and the persistence and reproduction of imperial diversity, on the other.[17] These opposite tendencies unfolded simultaneously, so that the empire's final nationalization and rationalization of its population policies never happened. "The imperial rights regime," to use Jane Burbank's excellent designation, persisted on the books and in practice, cultivating a sort of uneven "mosaic" citizenship in which particular population groups enjoyed varying rights and privileges and owed duties to the state through membership in legal estates.[18] In the political context of the early twentieth century, "the imperial rights regime," through which the state promoted confessional and social identities over national ones, worked as a pragmatic political strategy for slowing down the mobilization of imperial subjects along national lines. But in the Jewish case, especially since the late nineteenth century, a confessional group coincided with ethnicity and even race so that membership in a social estate and even baptism could not wipe off the "stigma" of Jewishness. All of these, reinforced by rising antisemitism, enhanced Jewish collective visibility on the public scene but did not automatically yield recognition of Jews' political claims as a nation. As Julius Brutzkus complained in the pages of a leading Zionist magazine, even the most progressive Russian intelligentsia, who readily supported other anti-imperial nationalisms, was not offering its support to the Jewish one because it did not conform to the normative standards. Brutzkus appealed not to the Russian public but to the Jewish political leaders and activists, whose task he saw as to urgently elevate "our own nation to a level equal in value to other nations."[19] It is important to note that this task of self-normalization and self-legitimation as a nation was to be accomplished by the Jews themselves, and it could not wait until (if) Jews would acquire a nation-state in Palestine. National self-normalization by means of national self-mobilization provided the broadest framework for Russian Jewish mass politics in the late imperial period. The largest Jewish socialist party, the Bund, embraced this agenda and began investing in steady nation-building through cultural and political work around 1908.[20] The Folkspartei, established in 1906, made Diaspora cultural politics its main objective, and concern with the form of the Jewish school and the Jewish language was shared by all Jewish parties in the 1910s.[21] But the political implications of this turn toward delimiting national "substance" remained contested and unclear, especially because the growing national-cultural awareness did not bring about the desired cultural and hence national uniformity, and because the impossibility of territorial Jewish autonomy in Eastern Europe had emerged as a significant handicap on the way toward normalization.

Among the most vocal opponents of Jewish nationality on the left flank of Russian oppositional politics were Joseph Stalin and Vladimir Lenin, who believed that "a nation without a territory is unthinkable." Having been generally sympathetic to the Jews of Russia and condemning antisemitism, Lenin in particular insisted that "not only national, but even racial peculiarities are denied to the Jews by modern scientific investigation."[22] The rejection of Jewish special interests underlined the conflict between the Lenin-led RSDRP(b) and the Jewish Bund. For his part, Stalin offered the most comprehensive analysis of the points of disagreement between the Bolsheviks and the Bund as well as the most detailed treatment of presumed Jewish national insufficiency in his seminal *Marxism and the National Question* (1913)—the only serious Bolshevik examination of the problem of nationalism before the revolution of 1917. Defending the principle of national self-determination, on the one hand, and treating nationalism as a temporal phenomenon characteristic of the capitalist stage of development, on the other, Stalin explained that the rise of popular nationalisms in the Russian Empire was the result of the "mounting wave of militant nationalism" from above and intensifying competition between national bourgeoisies from below. These structural factors explained "the spread of Zionism among the Jews, the increase of chauvinism in Poland, Pan-Islamism among the Tatars, the spread of nationalism among the Armenians, Georgians, and Ukrainians, the general swing of the philistine toward antisemitism—all these are generally known facts [of post-1905 political life]."[23] Stalin's general sociological definition of a nation reflected the normative ideas of his time and clearly delegitimized Jewish nationhood. He wrote, "A nation is a historically constituted, stable community of people, formed on the basis of a common language, territory, economic life, and psychological make-up manifested in a common culture."[24] Although his description of the "national character" (psychological makeup) exposed a clear racial bias, he insisted that nation is not a race and that all four attributes listed should be present for a nation to be recognized as such. For the Jewish case, this meant the following:

> Bauer speaks of the Jews as a nation, although they "have no common language"[25]; but what "common destiny" and national cohesion is there, for instance, between the Georgian, Daghestanian, Russian and American Jews, who are completely separated from one another, inhabit different territories and speak different languages? . . . But how can it be seriously maintained that petrified religious rites and fading psychological relics affect the "destiny" of these Jews more powerfully than the living social, economic and cultural environment that surrounds them? And it is only on this assumption that it is possible to speak of the Jews as a single nation at all.[26]

It was no wonder, Stalin observed, that Otto Bauer himself had to recognize that under capitalism it is impossible for Jews to continue as a nation and that they had no objective grounds for national autonomy.[27] Stalin's inconclusive theoretical fluctuation between support for national self-determination (especially in the context of Marxist criticism of colonialism and imperialism) and the rejection of nationalism (especially Jewish nationalism) as a bourgeois ideology, on a practical level resulted in strategic support for extraterritorial national autonomy for the Russian Jews.

After the revolution of 1905–1907, most of Russia's socialist and liberal parties came to endorse this idea as an inevitable compromise between recognizing national rights in general and denying the possibility of Jewish nationhood. But even the Jewish parties, including Dubnov's Folkspartei, had no clear vision of a Jewish national-cultural autonomy that would effectively prevent the mass-scale assimilation and internal differentiation of nonterritorial Jews.[28] As a result, the concept of autonomism became imbued with different meanings. It was understood in terms of acquiring linguistics rights, cultural autonomy, administrative autonomy, Jewish national assembly, or a ministry of Jewish affairs in a democratized imperial government, and, later, as Jewish (Yiddishist) Soviets. Different combinations of the above were possible, up to a federalist project allowing for partial territorialization of Jews in different regions. Austro-Marxism was the main source of all this theorizing. But as one can see from Stalin's *Marxism and the National Question*, it was obvious to contemporaries that Austrian advocates of the principle of national nonterritorial autonomy did not necessarily see the Jews as meriting or needing it. Otto Bauer, with whom Stalin polemicized, was himself a Jew and member of the official Jewish community (the Israelitische Kultusgemeinde). Nevertheless, as a theorist of nationality, he was a committed assimilationist and he specifically opposed granting autonomy to Jews. In his excellent study of "nationalism and autonomy" in Russian Jewish politics, Simon Rabinovitch reminds us of Bauer's suggestion that Jews were "an exception" to the theory of national minority autonomy in Austria, and that Jewish national autonomy and even separate Jewish schools "would harm the Jews' relations with their neighbors."[29] Victor Adler, the founder and leader of the Social Democratic Workers' Party of Austria, was born Jewish but converted to Protestantism shortly after his marriage. He opposed any kind of Jewish "national separatism."[30] And the position of Karl Kautsky, which partially inspired Lenin's original views on Jewish nationality, is well-known: "When the Jews shall have ceased to be persecuted and outlawed, the Jews themselves will cease to exist."[31] Russian Jewish politicians debated the interpretations and implications of Austro-Marxism, especially the role of territoriality in it, but could not offer an alternative language of Jewish political nationalism in the region.[32]

Against this background, it is not so hard to see why the politics of Jewish self-racializing seemed a helpful addition to the available political repertoire. The argument that Jewish nationality was based on biological race could offer a solid basis for all types of conversations about national Jewishness and normalize it scientifically and politically. Moreover, as we shall see, the politics of self-racializing empowered Jews as a politically disadvantaged subaltern nation by affording this nation statistical and eugenic control over its assumed racial/social body. What were the implications of such a proactive use of "race" in the imperial conversation about the modernized empire and the modern Jewish nation of the future? I further consider precisely this question in the book.

ZIONISM AS A TYPE OF SCIENTIFIC POLITICS

In historical scholarship, the politics of Jewish self-racialization has been firmly associated with Zionist politicians such as Max Nordau and Arthur Ruppin, the founder and director of the Berlin-based Bureau for Jewish Statistics, or race scientists such as Ignaz Zollschan.[33] Eastern European Jews have played little part in this drama of scientifically informed Jewish politics (except as objects of racialized and statistical projections). Ruppin famously located the majority of contemporary Russian, Romanian, and Galician Jews, together with Moroccan, Asian, and Turkish Jews at the first, premodern developmental stage, because they exhibited the level of cultural and social development that, Ruppin believed, characterized the Middle Ages.[34] Obviously, this orientalization of non-Western Jewry by western European Jews structurally replicated the orientalization of Jews in European cultural and political modernism.

Meanwhile, Russian Zionists shared many assumptions of scientific politics with Nordau, Ruppin, and other advocates of national statistics, sanitation, eugenics, ethnography, sociology, and so on. Many of them were neopositivists who believed in the objective power of science to assist Jews in their national struggle. Many understood Jewish modernity as developing "from the Talmud to Darwin," to quote Jabotinsky's remark from a 1904 article.[35] Against the examples of Russian Jewish race scientists and activists such as Samuel Weissenberg or the Moscow physician, statistician, criminologist, and journalist, Solomon Vermel', Ruppin does not seem unique or particular either in his eagerness to participate in the Alfried Krupp Prize essay competition (1899) under the suggested topic—"What do the principles of the theory of evolution teach us about the internal political development and legislation of the nations?"—or in his lifelong interest in physical anthropology (which Ruppin studied in Germany under Felix von Luschan).[36] Likewise, Max Nordau's ideas resonated with many contemporaneous statements by Russian Jewish intellectuals, especially their practical implications as summarized in Nordau's speech at the Fifth Zionist Congress in Basel in 1901: "We must know with greater precision about the national material with which we have to work. We need an exact anthropological, biological, economic, and intellectual statistics of the Jewish people."[37] One should only recall that at the Fourth Zionist Congress in London, it was the Zionist and physician from Kiev, Max Mandelstamm, who delivered a speech about Jewish physical degeneration, which he, like Ruppin, ascribed specifically to Eastern European Jews.[38] After 1905, Nordau, on a par with Otto Weininger, "earned prominent places on lists of the most-circulated works of philosophy" in Jewish public libraries.[39] The Bureau for Jewish Statistics, which had been established in Berlin in 1904 and over which Ruppin assumed leadership, had from the outset acquired branches in central and Eastern Europe.[40] And in general, at the turn of the century, the very understanding of politics, especially national politics, as based on modern scientific knowledge was already deeply entrenched in human minds everywhere: imperial regimes and nation-states, progressive social reformers and conservative activists, anticolonial resisters, and socialist revolutionaries all spoke in terms of biopolitics.

Simultaneously with Ruppin's assuming directorship of the bureau in 1904, a new Zionist monthly, *Evreiskaia Zhizn'* (*Jewish Life*, 1904–1907), was launched in the capital of the Russian Empire, St. Petersburg. "One can not exaggerate the importance [of *Evreiskaia Zhizn'*] for the propagation of Zionist ideas in Russia," Brian Horowitz insists. "Its readership rivaled the most popular newspapers in Russia."[41] *Evreiskaia Zhizn'* promoted a scientific agenda focused on the Jewish nation and gave voice to the leading representatives of Russian Zionism such as Daniel Pasmanik, Abraham (Avram) Idelson, Menachem Ussishkin, Vladimir Jabotinsky, Yehiel Chlenov, Yehude Leyb Katzenelson, and Julius Brutzkus.[42] The journal's contributors preached that

> in the end, all phenomena of public life could be reduced to one or another view of the reality of the national problem, to one or another evaluation of the influence of national and racial character on the historical process.... Parties that maintain national and racial platforms should openly and decisively state their understanding of the role of nationalities in the historical process and of the effects of hereditary racial characteristics on the formation of a national character. Otherwise [these parties] can be easily assigned to the reactionary chauvinist clique and [grouped together] with militant theoreticians of the "racial competition."[43]

Most contributors agreed that "race" was to be taken seriously and explained as a part of a Zionist political platform, but national politics itself had to remain immune to social Darwinism and racism. The author of the cited article advanced a habitual lament about a nation, "which, in the course of its historical existence, had lost one of the 'required basic' attributes. Such a nation would have to accept that it does not exist or [would have to] be satisfied with a pitiful right to be regarded an 'exception.'"[44] Alternatively, however, such a nation could embrace

race thinking and claim an objective biological basis for itself. The only other remaining option was a consistent constructivist position that framed nations as products of long- and short-term political and cultural influences. Such a nation would be defined by its members' shared subjective sense of belonging.[45] But Jewish nationalists were quite aware of the weakness of consistent anti-essentialism as a position on the competitive late imperial political scene.

Echoing these concerns, the author of the quoted article in *Evreiskaia Zhizn'*, like so many of his contemporaries, preferred a combination of the racializing (essentialist) and constructivist (anti-essentialist) approaches: "What makes a particular group a nation is not only objective kinship," he wrote, "but also a subjective, although not always conscious, positive evaluation of the group's affinity."[46] Still, in the latter case, the stress on the irrational (not "always conscious") nature of subjective belonging suggested the relevance of "race." And indeed, the concept duly appeared in the text signifying a biological anchor for the shared positive feelings of belonging that constituted the "national character."[47]

Another contributor to *Evreiskaia Zhizn'*, Daniel Pasmanik, defined a nation as a product of a particular racial composition, territory, language, and shared subjective consciousness.[48] When Pasmanik presented to "Jewish youth" an image of the Jewish nation as undying, lasting, and almost ahistorical in its permanency, he expected the young novices to Zionism to stay "true to the theory of organic evolution of being and thinking."[49] Vladimir Jabotinsky's texts in *Evreiskaia Zhizn'* were notable for the same symbiosis of racial essentialism with cultural constructivism, "idealism with materialism; individualism with collectivism; and the primordial and mythical with the historical and material."[50] A greater dose of socialism in Zionism (compared to that of Pasmanik and Jabotinsky) did not in principle alter this symbiosis of natural and social essentialism. Thus, Dov Ber

Borokhov, a founder of labor Zionism and a Yiddishist scholar, believed that the Jewish "national character" was immune to the forces of history: "We will try to prove that Jews possess such common and specific traits of mind that not only bring them together but distinguish them from other peoples. These qualities of the Jewish mind are absolutely distinctive and original; they were not planted from outside in the course of Jewish life among other nations. Quite to the contrary, other nations often borrowed these traits from the Jews."[51] The qualities of the Jewish mind that Borokhov called "national character" included "monistic subjectivism"; poor abilities for natural sciences, plastic and visual arts, and epics and odes ("Jews are devoid of creative ability"); a gift for music and lyrics; a high propensity toward public activism; and, finally, logical thinking but "mythical monism of feelings."[52] At the turn of the century such essentialization of the "national character" was commonplace in academic ethnography, Oriental studies, or history and philosophy, and it resonated widely in mass ideologies.[53] In the latter sphere in particular, the "national character" discourse extended to incorporate national and class instincts and stereotypes, and other forms of intuitive or rational belonging to or rejection of a group.[54] During the First Russian Revolution, psychiatric experts who diagnosed social crises and mass "agitation" and explained various manifestations of the "national character" joined the ranks of ethnographers and race scientists who had already been supplying political activists and ideologues with appropriate scientific idioms of degeneration, moral health and decline, and social norms and deviance.[55] As Macej Górny suggests, the power of the racialized national characterology was based on "its status as a science-without-institutions, combined with its long and rich tradition." Due to this, "characterology could serve as an intermediary between national (as well as other, e.g., gender) stereotypes and the human sciences. References to stereotypes 'dressed up' in this form could have allowed one to avoid the discomfort involved in directly translating one's ideological beliefs into the practice of an objective science."[56]

The results of the medicalization and "naturalization" of political discourse that accompanied the rise of science-based nationalism came as a surprise to the predominantly left-leaning, ideological Russian intelligentsia, who previously ignored nationalism as either a conservative slogan or a form of false consciousness. The intelligentsia cared about the happiness of "the people" as the laboring and exploited classes, not as Russians, Ukrainians, Tatars, and so on, and both populists and socialists were better prepared to discuss class instincts than some national instincts or character. The discovery of nationalism as a real mobilizing and uncontrollable force, a powerful agent of political change, was equally traumatic for all members of the Russian intelligentsia. In this transitional moment, Jewish nationalists who, since the late nineteenth century, had been tackling problems of Jewish national "insufficiency," imperial subjugation, and antisemitism, turned out to be better prepared to engage in the politics of race and nation and better equipped with the appropriate idioms than their non-Jewish counterparts.

TEACHING SCIENTIFIC NATIONALISM

"We, *'inorodtsy'* [aliens], . . . are responsible for explaining to others what we have known for a long time and what all Russia's political parties will have to accept sooner or later," Jabotinsky declared in the pages of the Ukrainian nationalist journal *Ukrainskaia Zhizn'* (Ukrainian life), published in Russian in Moscow by Ukrainian national activists. This journal was a Ukrainian twin of the Zionist *Evreiskaia Zhizn'/Jewish Life*, and Jabotinsky missed no chance to underline the ideological proximity of the two and their respective national causes. In acknowledging their parallelism, Jabotinsky went so far as to include Ukrainians in the category of inorodtsy, to which they, unlike Jews, never officially belonged. By rejecting the old legal definition of inorodtsy fixed in imperial law, and instead embracing a clearly national semantics equally applicable to all ethnic non-Russians, Jabotinsky was modernizing the very language of the "imperial rights regime." He saw the shared mission of the politically organized ethnic non-Russians in delivering the message that "the national question in this empire is a problem of ultimate, not secondary, urgency.... [It is] much more important than the agrarian or the labor question.... And no one else but we, '*inorodtsy*' should explain once and for all to liberal Russia that we do not agree to splitting a common struggle into two stages: 'Constitution'—first and 'national question'—second."[57]

Articles in the Zionist *Evreiskaia Zhizn'* provide many vivid illustrations of this expert position on the national question assumed by Jewish inorodtsy. One especially interesting article from a 1904 issue was penned by a close childhood friend of Jabotinsky, Korney Chukovsky, who would soon become a quite famous journalist and literary critic, and a talented writer of children's literature. But back in 1904, Chukovsky was at an early stage of his career and under the strong intellectual and political influence of his friend. In the article for *Evreiskaia Zhizn'* Chukovsky publicized views that both shared. He used a paper delivered by a member of the Odessa Literary Club at one of its meetings to ridicule the imperial democratic intelligentsia's position on nationalism. Chukovsky particularly engaged with the paper's refusal to accept the objective nature of nationality ("race is not a measure of nationality; religion is not a measure of nationality; language is not a measure of nationality"). If this is the case, Chukovsky reasoned, that is, if indeed the nation could not be objectively "measured," it did not exist as a scientifically verifiable reality.[58] This made no sense to Chukovsky. He insisted that social and cultural criteria were not good measures for the nation because it belonged to the world of nature rather than culture:

> Just imagine: a Mister appears before you and delivers a paper under the following title: "The Division of the Organic World into the

Animal World and the World of Flora Is a Fiction Existing Only in Your Brain"... Seaweed does not have roots, stalks, or leaves, so, why do we consider them plants?... A snake does not have limbs; worms cannot see or hear—so, why do we consider them animals?... Would my Mister be right or wrong? Of course, we would consider him right, a thousand times right, but only on one condition—that is, if he would not demand from us that, after having thrown away false divisions between plants and animals, we put a rose on a chain and begin smelling a dog.[59]

Denying the reality of nation, Chukovsky concluded, would be as unnatural and counterintuitive as smelling a dog, for nothing was more apparent and real than the feeling of group belonging shared by members of a nation. That such a level of theoretical abstraction seemed appropriate for a political magazine at a time of rising popular political mobilization is quite revealing about the contemporary perception of Zionism as a version of scientific politics. Moreover, this type of discourse was not unique to *Evreiskaia Zhizn'*. To the contrary, it was promoted by other new Jewish nationalist periodicals. For example, the Jewish monthly founded in 1904, *Evreiskaia shkola* (Jewish school), advanced a very similar interpretation:

> If one cannot express the nature of Jewishness either by means of religious idiom—Judaism, or by means of national [idiom]—Zionism, what then is this Jewishness? a reader can ask.... One may call it an instinct intrinsic in Jews. Or one can [describe it] as the essence of the spirit of a ten-million-strong group of individuals scattered all over the globe. Or one can [define it] as this people's psyche, which is hard to demarcate clearly, or some other way. This does not matter, for Jewishness is a form of connectivity between one Jew and another Jew (in whatever state they live at any given moment) that only a Jew can feel.[60]

Both Chukovsky in *Evreiskaia Zhizn'* and the writer for the Jewish pedagogical monthly implied that nationality was grounded in a deeper and often invisible yet objective reality of the primordial national body and soul. Chukovsky elaborated: "Pushkin, Tolstoy, and Dostoevsky were so boundlessly great because they felt behind their backs, behind their every step ... the will of someone huge, someone centuries old and extremely numerous, whose name was the people.... They could always see ahead a firm, unshakable, and unquestionable truth—not a class truth only, or the truth of their historical time only, but the truth of the people, of the nation. They felt its flesh and blood; there was nothing accidental in their [creativity], because everything about it was national."[61]

It is ironic that while writing for a Zionist periodical, Chukovsky borrowed his strongest illustrations of the reality of a primordial nation from the Russian, or, strictly speaking, the imperial literary canon, which he obviously meant as an ethnic/national canon. But whether Russian or Jewish, true cultural greatness was only possible for him as an expression of the collective national genius, and the true artists were particles of the "flesh and blood" of their "centuries-old" national bodies. Chukovsky conveyed this familiar romantic trope of literary geniuses as embodying the soul of their nations through a distinct neopositivist language and comparisons with the natural world. His system of proofs clearly prioritized natural sciences and social theories based on them.

Aspiring conscious Zionists—the readers of the new periodicals, the actors on the new emerging political scene—were expected to acquire scientific knowledge about the nation and problematize the terms of their own national belonging and hence their political goals. In the discourse of new nationalism, elaborated for the Diaspora or directed at the land that Zionists claimed as their national home, the most valuable fields of knowledge were history, geography (including practical data on climate and soils), statistics (anthropometric, medical, and social), and economics. Mass Jewish periodicals of the early twentieth century addressed these subjects in hundreds of articles that discussed the "nation" from philosophical, historical, political, and biological perspectives.[62] Education programs composed by Zionist intellectuals for popular Zionist circles, especially for young Zionists, reflected the same orientation toward modern knowledge. A typical program of this sort, put together by the Moscow-based Committee for the Organization of Theoretical Work in Jewish Youth Circles (Program for the Study of the National Question), was publicized in *Evreiskaia Zhizn'* in 1905.[63] It opened with the subsection "Nation from the Point of View of Anthropology." Under this rubric, young Zionists were advised to read Russian translations of *L'Anthopologie* by Paul Topinard (as a general textbook), *Les Lois psychologiques de l'évolution des peuples* by Gustav Le Bon (in which he developed a view of history as a product of racial or national character), and the third volume (*The Nature of Human Society*) of the three-volume work by the Russian positivist sociologist and historian Nikolai Kareev, *The Main Problems of the Philosophy of History* (Kareev understood sociology as a nomological science in relation to all other, phenomenological sciences; he also developed a theory of the "national character" rooted in the racial makeup of a group).[64] Kareev's volume was listed as a take-home reading, but one chapter, "Anthropological Data," which offered "a systematic treatment of the problems of race, cultural group, and nation taken together," was singled out for group reading and discussion.[65] Other important works mentioned and annotated in the program included Russian translations of Alfred Fouillée's *Psychologie du peuple français*, Vladimir Solov'ev's *The National Question in Russia*, Alexander Gradovskii's volume *Articles and Public Lectures on the National Question, The Slavonic Question and the War of 1877, The Polish Question*, and a few others. The list in its entirety signaled that the national question was a universal problem of humanity and the main format for modern political subjectivity as well as that in the Russian Empire, not only Jews but also Slavs, the state-bearing people, struggled with the difficulties and challenges of national politics. Building on these conclusions, the program culminated with a section somewhat awkwardly titled "The Question of the Existence of the Jewish Nation and Cultural Trends among the Jews."[66] Here, the recommended reading included works by Simon Dubnov, Ahad Ha'am, Moses Hess, and Daniel Chwolson, but the two works that opened the list were again by race scientists: Solomon Trivus, whose article in *Voskhod* asserted that Jews, scientifically speaking, were not a religious group and should be considered a nation, and Ignacy Maurycy Judt, the Polish Jewish Zionist author of the monographic study *Jews as a Physical Race* (*Żydzi jako rasa fizyczna*, in the original).[67] The instruction regarding Judt read:

> Content. In this wonderfully prepared work on Jewish anthropology the author arranges all that has been said on this question before him into a system; he also checks anthropological conclusions against historical data. Having thoroughly examined all this substantial material, he advances his own hypothesis (For the take-home reading).
> It is useful to check your knowledge [after the reading is complete] and formulate an independent point of view using the earlier general works [to reflect on Judt's study]. This can be done during the discussion [of Judt's work] (For the group discussion).[68]

It should be noted that the translation of Judt's work was one of the very first undertakings of *Evreiskaia Zhizn'*, which published the entire book in installments throughout 1904.[69] The choice of this scientific monograph by a mass political Zionist periodical must have signified its special relevance for the cause. The very decision to popularize a specialized scientific work among the ideologically motivated readers of *Evreiskaia Zhizn'* suggested their awareness regarding the role of modern science in Jewish nationalism and interest in "race" as a foundation of scientifically constructed nationality.

TWO

MEDITERRANEAN AS NEW EUROPEAN

Race and Europeanness in Zionism and Other New Nationalisms

> The goal of this essay... should be perfectly clear: an exposition and critique of the dominant theories, by means of an analysis of the anthropological data and relevant facts, so that in the end we can offer an answer to the following question: What does it mean for the Jews to be a pure race?
>
> Ignacy Maurycy Judt, *The Jews as a Race*, 1903

THE POLITICS OF EUROCENTRIC ZIONISM: IGNACY MAURYCY JUDT IN *EVREISKAIA ZHIZN'*

The editors of *Evreiskaia Zhizn'* did not even bother to adapt the Russian translation of Ignacy Maurycy Judt's work for a non-academic audience. It was hastily translated and published in serialized form in five consecutive issues in 1904. The text introduced readers to a respectable international academic tradition of studies of the Jewish race, critically engaging with different schools, theories, and authors. It considered Carl Vogt, Bernhard Blechmann, Josef Deniker, Constantine Ikow, and many other leading European anthropologists. An inquiry into theories was followed by a review of classifications of the Jewish race and by a meticulous analysis of the available anthropometric statistics assembled by the leading anthropologists. Measurements and indexes were grouped in tables according to Judt's understanding of the most stable attributes of race: skull index, height, and eye and hair color. Sometimes tables featured non-Jewish anthropometric statistics, too, which Judt needed for his conclusions about the purity of the Jewish race. The entire work embodied the ideal of scientific positivism and objectivity. Judt even exposed shortcomings of the anthropological method that could potentially compromise his conclusions. Thus, he admitted that anthropologists used different designations for color indicators. If some (for example, John Beddoe) distinguished "light," "chestnut" (*kashtanovyi*), "dark," and "black" types, others (for example, Bernhard Blechmann) classified "blonds," "light-chestnut," "dark-chestnut," and "black" types, and still others (for example, Samuel Weissenberg), "blonds," "brunets," and "transitional colors."[1] Moreover, all these categories underwent multiple translations from and to different languages: "One may assume that the English 'brown' and the German 'braun' are identical with the 'brown hair' type [*shaten*], and that 'black' and 'schwarz,' according to our understanding, are brunets. But what do we do with Majer and Kopernicki's system and where do we classify brunets if we have a special group of the black-haired?"[2]

Having honestly admitted these incongruities, Judt nonetheless proceeded with cataloging anthropometric data. He simply reduced the whole variety of color indicators to three basic groups: blond, brown-haired, and brunet. In a similar and obviously not entirely innocent manner, he homogenized all other anthropometric indicators. Judt was thus preparing his raw material for the book's main conclusion, which stated the homogeneity of the Jewish race.

Judt's study showed that contrary to the stereotypical image of a dolichocephalic Semite, Jews were predominantly brachycephalic (short-headed). In addition, he uncovered no statistical substantiation of the division of Jews into the Semitic Sephardic

ЕВРЕЙСКАЯ ЖИЗНЬ.

Въ library много разъ упоминается термінъ хеть—сынъ Ханаана, Кетчима, по словамъ легенды, были татарами Евpoпейца (Бытіе XVI, 3, 45). Авраамъ пріобрёлъ, свою и пещеру отъ одного хеттянина (Бытіе XXVIII) Исавъ и Галаамъ — жены Исава были родомъ изъ этого народа (Бытіе XXXVI, 2, 3). Тоцарь Давидъ Ахимелехъ былъ также хеттянинъ (I Самуил XXVI, 6). Есть и еще множество указаній на тот же родъ (II Самуил XI, 27; Бытіе XV, 15—20; Судей III, 5—6 и т. д.).

Антропологический типъ хеттянъ рисуется лучше, чемъ рисовали черты типовъ древнихъ евреевъ. Многіе памятники относятся и

Хеттейскіе солдаты, срисованные съ гробницы Рамзеса II, около Qurban (по Мадпорг 1887).

обозначены хеттейскіе древностей есть свидетельствуютъ объ исключительности этого племени изъ числа семитической организаціи. Можно, однако, признавать, что семитскіе кушитскіе предметы лежащихъ, представ чертамъ, карикатурными форм. Тыл ихъ были мы и съ наклонными чертами малаго устойчиво, что услово-отражены выступающія скулы, широкій носикъ, тестими губки, приминутыми волосами, низко приплюснутный передь, густыхъ волосяной покровъ и глазки, совпадающая внѣ коренящихъ птичьему носу, невысокій ростъ.

Каковы происхождение хеттянъ? Conjder усматриваютъ въ нихъ предковъ Туранской расы, т. е. явилась монгольской, получила это родство съ басками, ругусами и и всточными финскими племена. Между прочимъ, Cuturax усматривается на лицахъ всех хеттъ, какой предписывается таки Моисеевъ, т. е. выдающих скулахъ а длиннаго черепа, подобно

ЕВРЕИ КАКЪ ФИЗИЧЕСКАЯ РАСА.

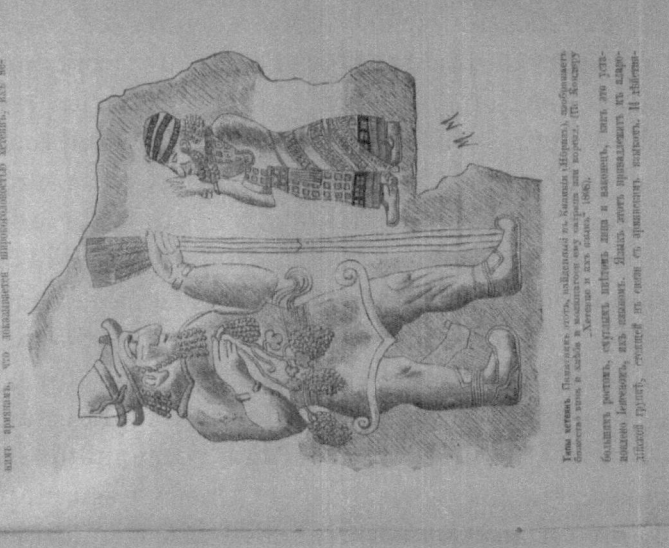

дней. Но Лешанъ (1894) доказываетъ, что имѣетъ это родственныя признакъ, что показываетъ широколицевостью черепа, какъ Константин и ихъ сыны" 1896).

Типы хеттянъ. Сложеніе ихъ, Папинамъ въ Кадышѣ (Египетъ), приближается ихъ и слабо и малогатлое ему острымъ для науки. (В. Мазеру болѣе рослое, сухая губы и кадончикъ, какъ ли установленное. Лицомъ, далее ихъ внимали. Плодъ лицо призывается въ спущеннымъ боковыхъ, въ скулистый. Лицо съ остатка по сами съ другимъ партий. И лицъявно какой бритъ, строгій но самъ съ другимъ партіи и другой на

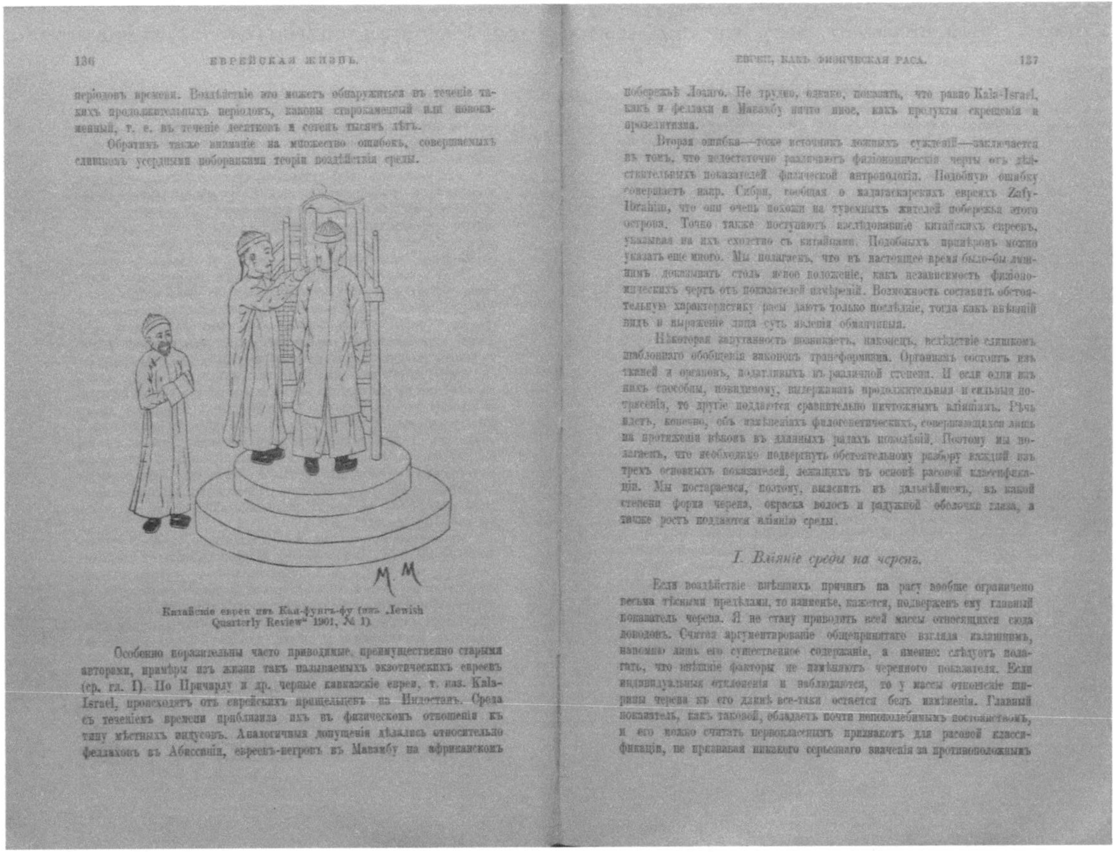

136 ЕВРЕЙСКАЯ ЖИЗНЬ.

періодовъ времени. Воздѣйствіе это можетъ обнаружиться въ теченіе такихъ продолжительныхъ періодовъ, каковы старокаменный или новокаменный, т. е. въ теченіе десятковъ и сотенъ тысячъ лѣтъ.

Обратимъ также вниманіе на множество ошибокъ, совершаемыхъ слишкомъ усердными поборниками теоріи воздѣйствія среды.

Китайскіе евреи изъ Кай-фунгъ-фу (изъ „Jewish Quarterly Review" 1901, № 1).

Особенно поразительны часто приводимые, преимущественно старыми авторами, примѣры изъ жизни такъ называемыхъ экзотическихъ евреевъ (ср. гл. I). По Причарду и др. черные кавказскіе евреи, т. наз. Kala-Israel, происходятъ отъ еврейскихъ пришельцевъ изъ Индостана. Среда съ теченіемъ времени приблизила ихъ въ физическомъ отношеніи къ типу мѣстныхъ индусовъ. Аналогичныя допущенія дѣлались относительно феллаховъ въ Абиссиніи, евреевъ-негровъ въ Маваибу на африканскомъ

ЕВРЕИ, КАКЪ ФИЗИЧЕСКАЯ РАСА. 137

побережьѣ Лоанго. Не трудно, однако, показать, что равно Kala-Israel, какъ и феллахи и Маваибу ничто иное, какъ продукты скрещенія и прозелитизма.

Вторая ошибка—тоже источникъ ложныхъ сужденій—заключается въ томъ, что недостаточно различаютъ физіономическія черты отъ дѣйствительныхъ показателей физической антропологіи. Подобную ошибку совершаетъ напр. Сибри, сообщая о мадагаскарскихъ евреяхъ Zafy-Ibrahim, что они очень похожи на туземныхъ жителей побережья этого острова. Точно также поступаютъ изслѣдователи китайскихъ евреевъ, указывая на ихъ сходство съ китайцами. Подобныхъ примѣровъ можно указать еще много. Мы полагаемъ, что въ настоящее время было-бы лишнимъ доказывать столь ясное положеніе, какъ независимость физіономическихъ чертъ отъ показателей измѣреній. Возможность составить обстоятельную характеристику расы даютъ только послѣдніе, тогда какъ внѣшній видъ и выраженіе лица суть явленія обманчивыя.

Нѣкоторая запутанность возникаетъ, наконецъ, вслѣдствіе слишкомъ шаблоннаго обобщенія законовъ трансформизма. Организмъ состоитъ изъ тканей и органовъ, податливыхъ въ различной степени. И если одни изъ нихъ способны, повидимому, выдерживать продолжительныя и сильныя потрясенія, то другіе поддаются сравнительно ничтожнымъ вліяніямъ. Рѣчь идетъ, конечно, объ измѣненіяхъ филогенетическихъ, совершающихся лишь на протяженіи вѣковъ въ длинныхъ рядахъ поколѣній. Поэтому мы полагаемъ, что необходимо подвергнуть обстоятельному разбору каждый изъ трехъ основныхъ показателей, лежащихъ въ основѣ расовой классификаціи. Мы постараемся, поэтому, выяснить въ дальнѣйшемъ, въ какой степени форма черепа, окраска волосъ и радужной оболочки глаза, а также ростъ поддаются вліянію среды.

I. Вліяніе среды на черепъ.

Если воздѣйствіе внѣшнихъ причинъ на расу вообще ограничено весьма тѣсными предѣлами, то наименѣе, кажется, подверженъ ему главный показатель черепа. Я не стану приводить всей массы относящихся сюда доводовъ. Считая аргументированіе общепринятаго взгляда излишнимъ, напомню лишь его существенное содержаніе, а именно: слѣдуетъ полагать, что внѣшніе факторы не измѣняютъ черепного показателя. Если индивидуальныя отклоненія и наблюдаются, то у массы отношеніе ширины черепа къ его длинѣ все-таки остается безъ измѣненія. Главный показатель, какъ таковой, обладаетъ почти непоколебимымъ постоянствомъ, и его можно считать первокласснымъ признакомъ для расовой классификаціи, не придавая никакого серьезнаго значенія за противоположнымъ

Fig. 2.2 Images included in Ignacy Maurycy Judt's "Jews as a Physical Race," *Evreiskaia Zhizn'* 2 (1904): 136.

Fig. 2.3 Images included in Ignacy Maurycy Judt's "Jews as a Physical Race," *Evreiskaia Zhizn'* 2 (1904): 138–39.

racial type and the Ashkenazi racial type: "such a distinction between their skulls does not exist."[3] And, finally, Judt's comparative data showed zero correlation between Jewish and non-Jewish skulls and color indicators. His general conclusion read: "Almost everywhere, Jews exhibit a predominance of the dark type over the light type. However, one cannot assume that this feature is typical of them as [representatives] of the Semitic tribe. Among Bedouins, for example, the blond type is very rare, but among Jews the proportion of blonds and light-eyed [individuals] reaches 30 percent, and of brunets—30–40 percent, while dark-eyed individuals make up close to 50 percent. These numbers testify to a substantial proportion of light-eyed and blond elements within those racial groups that made up the Jewish people."[4]

The only Jewish racial indicator that showed any correlation with non-Jewish indicators was height. Unlike many other race scientists, Judt considered height to be a racial indicator, but one that could change under the influence of environment. He readily admitted a wide range of fluctuations of Jewish height measurements (up to nine centimeters), as this fact did not threaten the otherwise clear picture of "uniformity of the Jewish physical type" as reflected in "uniformity that is evident in skull index (according to Judt, up to 80 percent of all Jews were short-headed, with a skull index of 80–83 - *MM*), and color of hair and eyes."[5] Judt did not classify his uniform short-headed Jewish race as Semitic: the real Semites populated Asia, whereas Jews were members of European racial families.

Even if accepted as accurate, Judt's ratios of color indicators hardly offered unconditional evidence of the uniformity of race, especially against such impressive scholarship arguing otherwise. Rather, Judt's calculations might convince readers who actively wanted to see them as objective proof of Jewish racial uniformity. It is obvious that many such readers were among the politically motivated *Evreiskaia Zhizn'* audience. Even Judt's ideological Eurocentrism would not be unfamiliar to Russian and European Zionists. The propensity to see Jews as Europeans—at least in cultural terms—was quite strong in Zionism, and Theodor Herzl himself was the leading proponent of such a view.[6] Moreover, Eurocentrism could also help Judt persuade the Jewish audience outside of Zionist circles. In fact, among his most qualified readers in Russia was the Moscow anthropologist Aaron (Arkadii) El'kind. Although El'kind never associated himself with Zionism, in Judt's synthesis, he sensed a kindred impulse toward imagining Jews as a European (read: modern) race/nation.

In his review of the original Polish edition of *Żydzi jako rasa fizyczna* (1902) in the leading Russian anthropological journal, El'kind praised his colleague for going beyond the usual admission of physiognomic uniformity of Jews and demonstrating the uniformity of their main physical traits.[7] He paid special attention to the way Judt protected this Jewish racial uniformity from being eroded by the measurements of Jews of the Russian Caucasus. Judt claimed that the Caucasian Jews had produced "confusion" "in the physical anthropology of their [i.e., Jewish] people.... The history of the stream of Jews who moved to the Caucasus and the conditions of their life among local traders greatly differs from the history of European Jews."[8] Allegedly, ancient ancestors of the contemporary Caucasian Jews had arrived in the region prematurely, at an early, still formative, stage of their development as a race. They mixed with the local population, which had detrimental consequences for their racial Jewishness. True Jews "did not racially mix with the indigenous population either through proselytizing or through mixed marriages. Individual examples of racial mixing did not affect the condition of the race. Caucasian Jews present the only exception to this rule."[9] El'kind was most certainly emboldened by Judt's conclusion when in his own dissertation he went as far as to declare the Caucasian Jews "allotypical," because they undermined the image of the physically homogeneous and essentially

European (urbanized, participating in industrial capitalism) Jewish race.[10]

The fact that El'kind's review embraced the theme of Europeanness without directly engaging the claim that Jews were not Semites is indicative of the range of possible interpretations of the Europeanness trope. According to Judt, Jews had already ceased to be Semites in biblical Palestine, where he admitted that racial mixing resulted in the formation of the Jews. "Purity" of race, therefore, meant not its monoracial composition, but preservation in the Diaspora of the initial mixture. Obviously, Judt was not the first anthropologist to assume the fact of racial mixing in ancient Palestine nor the first to deny that some groups within the Jewish people were Semites. For example, the German anthropologist Constantine Ikow distinguished three Jewish types and classified only one of them as Semitic—the dolichocephalic Jews of the Balkans, Turkey, Algeria, Spain, and Italy. Ikow assigned them to what he called the Semitic Mediterranean race (as we shall see, Judt used the same concept in a different sense). The two other types, according to Ikow, were the products of racial crossing in the Diaspora and hence were not Semitic and "original" Jewish: the brachycephalic Jews of Western Europe, who intermixed with native populations, and the Russian Jews, who showed no Semitic characteristics at all.[11] The French scholar Gustav Lagneau registered Semitic traits only among the Jews of North Africa. He claimed that the Jews of the Mediterranean had been transformed by mixture with Greek and Roman proselytes and the Jews of Eastern Europe were Slavs and Germans in terms of their racial makeup.[12] The result of such desemitization of Jews was the split of their collective body into two or three parts, to the effect of potentially denying their coherence as a race and legitimate nation. Judt's desemitization, to the contrary, worked to objectify the idea of Jews as a uniform European race and hence a legitimate nation. It is here that he went against the Zionist anthropological mainstream: the majority of Judt's Zionist colleagues would agree with him regarding the racial uniformity of modern Jews and the racial crossing that took place in ancient Canaan but would argue that Jews crossed primarily with members of other Semitic races, who were physically, culturally, and linguistically closer to them.[13]

Trying to scientifically justify his revisionism, Judt reconstructed the racial composition of the ancient Canaan population with great care. Once again he had to admit the limitations of his objective method: "It is not easy to apply the caliper and measuring tape of a modern scholar to an object [reconstructed] on the basis of historical-archaeological and legendary speculations."[14] Yet Judt engaged in precisely such speculations. He assumed the existence of a Jewish people with a certain racial makeup during the "Patriarchal period" before the Israelite kingdom, and he traced these Jews throughout the "period of Jewish statehood," at which time they actively mixed with local races in Palestine. In the end, "the long-skull Semitic [Jewish] individual" amalgamated into itself physical elements of alien racial types, especially of the "short-headed population of middle Asia."[15] In Judt's presentation, Jews were "race-conquerors" who racially absorbed the indigenous population. "Here, in Canaan, we meet one branch of the above-mentioned racial group—Hittites—who were originally from Central Asia. Besides, here we find Amorites, who arrived from Western Europe via Northern Africa, and also Kushites from Southern countries. [Their presence] explains the physical deviation of the ancient Jews from the initial type. This could have happened either through direct mixing [with representatives of each type], or through the mediation of other peoples, especially Canaanites who had already amalgamated with Amorites, Hittites, and Kushites."[16] By ascribing each group to a distinctive racial body that then engaged in mixing as collective entities, Judt mentally homogenized inhabitants of biblical Canaan just as he previously homogenized ancient and modern Jews. Moreover, he attributed the same racializing and

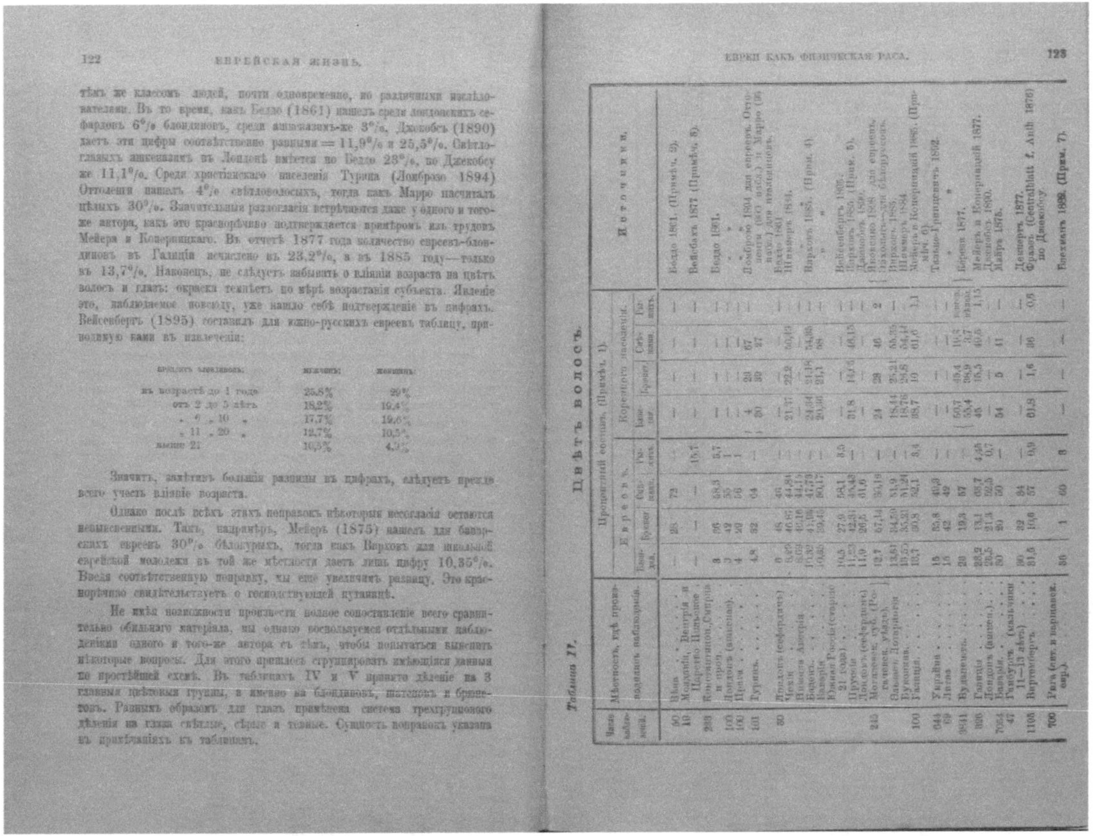
122 ЕВРЕЙСКАЯ ЖИЗНЬ.

тѣмъ же классомъ людей, почти одновременно, но различными изслѣдователями. Въ то время, какъ Беддо (1861) нашелъ среди лондонскихъ сефардовъ 6% блондиновъ, среди ашкеназимъ-же 3%, Джекобсъ (1890) даетъ эти цифры соотвѣтственно равными = 11,9% и 25,5%. Свѣтлоглазыхъ ашкеназимъ въ Лондонѣ имѣется по Беддо 23%, по Джекобсу же 11,1%. Среди христіанскаго населенія Турина (Ломброзо 1894) Оттоленги нашелъ 4% свѣтловолосыхъ, тогда какъ Марро насчиталъ цѣлыхъ 30%. Значительныя разногласія встрѣчаются даже у одного и того-же автора, какъ это краснорѣчиво подтверждается примѣромъ изъ трудовъ Мейера и Коперницкаго. Въ отчетѣ 1877 года количество евреевъ-блондиновъ въ Галиціи исчислено въ 23,2%, а въ 1885 году—только въ 13,7%. Наконецъ, не слѣдуетъ забывать о вліяніи возраста на цвѣтъ волосъ и глазъ: окраска темнѣетъ по мѣрѣ возрастанія субъекта. Явленіе это, наблюдаемое повсюду, уже нашло себѣ подтвержденіе въ цифрахъ. Вейсенбергъ (1895) составилъ для южно-русскихъ евреевъ таблицу, приводимую нами въ извлеченіи:

Процентъ блондиновъ:	мужчинъ:	женщинъ:
въ возрастѣ до 1 года	25,8%	29%
отъ 2 до 5 лѣтъ	18,2%	19,4%
„ 6 „ 10 „	17,7%	19,6%
„ 11 „ 20 „	12,7%	10,5%
выше 21	10,5%	4,3%

Значитъ, замѣтивъ большія разницы въ цифрахъ, слѣдуетъ прежде всего учесть вліяніе возраста.

Однако послѣ всѣхъ этихъ поправокъ нѣкоторыя несогласія остаются невыясненными. Такъ, напримѣръ, Мейеръ (1875) нашелъ для баварскихъ евреевъ 30% бѣлокурыхъ, тогда какъ Вирховъ для школьной еврейской молодежи въ той же мѣстности даетъ лишь цифру 10,35%. Введя соотвѣтственную поправку, мы еще увеличимъ разницу. Это краснорѣчиво свидѣтельствуетъ о господствующей путаницѣ.

Не имѣя возможности произвести полное сопоставленіе всего сравнительно обильнаго матеріала, мы однако воспользуемся отдѣльными наблюденіями одного и того-же автора съ тѣмъ, чтобы попытаться выяснить нѣкоторые вопросы. Для этого пришлось сгруппировать имѣющіяся данныя по простѣйшей схемѣ. Въ таблицахъ IV и V принято дѣленіе на 3 главныя цвѣтовыя группы, а именно на блондиновъ, шатеновъ и брюнетовъ. Разнымъ образомъ для глазъ примѣнена система трехгруппового дѣленія на глаза свѣтлые, сѣрые и темные. Сущность поправокъ указана въ примѣчаніяхъ къ таблицамъ.

ЕВРЕИ КАКЪ ФИЗИЧЕСКАЯ РАСА. 123

Таблица 17.

Цвѣтъ волосъ.

Число наблюденій.	Мѣстность, гдѣ производились наблюденія.	Процентный составъ (Примѣч. 1). Евреевъ.				Коренного населенія.				Источники.
		Блондъ.	Брюнет.	Шатен.	Рыжих.	Блонд.	Брюнет.	Шатен.	Рыжих.	

Fig. 2.4 A typical page from Judt's "Jews as a Physical Race," *Evreiskaia Zhizn'* 2 (1904): 122–23.

essentializing gaze to his sources, suggesting, for example, that "Egyptian artists were capable of distinguishing racial colors," and hence one could use Egyptian art as a source of objective information on skin, eye, and hair colors.[17]

We have to remember that this long academic and partially even esoteric narrative appeared in a political periodical for the masses at a moment of rising political tension. It vividly exposed the role of science in Zionism and the importance of education in becoming a conscious Zionist. Those readers of *Evreiskaia Zhizn'* who embraced the message and felt motivated to work through Judt's study until the end could derive from it a great admiration for physical anthropology that operated with mass data, mathematical calculations, and archaeological material evidence. They would learn that Jews had acquired their present racial composition, which was not Semitic, in Canaan through mixing with local racial types. The only Semitic heritage that contemporary short-headed Jews retained was their language. In the Diaspora, Jews preserved their racial wholeness and uniformity and did not mix. Readers might be surprised to learn that these same racial types that had transformed the Jewish race in biblical times also partook in the formation of European races. Therefore, Jews' proper place was not among Semites but in the Alpine-Himalayan branch of the Asiatic-European racial family and in the Mediterranean race, now reconceptualized as a core European race.[18] So, what was the immediate political utility of such a complex message?

MEDITERRANEAN RACE AND SUBALTERN NATIONALISMS

When Judt was working on his magnum opus, the Mediterranean race concept had just reached its peak of influence. It entered mainstream anthropological discourse in 1883, "when the term 'Mediterranean' was first used for Europe's short, 'sallow' southern and Atlantic dolichocephals."[19] In 1899, William Ripley, a professor of political economy at Harvard University and the author of one of the most influential turn-of-the-century scientific classifications of races, *The Races of Europe* (1899), had firmly established the place of the Mediterranean race on the anthropological classificatory map. Ripley distinguished only three European races: Nordic, Alpine, and Mediterranean. The latter race included African, Middle Eastern, and Southeast European elements. "Beyond the Pyrenees Africa begins," wrote Ripley, thus aphoristically encapsulating the transitional place of the Mediterranean race precisely at the imagined European border with blackness.[20] Writing ten years after Ripley, Judt was already able to safely state that "in the anthropological sense, Europe is divided into three main parts": the Mediterranean race ("Greeks, Italians, Sicilians, Sardinians, and Spaniards"), the Teutonic (Nordic) race ("the population of Scandinavia, Northern Germans, Danes, Flemish, English, Scotts, Irish, and others"), and the Alpine race ("French, Southern Germans, Swiss, and Slavs").[21] He went on to anchor Jews in two of the three main European races, but this was not at all what Ripley's classification had implied. William Ripley did not believe that Jews constituted a race. He referred to Samuel Weissenberg, among other authorities, to argue that Jews were everywhere transformed by racial mixture with the locals and that the Jewish initial racial composition was altered by wholesale conversions of gentiles to the Jewish faith, as was presumably proved by the cases of Khazars and the Falashas.[22] Ripley's physical description of the Mediterranean race as dolichocephalic, short in stature, and dark-skinned (which compromised the Europeanness of this race bordering on the world "beyond the Pyrenees") did not resonate with Judt's description of Jews.

It is absolutely fascinating to see how scholars such as Judt, advocating on behalf of peoples with questionable chances of being regarded as full-fledged "Europeans," claimed the Mediterranean race concept for themselves. The most famous representative of this cohort was the Italian (or rather Sicilian) scholar Giuseppe Sergi, the founder of the distinctive Roman anthropological school and Italy's first eugenics society. An Italian nationalist, Sergi not only classified Italians as a Mediterranean race and thus homogenized and ascertained as Europeans, he also distinguished them from the French Celts and German Aryans. Aryans, in particular, in his scheme of things, were barbarians who conquered and destroyed the superior Mediterranean civilization.[23] Richard McMahon has proposed viewing scholars such as Judt and Sergi as the new classifiers, who "invested superiority in the Mediterranean, Deniker's Easteuropean or Dinaric races, or 'European' type A blood," and who remained "far less hegemonic" than the academic mandarins of race science such as Paul Broca or William Ripley.[24] However, by appropriating the influential classificatory concepts from the margins of the international academic and geopolitical arenas, they had accomplished at least two important tasks: they promoted rival nationalist narratives, and they splintered hegemonic race classification discourses from within.[25] Judt's Mediterraneanizing of Jews confirms this observation and exposes yet another aspect of the revisionism of the new classifiers: they legitimized their narratives through embracing even more aggressive Eurocentrism. The Mediterranean as a site of race formation suited this purpose particularly well, for it embodied the idea of Europe as a borderland, an epitome of modernity, development, dynamism, and change. Sergi introduced the Mediterranean basin as a cosmopolitan space between Europe, Asia, and Africa (and simply "one of the happiest habitable regions of the globe"); an "anthropological unit" that has become "the center of civilization and of dispersion."[26] His Mediterranean was a hybrid space defined by contacts, movement, crossing, and diffusion, a space that allowed "provincializ[ing] Europe" without really decentering the European civilization narrative.[27]

This type of Mediterranean revisionism was not entirely new. It can be traced back to the founding father of modern geography, the celebrated naturalist and traveler, Alexander von Humboldt. Among his many contributions to modern scholarship was a thirty-volume account of his 1799–1804 travels in the New World, to which he applied the neologism "American Mediterranean." Humboldt Mediterraneanized America in much the same terms as Sergi would later Mediterraneanize Europe, and hence, as Susan Gillman writes, "Humboldt's American Mediterranean reinvented Europe as much as it rediscovered America."[28] Humboldt approached the Mediterranean as a structure, which enabled comparison and inclusion of new places in the sphere of civilization, and simultaneously served as a paradigmatic model of the cosmos ("the Mediterranean considered as the starting point for the representation of the relations which have laid the foundation of the gradual extension of the idea of the cosmos").[29] Writing almost a century after Humboldt, Judt, Sergi, and other new classifiers still believed that the cosmos was centered on Europe and, like Humboldt, perceived the Mediterranean as a place and a structure. This Mediterranean performed the demiurgic and transformative function of allowing the reinvention of Europe through rethinking comparative frameworks, connections, and racial mixing and crossing and positing a new logic of inclusion and exclusion.

Being an example of such a revisionist narrative, Judt's *Jews as a Physical Race* operated within the Eurocentric civilizational discourse and extended Europe's frontiers instead of narrowing them. It claimed Europe for the Jews instead of advancing a politics of exclusion. Moreover, unlike Sergi, Alfredo Niceforo and other promoters of the long-headed Italian Mediterraneans, Judt had accomplished his Mediterraneanizing of the Jews without claiming racial superiority. This difference between the Jewish and Italian Mediterranean counternarratives appears to be purely political, having nothing to do with the concept of the Mediterranean race itself and everything to do with the politics of race embraced by individual scholars, politicians, and their mass followings. Indeed, the analytical language of the new classifiers, and especially the terms that they invented to convey the dynamic nature of the Mediterranean, were composite or even hybrid, and could theoretically work both ways—extending the civilizational borders of Europe or narrowing them through the politics of exclusion. Thus, Sergi built his theory on the assumptions that the three main human varieties (African, Mediterranean, and Nordic) all extended "from the great African stock" and formed "one *species*, which I call *Eurafrican*" and that "the primitive civilization of the Eurafricans is Afro-Mediterranean, becoming eventually Afro-European."[30] His language and vision here appear extremely inclusive and bear no trace of exclusive Italian nationalism or colonialism.[31] Sergi's theory was also tolerant toward Jews, whom he, however, classified as Semites and viewed as a branch of the Eurafricans—a racial group closely related to the Mediterraneans. As he wrote in 1895 in *Origine e diffusione della stirpe mediterranea*: "In the Mediterranean, it is almost impossible to distinguish the Semitic heads of the Phoenicians and the Jews from other non-Semitic heads.... Moreover, where can one find an antique or a modern people who are not a composition of various elements?"[32] Finally, Sergi explicitly counterposed his understanding of the Mediterranean race to a more restrictive French interpretation: "The term 'Mediterranean,' as I use it, has not the extension given to it by French anthropologists.... I understand by it all those primitive peoples who have occupied the basin of the Mediterranean and have such fundamental physical characteristics in common as to enable us to assign to them a single place of origin, which must be in east Africa and to the north of the Equator. The French give the race as they term it, a more restricted and partial sense, so as to exclude many of the populations which belong to it."[33]

All Sergi's Eurafricans, Afro-Mediterranean, and Afro-Europeans hybridized not just the hegemonic classificatory discourse of race science, but the very scientific foundations of European nationalism and colonialism. But if this was the case, how did Sergi eventually arrive at the unequivocal propaganda of Italian national superiority? A comparison with Judt's Mediterranean theory suggests an explanation: Judt's Mediterraneanizing and Europeanizing of Jews occurs from beginning to end on a transnational scale. In Judt's narrative, the Mediterranean could signify the Canaan or indeed the entire Mediterranean basin, but it could not be reduced to any past or present nation-state. In other words, it retained its status as a superstructure, a symbol, or a model of the ideal Europe. Politically, Judt was satisfied with the opportunity to scientifically challenge the consensus that denied Jews the status of a civilized (that is, a European) complete nation. Sergi's political context and intentions were different and his nationalism was territorially grounded, thus motivating him to engage in direct national competition. The diminishing hybridity of his conceptual language was proportional to the rising degree of politicization of his discourse. When the target was specifically the northern German—the "Aryan" neighbor—Sergi's conclusions were clear and straightforward: "The two classic civilizations, Greek and Latin, were not Aryan, but Mediterranean. The Aryans were savages when they invaded Europe: they destroyed in part the superior civilization of the Neolithic populations and could not have created the Greco-Latin civilization."[34]

Regardless of these important differences between Sergi's and Judt's positions, the Mediterranean race concept could accommodate both the Jewish and Italian national projects, exposing the most essential connection between them—the European connection. Moreover, the same European connection brought the least obvious "new classifier," W. E. B. Du Bois, to the Mediterranean race. Du Bois's discourse on Negritude revealed the same tensions between the "double consciousness" complexity and nationalist simplicity, between the Mediterranean as a model of an alternative, dynamic, and inclusive Europe and unequivocally ethnocentric claims. In his address to the Omaha Philosophical Society in April 1917, provocatively titled "The African Origin of the Grecian Civilization," Du Bois directly quoted Sergi to reinforce his own argument about the African origin of Mediterranean civilization and the key role of African races in European history:

> Professor Sergi, of the University of Rome, has founded a new study of the origin of European civilization upon the remarkable archeological finds, entitled "The Mediterranean Race." From this masterly work I choose the following: "Until recent years the Greeks and Romans were regarded as Aryans, and then as Aryanized peoples; the great discoveries in the Mediterranean have overturned all these views. Today, although a few belated supporters of Aryanism still remain, it is becoming clear that the most ancient civilization of the Mediterranean is not of Aryan origin. The Aryans were savages when they invaded Europe [see the next part of the quote above]. . . . The primitive populations of Europe originated in Africa and the basin of the Mediterranean was the chief center of movement when the African migrations reached the center and north of Europe."[35]

Du Bois's interpretation of Sergi's *Mediterranean Race* in the address revealed not only that the notion of a Mediterranean margin had no exact limits but also that the concept itself could be appropriated by the actors speaking on behalf of those "beyond the Pyrenees." Paul Gilroy's brilliant reading of Du Bois's "double consciousness" helps clarify why Du Bois dwelled on such a Eurocentric concept in his efforts to define Negritude as an identity. Gilroy goes beyond the duality articulated by his protagonist and deeply resonates with the duality of the Russian Jewish identification ("one ever feels his twoness,—an American, a Negro; two souls, two thoughts, two unreconciled strivings") to recover a three-part structure underlying Du Bois's thinking: "The first is racially particularistic, the second nationalistic in that it derives from the nation state in which the ex-slaves but not-yet-citizens find themselves. . . . The third is diasporic or hemispheric, something global and universalist."[36]

Gilroy calls this the "unhappy symbiosis," but its "unhappiness" does not imply uniqueness. Judt and those who shared his views were facing much the same three-party deadlock when he desemiticized the Jews and traced their origin to the two main European races: he tried to introduce a racially particularistic view of Jewish groupness while at the same time preserving its transnational scale; he aspired to claim equal status for the Jews who deserved to be citizens based on their status as civilized Europeans; and he wanted to minimize the importance of the nation-state by promoting the Mediterranean as a space of communication, exchange, and movement.

In other words, the impossibility of thinking beyond the European civilization model and the shared aspiration to redefine the borders of European civilization, recenter its core, and revise the list of key actors brought intellectuals and scholars such as Judt, Du Bois, and Sergi to the Mediterranean race concept. The divergences of their Mediterraneanizing national projects told the most about the context and position from which the new classifiers spoke. Sergi's rhetoric was the most radical because Italian nationalism had just accomplished the task of establishing a nation-state, and Sergi had less interest in minimizing its centrality for his nationalist vision. Judt avoided any direct discussion of the relationship between a nation and a state, operating instead with terms that were indifferent to any national borders but stressed the normativity and Europeanness of the race. In his anthropological narrative, Canaan remained the most important part of the Mediterranean but not the place where the Jewish race would necessarily complete itself as a nation. The core element in his model was not the state but the cultural text to which he referred, the Hebrew Bible, which was also the founding text of Western/European civilization. And Du Bois had neither of these—a state nor a particular textual tradition that could be identified as a source of Western civilization. His main cultural reference, therefore, became classical heritage, especially Greek mythology, which he claimed for the pan-African race: "The Great Grecian epics are epics of an African people and Helen, the cause of the Trojan war, must henceforth be conceived as a beautiful brown skin girl.... The heroes of Homer shall, like the Prince of Morocco, wear the livery of the burnished sun and be knit by binding ties of the blood of Africa's clime from whence civilization took its primal rise."[37]

Whereas Judt's Zionist anthropology aimed at presenting Jews as a separate and uniform nation of European origin, Du Bois searched for ways to express double-belonging and double consciousness in terms of the racial hybridity that was so conveniently epitomized by the Mediterranean race concept: "Again we must admit, no matter how bitter the taste, that the mixed race has always been the great race—the pure race always the stagnant race."[38] This admission of Du Bois in the concluding part of the address summarizes the very essence of his deployment of the Mediterranean race concept and validates Gilroy's praise of him as a paragon of hybridity. Du Bois's and others' versions of racial Mediterraneanizing undermined modern territorial nationalism as based on a narrow and linear origin argument and the political subjectivity that was derived from it. In this sense, they predicated many later epistemological and ideological trends that today manifest themselves in projects such as Martin Bernal's "Black Athena," organized around the claim that "there are no simple origins.... The past... is better imagined as a river in which currents come together to form a unity, then diverge and combine with others to form new unities and so on. The uncertainty of this image should not lead to despair or paralysis. The fact that the chase is endless adds to, rather than detracts from, its fascination."[39]

VLADIMIR (ZEEV) JABOTINSKY'S MEDITERRANEAN ZIONISM

Who among the Russian Zionists shared such visions of origin and of Europe and considered the conversation with Sergi, Judt, and indirectly with Du Bois and other new classifiers and political thinkers and activists to be momentously relevant? It was Vladimir Jabotinsky, who at the time was a member of the *Evreiskaia Zhizn'* editorial board. Twenty years after *Żydzi jako rasa fizyczna* had appeared in Russian, Jabotinsky reproduced quotations from it almost verbatim in his exemplary Zionist novel *Samson the Nazarite* (originally written in Russian and published in installments in the Zionist journal *Razsvet* in 1926 and as a separate edition in Berlin in 1927).[40] This incorporation gives us a glimpse of the profound and lasting influence of Judt's anthropology on Jabotinsky.[41] Jabotinsky made the theme of initial racial mixture—the dilution of "local races" of Canaan in the "savory and dense blood of the gloomy [Jewish] colonizer"—the central theme of his novel. In one characteristic exchange, a Jewish (Danite) protagonist of the novel remarks, "Our blood is the blood of the chosen. It is like water from a well and must not be poured out in the street-puddles," but Samson corrects him: "We are not water, we are the salt. The others are the water. Strike the water with your hand and it flies asunder, but throw a handful of the salt in a cask of water and it will not be lost, for all the water in the cask will be made salty."[42]

In *Samson*, racial mixing was presented as a hierarchical racial colonization—justified in ancient times and when Jews were colonizers but unacceptable as a modern practice and especially with Jews as the colonized (Samson: "Your blood is a cup of wine; the other a cup of poison. Suppose they were mixed, what is left of the wine now? I am not one of you!").[43] Samson himself symbolized not the mixing and colonizing moment but its proud and self-conscious result. His unhappy relationships with two Philistine women, Semadar and her sister Elinoar (Delilah), permeated with treason and deception, were highly instructive warnings against any further racial mixing. Except for these complicated relationships, Samson was an ideal self-conscious Jew with the eye of a professionally trained race scientist, who could distinguish racial colors, head forms, and other anthropometric characteristics of the peoples of Canaan: "[Samson] not once visited the towns and villages of the Jebusites, the Girgasites, [and] the Hivites, and could distinguish between them at first sight, while he recognized Hittites by their backward-sloping foreheads, and narrow-lipped Amorites by their proud stature even from afar."[44] In a town square, he would observe "numerous aborigines, residents of Zorah. From their [spatial] arrangement, poses, and mood an attentive observer could reconstruct a complete picture of relationships between the two races."[45] "Among the Danite women were a number of ['quite typical'—omitted in the translation] Canaanite faces belonging to second and third wives, concubines, mothers-in-law, and sisters-in-law—forerunners of the process now beginning by which the heedless native stock was absorbed in the sharp strong blood of the sullen colonizers."[46]

Samson made his choice in favor of the Jewish nation following the call of his "sharp strong blood," being aware of his particular racial origin.[47] Jabotinsky made a similar choice around 1903, and we will follow his transformation in the next chapter. For now, it is important to keep in mind that Jabotinsky was working on his theory of nationalism simultaneously with the appearance of Judt's "Jews as a Physical Race" in *Evreiskaia Zhizn'*. Until his last days, Jabotinsky remained true not only to Judt's interpretation of the formation of the Jewish race but also to the understanding of Jewishness and nationalism that he had formed back in 1903–1904 and then continued to perfect in the course of the 1910s. In 1939 Jabotinsky personally translated into English his original definition of the normative nation from the early 1910s, retaining the "original racial spectrum" as the first condition of real nationhood.[48] Territoriality was second in importance, as was stated in the original 1911 definition. The 1939 version differed only in that it stressed the significance of having clearly designated "frontiers" (of a national territory), and in its consistent usage of the "minority-majority" language. Otherwise, according to Jabotinsky's 1911 definition (based on his earlier definitions), a complete ideal nation

> would have to be distinguished by a specific racial spectrum, sharply differentiated from the racial nature of its neighbors. It would have to inhabit continuous and clearly bounded territory from time immemorial; it would still be better if there were not alien minorities on the nation's territory that would thin out its national unity [in the 1939 English translation by Jabotinsky that had later been edited for publication: "inhabit from time immemorial a territory with clear cut frontiers, preferably an island, and that the territory should harbor all the members of the nation, so that there would be no scattered minorities abroad"].[49] It [the nation] should speak an original language, a native language that is not borrowed from anyone—at least, the fact and moment of borrowing would be impossible to trace. [1939: "It should speak a language entirely unlike that of any neighbor across any frontier; better still, a language unlike any other in the world, a language created by the nation itself and reflecting all phases of its thought and emotion"].[50] ... It should practice a national religion, not a borrowed one [1939: "like Islam in Persia"], but one of its own creation from the earliest times such as the religion of the Hindus [1939: "Buddhism in India"], or, at least, Judaism of the Jews.[51] And finally, it should possess a historic unbroken tradition common to all its parts, that is, a complete commonality of historical emotional experiences from the remotest antiquity.[52]

Throughout Jabotinsky's turbulent life, pragmatic considerations may have altered the ideal image, but racial self-preservation always remained at its basis, together with territoriality and cultural authenticity.[53] The importance of Palestine in this discourse, just as in Judt's narrative, rested on anthropological and historical foundations: it was the land where Jews acquired their unique racial spectrum and became the nation of Samsons. This learned, scientific appreciation of Palestine gradually developed into a real emotional attachment, which, however, never completely replaced Jabotinsky's original deep emotional and cultural attachment to Europe.[54] "I consider 'the East'—in the spiritual and common-life sense—the most offensive of all swear words, and I think that the Jew is the most ancient European," he admitted in *The Story of the Jewish Legion* in 1928.[55]

In 1930, four years after the publication of *Samson*, Jabotinsky revisited the anthropological story of Jews' racial transformation in Canaan and of Mediterranean race theory in the brochure *The Hebrew Accent*.[56] He reminded readers about the old lesson of Judt: although Hebrew was a Semitic language, Jews themselves were not Semites but a Mediterranean European race. "The language of Arabs developed in a climate and natural conditions that drastically differ from the conditions in our country.... And racial origin differs, too."[57] Echoing Judt once again, Jabotinsky wrote:

> At the beginning of the Jewish conquest Canaan was teeming with various tribes: Jebusites, Hittites, Amorites, Philistines, and many others; some of them were bits of European and Anatolian peoples, others were Hamites. But by the end of the Kings' period these tribes were no more or almost no more; most of them had dissolved within the tribes of Israel. This is how the Jewish race came into being—the "Mediterranean race," in which the blood and soul, and the features and tastes of the entire line of Northern and Western peoples, mixed and merged.... Although Hebrew and Arabic are Semitic languages, it does not mean that our Fathers spoke with an "Arabic accent."... We are European and our musical taste is European—the taste of Rubinstein, Mendelssohn, and Bizet.[58]

One had to look for musical kinship, Jabotinsky continued, not in the Arab language, but "in the languages of the West, especially in those that were also born and developed on the Mediterranean shores."[59]

By 1903, Jabotinsky, whose first language was Russian, had acquired fluent Italian (before he made a conscious decision to embrace Jewishness and Jewish nationalism and master Yiddish and Hebrew). Italian "Mediterranean shores" always remained his favorite European destination. As a young man, from 1898 to 1901, he lived in Rome, mingled with Italian nonconformist, syndicalist intellectuals, and studied at the University of Rome. He took classes with Enrico Ferri, a student of Cesare Lombroso, the proponent of an anthropological approach to social reality and a member of the Italian Socialist Party.[60] According to Eran Kaplan, Ferri's version of criminal anthropology and his view of human history through social statistics and natural laws exerted a strong influence on Jabotinsky.[61] Raphael Falk, a student of eugenicist thought in Zionism, agrees: "Jabotinsky was strongly affected by the nationalistic and futuristic ideals prevalent during his years as a student in Italy."[62] Indeed, Jabotinsky's feuilletons for the Russian newspaper *Odesskie Novosti* (Odessa news), especially those written during his stay in Rome and immediately after, were peppered with references to Italian social theories and "new Italian criminalists."[63] Svetlana Natkovich argues that although specific names of the Italian social scientists were rarely explicitly mentioned in these and other writings of Jabotinsky, "their ideas and terminology frequently appeared in his rhetoric and shaped it to some extent."[64] Cedric Cohen Skalli and Natkovich have established the influence of Ricciotto Canudo, another friend of Jabotinsky, on his thinking. Canudo, a French Italian theoretician of the arts, developed the "Mediterranean" aesthetics theory that assumed harmonization in the Mediterranean race of "all the powers of a race, positive and negative." His understanding of race was not purely biological. In the context of Italian empire building, he emphasized "the imperial capacity to amalgamate different national energies and cultures into a political and spiritual harmonization."[65]

Canudo, Ferri, Antonio Labriola, Benedetto Croce, and others among Jabotinsky's Italian teachers, acquaintances, and friends, like most Italian antiliberal intellectuals of their time, shared the myth of a national regeneration and "succumbed to the verities of racial science flooding Italy's universities."[66] Canudo's imperial race coexisted in these Italian circles with social Darwinism, proto-eugenics, cultural futurism, and political nationalism. Mediterranean race theory and a new aggressive Eurocentrism were elements of the ideological mix to which Italy exposed Jabotinsky and which found a receptive environment among the Jews of the Russian Empire who were struggling for recognition as a modern and civilized nation in a polity whose Europeanness and modernity were likewise questionable in the eyes of the "proper" West.[67]

—⁂—

Obviously, Jabotinsky's own discovery of "race" was quite distinctive, and his racialized Jewish nationalism was not representative of the entire ideological spectrum of Russian Zionism, which embraced religious and secular worldviews, socialist and liberal political programs, and members and supporters from diverse social and economic backgrounds. But, to some degree, the same can be said about any other modern mass nationalism. Russian Zionism became a truly mass political movement when the empire was transitioning from a particularistic regime to a nationalizing regime that tolerated some forms of liberal representation and mass politics. Invigorated by these changes, proponents of scientific politics among the imperial intelligentsia made the irregular imperial hybridity a subject of their own scrutiny and criticism. Against this background, the choice of Judt's anthropology over, say, the more straightforward Zionist anthropological narrative of Ignaz Zollschan seems very interesting.[68] Judt's version of Jewish self-racializing was not completely exclusivist; it retained a creative impulse that allowed the reimagining of Europe's borders as more inclusive and the positing of the hybridity of cultures, languages, and identities. One can see why the "Mediterranean race" concept could inspire Jewish politicians whose political imagination, language, and visions were never monological and unidirectional. But one can also see that this type of self-racialization was not sustainable from a long-term perspective. Sergi's notion of the Mediterranean race ended up in Italian fascism, Du Bois's double consciousness remained politically inconclusive, and Jabotinsky's views on the nation-state in Palestine as a means and the end-goal of modern Jewish politics became much more straightforward.⁶⁹ Moreover, as the next chapters will show, Jabotinsky assumed an uncompromising critical position vis-à-vis imperial hybridity: he fought it with the fury and dedication of someone who saw himself as a hybrid and as someone who performed an act of exorcism of this colonial evil (as he understood it) from his own and the collective Jewish body.

As it turned out, the potential of hybridity that made the Mediterranean concept look so promising and attractive to the new classifiers and their followers was credible only in the structural imperial situation, which was characterized by inequalities and hierarchies, but also by the "strategic relativism" of double consciousness, identity politics, participation, and belonging.⁷⁰ It is this structural imperial situation that invited reinterpretations along the lines of inclusion and growing complexity; triggered counternarratives of open, dynamic, and multilingual borderland spaces (instead of rigid borders); and allowed the reimagining of marginality as a paradigmatic state of development and newness. Therefore, the Mediterranean race concept, which responded to the challenge of nationalism by envisioning "Europe" as a fairly open-ended contact zone with a moving core, remained a phenomenon of the late imperial moment. It had lost its political rationale in the clearly monological and normatively national postimperial and post-Wilsonian sociopolitical context with its cult of pure forms.

THREE

RACIAL PURITY VERSUS IMPERIAL HYBRIDITY
Vladimir Jabotinsky against the Russian Empire

Natural factors produce *race*. A complex, roaring mishmash of economic factors distorts and changes racial traits to such an extent that the impact of race historically disappears; [its influence becomes so negligible] that modern science almost completely ignores race. However if progress eventually brings some order into this maelstrom of multiple and diverse economic interests . . . then the race principle, which hitherto has been overshadowed by other influences, will draw itself up and blossom.

Altalena [Vladimir Jabotinsky], "Vskolz': O natsionalizme," 1903

A nation [*narod*] develops its distinctive psychological constitution [*uklad*] because this constitution alone corresponds to its physical-racial type, and no *other* psyche could be formed on this basis.

Vladimir Jabotinsky, "Pis'mo ob avtonomizme," 1904

"NATURAL FACTORS PRODUCE RACE"

Vladimir Jabotinsky (1880–1940) recorded the thoughts selected as epigraphs for this chapter at the very beginning of his career as a Jewish politician and a Zionist. They reveal the extent of racialization of Jabotinsky's understanding of history and politics already at this early stage of his political life. In addition, the epigraphs effectively summarize one of the key Russian public debates of the early twentieth century—the debate about empire, colonialism, and capitalism as forces distorting the natural evolution of human collectives such as nations and classes. With time, Jabotinsky came to firmly prioritize nation over class but remained a vigorous enemy of the old-style prenationalized, imperial political order. Two things about it bothered him the most: (1) colonial domination that did not allow subaltern peoples to properly nationalize, develop politically, and determine their own collective destinies and (2) the perpetuation of what he regarded as an unnatural imperial complexity and hybridity of identities and loyalties that was opposed to naturalness, simplicity, and purity of national forms.

"Natural factors produce *race*. A complex, roaring mishmash of economic factors distorts and changes racial traits." Jabotinsky insisted that the dialectical return (at a new, higher, developmental stage) was necessary to the initial "natural" condition, achievable through the uncompromising nationalization and racialization of politics.[1] In this, he anticipated the post–World War II wave of postcolonial thought that regarded nationalism and the politics of racial purity as answers to imperialism and the colonial suppression of freedom and authenticity of the colonized. Like the post–World War II generation of colonial intellectuals, Jabotinsky advanced his powerful critique of the imperial order from the clearly articulated position of an imperial subaltern, but he did this in an empire that never consistently relied on a racialized politics of difference. In this chapter, I argue that Jabotinsky and the "brand" of Zionism that he represented played a very important role in racializing the language of official politics in the Russian Empire.

With the advance of parliamentarism after the October Manifesto of 1905, Jabotinsky began propagating the idea of *Nationalitätenstaat* (a term borrowed from Karl Renner) "for all tribes and all regions."² He appealed to the deputies of the newly created Russian parliament, the State Duma, to embrace the sole principle of political representation that he deemed legitimate in the imperial situation, that is, representation by nationality. "In our political narrow-mindedness [*obyvatel'shchina*]," he wrote, "this is called nationalism, sometimes even 'narrow' nationalism . . . I have never been ashamed of this label."³ Writing almost fifty years later, Frantz Fanon expressed a similar demand, revealing a deep-rooted structure of the anti-imperial, nationalist logic: "A good many colonial subjects are active members in branches of metropolitan political parties. These colonial subjects are militant activists under the abstract slogan 'Power to the proletariat,' forgetting that in their part of the world slogans of national liberation should come first."⁴ Jabotinsky tirelessly repeated the same idea to members of Jewish and non-Jewish socialist parties and movements. He did not necessarily imply that national liberation had to triumph in the establishment of a sovereign nation-state, but he absolutely believed in a decisive shift toward national politics as the first evolutionary step toward reestablishing the natural developmental norm.

Jabotinsky envisioned turning empires into Nationalitätenstaaten, with political agency resting exclusively with self-organizing, autonomous (and when possible—territorial) nationalities. In cases when a projected state accommodated a heterogeneous population and the freedom of less developed or nonterritorial nationalities was threatened, he preferred a composite state to a nation-state model. In *Beyond the Nation-State* Dmitry Shumsky argues that this was not merely a tactical move on Jabotinsky's part but an ideological preference shared by many prominent nationalists of his generation, whose political imagination was formed in a world dominated by empires: "Like Pinsker in *Autoemancipation!* and Herzl in *Altneulad*, and like many leaders of national movements among non-dominant nationalities in the imperial spaces of Eastern Europe, Central Europe, and the

Mediterranean basin, Ahad Ha'am saw the future Jewish national entity in Palestine as a 'state within a state,' an autonomous country within an existing imperial structure."[5] Similar to these renowned older Zionists, Jabotinsky accepted the possibility of a national "autonomous country" within an imperial state ("the uniqueness of Zionism... is that it is explicitly social in character.... Its goal... is not a Jewish state but Jewish collective life"[6]), but in contrast to many like-minded political thinkers, he did not shy away from exposing and dealing with internal contradictions and the logical implications of such a political arrangement.

One obvious contradiction, at least in Jabotinsky's vision of Jewish national self-determination, was between the endorsement of a composite statehood and the decisive rejection of the concept of hierarchical or composite citizenship. Locating sovereignty and citizenship exclusively within the nation left the composite state without any special function or meaning. As Jabotinsky explained in 1906, "to be a citizen means to recognize that you are a part of an organic whole; this whole is not a territory but rather a nation. Therefore... it is impossible to be a 'citizen of your state'; it is only possible to be a 'citizen of your nation' and through your nation... to be a citizen of the place in which the nation lives."[7] The Habsburg Empire, in his view, was moving rapidly toward the state-of-nations ideal that Jabotinsky saw as a precondition for the implementation of national citizenship. And he welcomed the Young Turks' revolution in the Ottoman Empire as a crucial step in the same direction (a hope that had evaporated by 1912).[8] In other words, Jabotinsky valued modern nationalizing empires not as polities endowed with objective advantages over the nation-state, but as transitional forms in moving toward the Nationalitätenstaat and, eventually, toward the triumph of the national principle in all spheres of life.[9] With the imperial state being delegitimized as a political and economic aberration, and the composite state (call it empire or federation[10]) de facto stripped of its statehood, possessing no sovereignty and no supreme authority in any sphere without the sanction of participating nations, nation remained the only legitimate political subject. Revitalized and strong postimperial nations were expected to purge everything "imperial" from the composite political framework inherited from old empires. Structural conditions that enabled colonial domination were to be obliterated together with the hybrid, nonnational, situational, layered, and complex identifications and forms of belonging. Decades later Fanon summarized the goal of such a purge in one aphoristic sentence: "Decolonization unifies this world by a radical decision to remove its heterogeneity, by unifying it on the grounds of nation and sometimes race."[11]

Jabotinsky had arrived at a similar realization in the context of Russia's deepening revolutionary crisis that undermined the credentials of the imperial state and mobilized mass politics from below. He hastened to use the chance to nationalize the emerging democratic political sphere, hoping to push the Russian Empire onto the right evolutionary track, as he understood it.[12] Internally, he attacked Jewish socialists for accepting that Jews shared class interests with the Russia's proletariat. "We live in a foreign country," he insisted in 1906, "we are in the hands of a foreign people.... But one thing is in our power: we can summon the Jewish people, separate them from the surrounding peoples, shape the [Jewish] people into a beautiful whole and cultivate in it a sense of national obligation and work."[13] Not class but parliamentary politics was the right political choice of such a Jewish nation, because only in the State Duma the contours of the future Nationalitätenstaat could be elaborated.

In *Story of My Life*, Jabotinsky's autobiography originally published in Hebrew as *Sippur yamai* in 1936, Jabotinsky recounts how the leaders of the Russian Jewish public disagreed on the politics of twelve Jewish deputies, five of them Zionists, to the First Duma (lasting from April 27, 1906, to July 8, 1906). Whereas Jabotinsky's circle of Zionists demanded that they create a separate

Jewish faction, their liberal opponents defended the principle of affiliation, especially with the left-liberal party of Constitutional Democrats (Kadets).[14] To resolve this dispute, a congress of the Society for the Attainment of Full Rights for the Jewish People in Russia gathered in St. Petersburg in 1906, at which Jabotinsky articulated his vision of the nationalization of Duma politics and the creation of a Jewish national faction. Moisei Ostrogorsky, a well-known constitutional scholar—whose main works focused on North American and British party politics—and a sympathizer of the Constitutional Democrats Party, spoke on behalf of Jewish liberals.[15] "Never, either before that day or after it, did I experience such fear while preparing for a public debate," Jabotinsky recounted in his memoir, "What should I say?—how could I oppose an expert and a specialist with scientific arguments?" Ostrogorsky was indeed an expert, a professional political scientist by our contemporary criteria, who in 1905 was even offered a chair in political science at Cleveland University in the United States but preferred to remain in Russia and "run the electoral campaign as a 'democrat' and a 'Jew' in ethnically mixed Grodno province."[16] Nonetheless, during the debate, as Jabotinsky recorded in the memoir, Ostrogorsky's arguments struck him as unscientific. He never elaborated on what was exactly wrong with his opponent's views, but from reading Ostrogorsky's major work, *Democracy and the Organization of Political Parties*, one can easily grasp the reason for Jabotinsky's disappointment.[17] Ostrogorsky criticized the bureaucratization of party machines in Britain and the United States, narrow party representation, and majoritarian rule as mechanisms leading to the closure of political life in modern democracies. His political sociology of the imperial parliament exposed such a rigidly structured politics of representation as unsuitable for the mixed and hybrid imperial society. As a member of the first State Duma, Ostrogorsky worked on the Committee on Rules and Regulations, where, as the historian Alexander Semyonov writes, he was able to preempt "the emergence of majoritarian political culture and impact of party machines." Instead, Ostrogorsky advocated multiple membership in parliamentary groups, and promoted the politics of situational alliances and compromises to which Jabotinsky was passionately opposed.[18] As Semyonov explains, Ostrogorsky, the MP, conducted in the Duma a scientific experiment aimed at locating and theorizing a different modality of a representative system suitable for mass politics in the imperial society. And in pragmatic terms, "his own successful bid for an elected office proved that there was a room for practicing democratic politics without an exclusive party or ethnic affiliation."[19] Both experiments embodied for Jabotinsky an amateurish, unscientific approach and convinced him "that there exists as yet no 'science' of Jewish politics." "My generation is one of beginners, and we must create the science of politics in Israel from A to Z; the same applies also to Zionism, especially to Zionism," Jabotinsky wrote in the memoir, recalling his thoughts after the debate with Ostrogorsky.[20]

Following his vision of modern Jewish politics, in 1907, Jabotinsky went to Vienna specifically to study the social and political theory of the "national question." He then used this knowledge in a thesis that earned him the equivalent of a university diploma from Demidov College in Yaroslavl (1913), and, more important, in his political writings on Zionism and the Russian Empire.[21] Jabotinsky's selective canon of the "science of Jewish politics" included race scientists such as Ignacy Maurycy Judt, Italian criminal anthropologists, and the French Orientalist Ernest Renan; ideologues of Austro-Marxism (the most popular being Karl Renner [Springer]); "a new science that Germans call Natioalitätenrecht"[22]; and various studies in law, linguistics, psychology, economics, and history. In the latter category, two Ukrainian historians, Nikolai Kostomarov and Mikhail (Mykhailo) Hrushevskii, were his favorites. Among "Austrians," his most favored authors also included the legal scholar Rudolf von Herrnritt, the Austrian

German professor and premier expert in public law George Jellinek, and one of the leaders of the National Romanian Party and a theorist of federalism, Aurel Popovici. Being the ultimate "natural factor," a concept that simultaneously engaged natural and social sciences, "race" helped synthesize this diverse knowledge.

"Natural factors produce *race*. A complex, roaring mishmash of economic factors distorts and changes racial traits. . . . However if progress eventually brings some order into this maelstrom of multiple and diverse economic interests . . . then the race principle, which hitherto has been overshadowed by other influences, will draw itself up and blossom."[23] Between 1903 and 1913, this initial concise statement had evolved into a comprehensive theory of race and politics, the most complete version of which one can find in the essay "Race" (1913). In it, Jabotinsky introduced the phenomenon of race as a product of the initial mixture of physical types in antiquity. The original mixture constituted the "pure race"—the basis of a nation. "Ethnic groups differ from each other by their racial spectrum, and it is in this sense that the word 'race' acquires a very distinct and scientific meaning," Jabotinsky explained.[24] Race was omnipresent in all spheres of human life, including economics, because the mode of production depended on "natural conditions" such as climate, landscape, and human psyche. The latter, in particular, was "the chief instrument of production" (*verkhovnoe oruzhie proizvodstva*) and a direct expression of a race. Hence, race directly defined the mode of production:

> Under the ideal equality of all the other conditions such as climate, landscape, soil, and history, the two "races" would still produce different types of economy. A Marxist would claim that, by definition, different economic systems produce different types of culture. For a non-Marxist, who recognizes the autonomous nature and primary significance of ideological factors, this same conclusion should be even more obvious. If even economic systems and social regimes bear marks of "racial" psyche, its influence on religion, philosophy,

literature, and, to some degree, law is even more apparent. This applies to the entire sphere of spiritual culture that is so evidently connected to national psyche.[25]

In summary, everything, from spiritual culture to political forms to modes of productions rested in the "physical nature" of a nation, "in the recipe of its racial composition."[26] Jabotinsky wrote "Race" on the eve of World War I, not long before he had departed from the Russian Empire for good and the empire itself ceased to exist in 1917. One important legacy of the epoch of Russian Zionism that Jabotinsky took with him into his postimperial life was an elaborate philosophy of a return to natural forms of political, economic, and spiritual existence as determined by race.[27]

JEWISH *BILDUNG* AND THE FULFILLMENT OF RACIAL DESTINY

What, if any, was a natural form of Jewishness for Vladimir Jabotinsky? He was born in 1880 to an integrated Jewish family in the cosmopolitan port city of Odessa, which had preserved the feel of a borderland and the somewhat uprooted existence of its diverse population until the end of the old empire.[28] After the death of his father in 1886, his mother still found the means to send him and his sister first to a Russian elementary school and later to the best secondary educational establishment in Odessa—the Richelieu gymnasium. As a boy, he never attended heder, and their home language was Russian. Jabotinsky's multilingualism and his preference for Hebrew came later, around 1903, after his self-reinvention as a Jew and Zionist politician.[29] In this regard, Colin Shindler's surprising comparison of Jabotinsky to Trotsky as sharing a "remoteness and unawareness of Jewish life" is, in fact, quite precise and revealing. It underscores the absence of any determinism in their eventual political trajectories: both "came from a bourgeois background and also went to school in

Odessa.... Both Trotsky and Jabotinsky sought a clarification of identity and an intellectual anchorage. Both attended the Sixth Zionist Conference in Basle in 1903."[30]

Retrospectively, especially in *Story of My Life*, Jabotinsky, unlike Trotsky, reconsidered his life as a version of the Jewish *Bildung* culminating with the revisionist Zionism that he embraced in the 1920s.[31] And in an earlier autobiographical text, *The Story of the Jewish Legion*, originally published as a book in Russian in 1928, he suggestively presented Zionism as the fulfillment of the Jewish racial destiny. This revelation came to Jabotinsky, the reader learns, suddenly, while he was thinking about the Jewish volunteers of his admired brainchild—the Jewish Legion fighting in the British army against the Ottoman Empire during World War I. Observing the Jewish Legion fighters in action caused Jabotinsky to realize that "Zionists comprise a special 'race' with a special, inborn type of soul, and may even have some special blood composition." Just as one cannot pick a race, one cannot simply turn into a Zionist, and even "contact with Palestine" does not make one into a Zionist, that is, into a modern, strong, nationally conscious Jew. Zionist "poison," Jabotinsky concluded, should be present in Jewish blood from the outset, and none can "either inculcate or forge this trait."[32] His mother and the people he admired most as a child in Odessa all turned out to be "poisoned." In *Story of My Life* we read: "Of course, I knew that ultimately we would have a kingdom, and that I too would go to live there—my mother knew that too, as did all my aunts, and Ravnitsky; yet this was not a conviction but so to speak just a natural thing, such as washing one's hands in the morning and eating a bowl of soup at noon."[33] Every word in this seemingly artless description is intentional: if Zionism was not a conviction but a way of life, a natural thing, then Jabotinsky's late awakening to Zionism was not a calculated choice but a destiny. Even some of his fellow Odessans, who knew the pre-Zionist Jabotinsky, succumbed to this powerful vision of a naturally lived life. One of them, the journalist Petr Pil'sky, who worked with the young Jabotinsky at the liberal newspaper *Odesskie Novosti* (Odessa news), in 1921 wrote: "In the person of Jabotinsky we have a truly logical life—a life as a theorem, a life as a syllogism, in which causes and consequences and premises and conclusions are tightened and twisted into a springy spring."[34]

In reality, Jabotinsky's Jewish Bildung began in 1903, after his trip to the Sixth Zionist Congress in Basel (August 23–28, 1903). By that time, he was a successful twenty-four-year-old journalist at *Odesskie Novosti* who aspired, not very successfully but nonetheless vigorously, to become a recognized Russian playwright and writer. At sixteen, he embarked on translating into the Russian language the texts of stars of modernism and their precursors such as Paul Verlaine, Sándor Pétofi, and Edgar Allan Poe. His own literary works were often rejected by the publishers, but he did not give up and sent them to venerated Russian writers such as Vladimir Korolenko, Ivan Bunin, and Maxim Gorky seeking their approval and support. His true place was to be among the progressive-minded Russian intelligentsia and its literary elite.[35] In 1899, in a letter to Vladimir Korolenko, Jabotinsky expressed confidence that leading Russian liberal periodicals rejected his poems not because of their poor language or aesthetic form. The literary "generals" were simply ignoring a provincial author who lacked a powerful "patron." Thus, while feeling underappreciated in Russian literature, Jabotinsky never claimed that this was because of his Jewishness and he never doubted his right to belong to the community of Russian writers. To the contrary, he aggressively demanded explanations from the Union of Russian Writers: "I believe I have an undeniable right to turn to the Union with requests pertaining to the business of literature and that the Union absolutely must provide me with a response."[36]

Michael Stanislawski describes this early Jabotinsky as a cosmopolitan intellectual who could have called his spiritual motherland Russia or Italy, and whose love for European modernism was yet another reflection of his cosmopolitanism.³⁷ It is important, however, to remember that before he actually got a taste of the short-lived fin-de-siècle European cosmopolitanism, Jabotinsky had experienced imperial Russian cosmopolitanism of the kind that promised integration into the imperial nation through adopting the Russian cultural idiom. As Jabotinsky's lifelong engagement with Russian journalism and literature suggests, this idiom was never exclusively ethnonational. Secular intellectuals such as Jabotinsky often carried out their Jewishness as an external stigma almost unrelated to their actual upbringing, religious observance, education, and linguistic limitations or preferences. Many urban, educated Jews in the Russian Empire did not have a distinct, one-dimensional, stable identity, and their belonging to the Russian imperial discursive ("imagined") community did not connote the betrayal of some inborn identity of the colonized in favor of the ethnically Russian colonizer.³⁸ The case was the same for such Jews in the Habsburg Empire—another breeding ground of Zionism. As Adi Gordon points out, a "remarkable aspect of the pursuit of Jewish revival by [Hans] Kohn and his highly educated young friends" was that all of them had extremely limited knowledge of Jewish things. It is this Jewish illiteracy, Gordon believes, that explains their unique creativity in appropriation of Jewish texts, history, and, eventually, politics. On the other hand, the same Jewish illiteracy resulted in "an abundantly essentialist discussion of all things Jewish."³⁹

Gordon's pertinent observation is fully applicable to Jabotinsky and his generation of Russian Jews. It helps our understanding of their predisposition to race thinking and suggests an explanation as to why Jabotinsky's *Story of My Life*, his retrospective construction of the normative Zionist biography, turned out to be so profoundly essentialized. Jabotinsky's narrative streamlines the inherent contradictions of the turn-of-the-century Jewish imperial condition, resolving them by means of the "abundantly essentialist discussion of all things Jewish" (Gordon). This is particularly obvious in the chapters that cover the pre-1903 period, when Jabotinsky's Jewishness and Russianness were nothing but contextual and hence evolving notions. We learn from the memoir that Jabotinsky and his Jewish classmates were never segregated as Jews in school, and they freely socialized with non-Jewish students. In other words, they were completely accepted and lived in a world that could hardly be described as "Jewish" in cultural or social terms. Nonetheless, for some unstated reason, they maintained an additional, exclusively Jewish circle for themselves. Jabotinsky clearly wants his readers to pause and ask: Why? What motivated these young Odessans, who, according to Jabotinsky's testimony, never discussed any Jewish-related matters because they were not interested in or knowledgeable about such topics, to socialize among themselves? Jabotinsky does not openly articulate the answer in the text, but the narrative prompts the reader to assume that this was their deep-hidden Jewishness. To preclude any alternative interpretations, Jabotinsky clarifies that "the spirit of anti-Semitism was almost entirely absent from these government schools: perhaps because in those days public opinion generally was dormant in Russia, left-wing as well as right-leaning."[40] The tension is obvious here, for while constructing the essentialized Jewishness, Jabotinsky describes Russianness as still an open phenomenon, not yet politicized and properly nationalized. Moreover, his own choices in those early years suggest that embracing the Russian imperial idiom was not perceived in racial terms, but as a chance to join a higher, anational intelligentsia culture. This universalist and modern culture engendered the imagined all-imperial intelligentsia community of common values and social ideals and a shared language of political and cultural self-expression and communication.[41]

Rising antisemitism was only one expression of the more fundamental crisis of old imperial universalism and hybridity in a nationalizing and modernizing empire that was entering an era of mass politics. This tectonic shift motivated Jabotinsky and like-minded intellectuals to embrace a radical anti- and potentially postimperial national agenda that recognized neither the legitimacy and reality of hybridity nor the fluidity of social and cultural forms. In the introduction to the English-language edition of *Story of My Life*, Brian Horowitz perceptively observes that Jabotinsky was serious about "bending life to his will" in the Nietzschean sense and that his Zionism was "the Jewish version of striving for the transformation of reality."[42] A clarification is needed here that it was not just any reality that he meant. The reality he was striving to transform was the crumbling old imperial social order. In this respect, individual biography and evolution of sociopolitical institutions are inseparable. Whenever the young Jabotinsky talks about Jewish nationality as being based on race, or discusses the danger of biological contamination in the imperial situation, or struggles with epistemological domination of the Russian culture, he always keeps in mind his own belated acceptance of Jewishness, compromised by imperial complexity and messiness. His becoming a Zionist and Zionism's becoming an influential political ideology during Jabotinsky's lifetime were tightly intertwined processes rooted in the specific late imperial moment. The race concept connected the two planes of this transformation and the two bodies involved—individual and social. The race thinking that Jabotinsky developed was a radical and novel type of essentialization of everything Jewish. It embraced clear-cut postcolonial oppositions: authentic versus foreign/colonial; natural versus artificial; pure versus contaminated; simple versus hybrid; Russian versus Jewish; and nation-race versus empire.

SEEKING A LANGUAGE OF ANTI-IMPERIAL NATIONALISM

As Jabotinsky insists in his autobiographies, his Zionism was intuitive before it became ideological and political. However, his early twentieth-century writings tell otherwise: they reveal a persistent and conscious search for the precise language of an anti-imperial Jewish nationalism.

His earliest attempt to find an appropriate national idiom can be traced to an April 1903 newspaper column, "An Apocryphal Story." This parable about a man and his two wives, Mirra and Mira, is set in biblical times. The gendered nature of Jabotinsky's social imagination reveals itself in the portrayal of the Man-the Husband-the God as embodying the will and wisdom of the nation.[43] Similarly to the way that Man perceives Mirra and Mira, his two wives, all nations are equal before the God, Jabotinsky teaches, but he values most their unlikeness and distinctiveness: "A Greek has always remained a Greek, and a Jew [has always been] a Jew—as for me there is neither Greek nor Jew."[44] The inversion of the meaning of this famous line (Galatians 3:28) is obvious here: instead of quoting a canonical "for you are all one in Christ Jesus," Jabotinsky adds a prescriptive statement about cultivating national differences. Biblical allusions serve as superficial stylistic instruments for conveying a modern nationalist wisdom, a story about the old imperial diversity (you are all one to the dynastic authorities) redefined in the light of a modern postimperial nationalism (you have always been distinct and different and should remain so).

In June 1903, Jabotinsky published another column-parable, this time experimenting with the discourses and imagery of belonging and nonbelonging. The protagonists of the parable are rats. A pack of Alexandria rats from Egypt secretly lands at Quarantine harbor in Odessa and settles in the house of a certain Zhus'. Local Odessa rats (here Jabotinsky uses the Ukrainian word for rats—*pasiuk*, to stress their deep local roots as opposed to the newcomers) decide not to drive them away as long as they agree to stay in the house of Zhus' (Zhus' is another clearly Ukrainian-sounding name, which may be interpreted as a reference to the Pale of Settlement where the Russian-speaking population was a minority). However, gradually the Alexandria rats start spreading into the city, occupying holes at the Odessa *Tolchok*—its main marketplace. Moreover, they begin intermixing with the local pasiuks! So, the Odessa rats order them to go back to the house of Zhus' and stay there. Of course, the Alexandrian rats become upset. And only one old rat turns to her brethren with the following words: "Foolish rats you are! ... Why should Odessa holes be for Alexandrian rats?" These holes are for Odessa pasiuks, while Alexandrian rats must live either in the house of Zhus' or in Alexandria. "We have toured enough here. It is time to go home: we came from Alexandria, and it is to Alexandria that we have to return." And so they do. "Sometimes rats can be wiser than humans," Jabotinsky concludes his parable.[45]

Clearly, this column was intended as a didactic Zionist parable about Jews as eternal strangers outside of their native Palestine. They came to a strange land and were tolerated there as long as they lived in seclusion (the house of Zhus') within the Jewish Pale of Settlement. The very moment they started penetrating the host society and mixing with the locals, the latter showed Jews the door. The parable preached a Zionist lesson: it is time to return to the Jewish national home. Jabotinsky used Odessa as a symbol of empire where dangerous mixing could occur, which seduced the "Alexandrian rats" into behaving as if they belonged here. Deeply hidden in this text was Jabotinsky's personal story as an Odessan, an urban imperial intellectual without a distinct national identity who is learning the lesson of Jewish ultimate difference, separateness, and foreignness.

In 1903 for the first time, Jabotinsky tried another metaphor serving the same purpose: an orchestra performing a symphony and producing "endless harmony" due to the willing collaboration of different instruments—a metaphor that would soon be translated into the state-of-nations concept.[46] The fact that in 1903 Jabotinsky spoke in a language of parables and literary metaphors suggests that his transition to becoming a politician was not momentous and self-evident. Moreover, the topics of his newspaper columns in 1903 reflected none of the most pressing issues of Russian Jewish life at the time, not even the Kishinev pogrom (April 6–9, 1903). Stanislawski was the first to note that contrary to the official biographical narratives, in 1903 Jabotinsky the journalist did not comment on this tragic event.[47] Instead, a great number of his publications were centered on Italy—his spiritual homeland ("If I have a spiritual homeland, it is Italy rather than Russia"[48]), the place where he had experienced his most important intellectual influences, the symbolic "Mediterranean"—the inclusive and dynamic Europe. Now he was revisiting and reworking his Italian lessons from the perspective of a newborn nationalist.

From 1898 to 1901 Jabotinsky spent three happy years in Rome as a university student, an active observer of Italian political life, and an Italian correspondent for *Odessa News*. In his correspondence he described the Italian parliament, theaters, and the hospitable homes of ordinary Italians, reflected on the dialectics of Rome's ruins and modernity, and told funny and tender stories about his student friends, their lovers, and their acquaintances. One theme he never mentioned in this correspondence was Italian Jews, whose presence in Rome he did not even notice. Only when he visited the city again on the way back from Basel, did he discover old Rome's ghetto quarters and the Italian "Jewish question." Like his Odessa columns, Jabotinsky's 1903 Italian essays reflected the recently initiated search for a language of Jewishness and Jewish politics.

The first Italian essay (*Odessa News*, October 12, 1903) described a walk through Rome's former Jewish ghetto—a district that Jabotinsky knew from his student years but had never noticed how strikingly different it was from the surrounding urban landscape. Now his eyes registered only differences in the ghetto's architectural and human landscape. Even children playing on the streets resembled not their Italian peers but "those greenish (*zelenovatykh*) little Jews from Lithuania who come to Odessa to pass school exams for six grades, and their fathers." Jabotinsky shared his observations with a friend, a "native Italian and Catholic."

> "You know," I told my friend, "you can still see by their faces that they are not Italians."
> My companion ... did not understand.
> "What do you mean, they are not Italians?" he asked again, "and who they are, in your view?"
> Jews.
> And what does it mean? There are Italians who are Lutherans or Methodists, or belong to other confessions, but they are all Italians.
> But does it mean that Jews belong to the same race as your people?
> This he understood and replied:
> "In such a case you probably wanted to say that they are not of a Latin blood. This is correct. Jews are not Latin, but they are Italians."[49]

In this chain of misunderstandings, Stanislawski sees the reflection of Jabotinsky's characteristically Russian sense of Jewishness: "Consciously extrapolating from the Russian reality to that of other European countries, he believed that Russianness, Italianness, and Germanness were national categories that could not include Jews, regardless of the existence or degree of anti-Semitism in any given society."[50] But this was exactly a new and troubling discovery that had provoked Jabotinsky's Jewish awakening. The Russian Empire was not yet a state of nations the way Jabotinsky preferred it to be, and Russianness was not yet an exclusive national/ethic category, although its meaning was becoming more rigid and nationalizing pressure was growing. The dialogue enacted by Jabotinsky in his first Italian essay was, in fact, an internal conversation between the Jabotinsky of the Italian period, who felt very Italian (and Russian) himself, and the Jabotinsky who was in the process of becoming a nationally conscious Jew and a Zionist. When his old Italian "self" suggested that in Italy, "a Jew is accepted as a citizen not only on paper, but de facto,"[51] his new Zionist "self" rejected this as a logical impossibility because only primordial races/nations could be political subjects.

Predictably, the next essay in the Italian cycle exposed the false sense of Italianness among the Jews of Rome. They deceived themselves by hiding behind Italian names and refusing to admit that the true Italians of Latin blood treated them with contempt.[52] Jabotinsky condemned Italian Jews for calling Russian Jews "coreligionists" instead of stressing their racial unity (*soplemenniki*). This was not their authentic voice, Jabotinsky claimed. Italian Jews were "prohibited from loudly loving their race and loudly expressing their brotherly sympathy to the distant members of their kin."[53] Instead of fighting their colonial condition they accepted it, and thus betrayed their race and their national future.

The Italian essays were significant for Jabotinsky's political evolution: in them he tried his hand at exposing the hidden structures of colonial domination and false identities and loyalties. From then onward, this deconstruction became the most essential element of his "science of Jewish politics." Like Fanon, who in *The Wretched of the Earth* wrote that "the colonized, underdeveloped man is today a political creature in the most global sense of the term,"[54] Jabotinsky deemed it important to establish a direct connection between demonstrating the Jews' status as colonized and legitimizing and empowering them as political creatures.

THE "SCIENCE" OF POLITICAL LEADERSHIP

Another theme that consumed Jabotinsky in 1903 was the Sixth Zionist Congress in Basel, the first that he attended and the first serious event that introduced him to political Zionism. Jabotinsky's reports from the congress published in *Odessa News* were full of curious observations and descriptions—addressed to the broad public and not necessarily only to Jewish readers—and were clearly written from the perspective of a complete outsider who knew very little about Zionism and Jewish politics.[55]

One of Jabotinsky's strongest Basel impressions was Theodor Herzl himself—the leader of the Zionist movement. In Jabotinsky's correspondence, the theme of Herzl's undeniable and unique charisma completely overshadowed the discussion of his ideological views or political tactics. Herzl emerges in Jabotinsky's writings as a supermasculine, aristocratic figure: "[Herzl has] the most interesting appearance of all I have ever seen: there is something substantially manly, firm, and at the same time refined about him. He has the profile of an Assyrian tsar as they are depicted on ancient plaques."[56] In the poem "Hesped" (1904), written in Russian on the occasion of Herzl's death, Jabotinsky deployed the same combination of masculinity and aristocratism: "A giant! One who would not bend; An eagle with eagle eyes, proud and radiant; And he was tall, a man of might...; He wrapped our sufferings in majesty..."[57]

"So rest in peace, our eagle—our sacred kingly tribune."[58]

Today this description may seem hyperbolic and imaginative, but in fact, it was framed from beginning to end in the anthropological stereotypes of its time. The idea that the type of masculinity and royalty embodied in Herzl's figure reproduced Assyrian images of the ancient Israelites rested on a perception of the Jewish race as retaining its unique racial composition since its formative times. On a popular level, this stereotype circulated as a belief in the universal recognizability of the "Jewish physiognomy," and it was as widespread in Russia as elsewhere.[59] According to the Russian Jewish race scientist, Arkadii El'kind, his mentor, Dmitry Anuchin, the Moscow university professor and dean of Russian liberal anthropology, recognized "the Jewish prototype in Jewish images [portrayed] on Egyptian and Assyrian monuments, where Jews are easily distinguishable from the images of other Asian and African tribes."[60] Jabotinsky's gaze was very similar to Anuchin's: he "recognized" in Herzl an ancient Jewish prototype but with accentuated aristocratic and masculine features (this imagery, obviously, correlated with the Zionist art nouveau aesthetics, for which Stanislawski has found a fine definition: "from Jugendstil to 'Judenstil'"[61]). Herzl, just as another Zionist leader adored by Jabotinsky, Max Nordau, was a deeply assimilated fin-de-siècle European Jewish intellectual, but this did not prevent Jabotinsky from constructing a royal Jewish lineage for Herzl that stressed his otherness. Herzl thus appeared to belong to the Jewish nation and Jewish national movement not by choice alone but by the power and even the destiny of race, as manifested in his "profile of an Assyrian tsar," which also marked him as a natural leader.

Jabotinsky deployed a similar racialized reading of Herzl's psychological profile: "He is not at all a first-rate writer, but he is an excellent stylist, who expresses in a clear and sharp manner what he needs to convey. He is not a public speaker, but he says exactly what he needs to say.... He is amazingly harmonious and self-restrained.... Taking in the fine points, he is a gentleman of mediocre abilities, but in general he is a big figure, big personality, who needs big levers—perhaps, not a talented [figure], but probably a genius."[62]

This puzzling back-and-forth between "mediocre" and "big," and "not a talent" but "probably a genius" may seem confusing. But a contemporary reader of Jabotinsky would know how to connect this description to another widespread stereotype that was especially popular among modern antisemites—the stereotype of the Jews as lacking creative abilities, as a parasitic race that produced many able individuals and even talented imitators but no real creative geniuses. The pervasiveness of this trope even in Jewish turn-of-the-century literature is astonishing. Jabotinsky, who perceived modern Jewish politics as a radically new creative and scientific project was determined to prove that the Jewish race could produce its own original and creative genius.

Fig. 3.1 Portrait of Theodor Herzl in a 1904 issue of the Zionist periodical, *Evreiskaia Zhizn'*, commemorating his recent death.

Hespêd

Онъ не угасъ, какъ древле Моисей,
на берегу земли обѣтованной
онъ не дошелъ до родины желанной
ея видѣвъ тоскующихъ дѣтей;
онъ смѣетъ себя, и жизнь отдалъ святыню,
и „не забудъ тебя, Ерусалимъ,"
но не дошелъ, и пять сыновъ пустынѣ,
и въ лучшій день, родимой Палестинѣ
мы только прахъ трибуна прежнихъ...

И понялъ я загадку странныхъ словъ,
прошданныхъ изъ Агатъ Бени-Бархавой,—
что потребенъ, пустыню песчаной
не только ролъ трусливыхъ, бѣглецовъ,—
интересный ролъ, рабы, въ чей духъ и спины
вожди клеймо египетская шлетъ—
но кромѣ нихъ среди нѣмой равнины
въ сухомъ пескѣ зарыты исполины,
ихъ сердце стало, и тѣло ихъ какъ мѣдь.

Да, пойми, и смѣлые мудрецы:
весь міръ костями нашими усѣянъ,
не сорокъ лѣтъ, а сорокъ юбилеевъ
блуждаемъ мы въ пустынѣ безъ конца,
и не рабы, воскормленные банями,

зарыли мы въ сухой чужой землѣ:
то были титаны, съ гранитными плечами,
то были орелъ съ орлиными очами,
и лицо ихъ жизни, полной силъ,
съ орлиною печалью на челѣ.

И былъ онъ гордъ, и мощенъ, и высокъ,
и звонъ его гремѣлъ, какъ звонъ металла,
и прогремѣлъ: но чтобы то ни стало
и насъ дошелъ впередъ и на востокъ,
и десять концовъ былъ день его распятія,
въ иномъ краѣ, свободномъ и своемъ,—
и грянулъ громъ, и пѣснь не могла.
Но за него ли пѣснь нашихъ?

Пусть мы снесемъ подъ муками ярма,
и вѣтру, утихъ ключи свяшенной Торы,
пусть сыновей убьютъ ихъ вечные воры,
и двери въ позорные дома,
и въ мерзости настѣнникахъ дѣлаю
да снесемъ мы ихъ тотъ, черный день и часъ,
когда тебя и пѣснь твою забудемъ
и посрамимъ погибшихъ за насъ...

Твой голосъ былъ, какъ манна съ облаковъ,
и безъ него томитъ насъ скорбь и голодъ
изъ рукъ твоихъ упалъ могучій молотъ—
но грянемъ мы въ сто тысячъ молотковъ,
и стиснетъ скорбь отъ ихъ живого гула,
и голосъ вашъ умретъ среди разгула
и торжества работы напролетъ;
мы прорвемся утесы на дорогъ,
мы прополземъ, гдѣ намъ шагнуть нельзя,
но—chaj ha Sem!— мы пѣснь допоемъ.

Fig. 3.2 The first publication of Jabotinsky's poem "Hesped." *Evreiskaia Zhizn'* 6 (1904): 8–9 and 10.

10 ЕВРЕЙСКАЯ ЖИЗНЬ.

Такъ изъ оны дни отецъ нашъ Израиль
свой станъ придетъ къ родному порогу —
и прерядилъ Самъ Богъ ему дорогу
и бился съ нимъ, но Яковъ побѣдилъ.
Грозно билъ, какъ листья, размѣтая,
но мы тобой погонни, Богоборъ;
мы побѣдимъ ...но что бы то ни стало —
пусть божій жезлъ на странѣ перешанъ,
но мы пройдемъ ему навстрѣчу!

Сядь, вашъ орелъ, вашъ партенный трибунъ.
Наслышатъ день — услышишь гулъ походъ,
и скрипъ телегъ, и громъ цыганъ народа,
и путь назадъ, и звонъ веселыхъ струнъ,
и въ этотъ день отъ Дана до Барцена
благословятъ сказенный народъ,
и запоютъ свободные напѣвы
и поведутъ изъ Сіонъ чаши вина
передъ гробницей моровой...

Владиміръ Жаботинскій.

20 таммуза.

Нашъ свѣтъ, нашъ день угасъ, и солнце отвеже
Сокрылось прочь...
Поѣзда тамъ его — и все покрылось тьмою,
И снова ночь.

Я знаю: нѣтъ его. Но радугъ мой въ разорѣ
Съ моей душой,
И ноже мучительное горе
Я не могу загасить, глубокое, какъ міръ,
Въ груди больной.

Я убѣгу одинъ, куда—не знаю,
Какъ раненный блѣднѣть,
Зубами скрежеща и рану зажимая;
Вдали застынетъ, Кого-то проклиная,
И замолчу...

Но вспомнилъ народъ, скушенный страшнымъ звонкомъ,
О, братья и други,
И я, чистый печальныхъ покоренныхъ,
Предамъ ихъ, скорбь свою съ разсказовъ и стонахъ.
Глубоко затая.

Прошлое я скажутъ: въ разгарѣ боя
Мужай вождь упалъ,
И близкие къ нему упрям смерть героя
Нѣтъ тросить образа.

Въ его войскѣ ты ссть, какъ искра, пробѣгая, —
И была жестокій бой,
Когда солнце уже остывающее
Сердечной головой.

Moreover, he remained obsessed with this theme long after the fateful (for him) year of 1903. In *Story of My Life*, written three decades after the Basel essays, the dialectics of talent and genius surfaces at least twice. First, in a portrayal of Avram Idel'son, a fellow Zionist and editor of *Evreiskaia Zhizn'* (later *Razsvet*): "The word 'talent' is inadequate to describe Idel'son. That man stood on the threshold of genius."[63] Then, in describing Ber Borokhov as "the spiritual leader of Poale-Tsion, who also stood on the threshold of genius."[64] In Jabotinsky's nostalgic and also autobiographical novel *The Five*, written in Russian and published as a book in Paris in 1936, one of the protagonists, an assimilated Jewish "litterateur from the capital," who "was not a real talent, but who bore sparks of true genius,"[65] offers a full articulation of the "lack of genius" theme: "On the heights, Russians ignite incomparable universal fires, but in the flats, splinters flicker. This is the token of their greatness: the sluggish slow-wittedness of millions—so that the spirit of the race would be concentrated more brilliantly in a chosen few. It's the complete opposite with us Jews: among us talent is widely distributed; everyone has some gifts, but there are no geniuses; even Spinoza was only a jeweler of thought, and Marx was simply a conjurer."[66]

That the pervasive "lack of geniuses" theme had premiered in Jabotinsky's first essay on Herzl suggests that for him it was connected to the problem of political leadership. He accepted that the leaders of Zionism and Jewish intellectuals such as Herzl, Nordau, and Idel'son may have had no apparent talents, and in this they differed from regular Jews who were generally talented. As we have seen, Jabotinsky associated the "talents" of Diaspora Jews with mimicry. But the leaders of Zionism were inventors of new political forms, new solidarity, and new ideas, and in this they were geniuses or almost geniuses. Herzl in particular was the prime example of a "genius of the race." This perception did not necessarily square well with how some Russian Zionists felt about Herzl in 1903. For example, Ahad Ha'am and his followers accused Herzl of lacking the true Jewish spirit and doubted his exclusive emphasis on political Zionism.[67] As if responding to this criticism, after Herzl's death in 1904, Jabotinsky further developed his psychological portrait, now adding the requirement of authenticity to the template for the leader of a modern/old nation. Because he did not yet have an appropriate language of authenticity to rely on, he again turned to historical analogies and romantic allusions. In a "real" Jew, Jabotinsky wrote,

> one should feel the great and peculiar sorrow of the Jewish prophets, the Jewish dreamy lyricism, the Jewish fantasy [allowing one] to predict the future, the Jewish belief in the living God ... the Jewish practical genius, the Jewish indigeneity of speech and the authentically Jewish, unmatched by any other people, love of his own tribe. ... In reality, all of these had amalgamated and realized in one living man, and that man was Herzl. ... Herzl was a perfect and complete example of the Jew from top to bottom, the Jew to the marrow of his bones.[68]

It was Herzl's primordial, all-embracing, complete Jewishness that endowed him with power and charisma.[69] To be more like Herzl, Jabotinsky engaged in a rigorous personal decolonization in order to liberate his own authentic Jewish self as a prerequisite for successful political leadership in the national-liberation movement.

In the 1930s when the recognized leader of revisionist Zionism, Vladimir (Zeev) Jabotinsky, revisited in *Story of My Life* his first encounter with Herzl, he kept the original psychological portrait intact. Moreover, by insisting on being a true heir to Herzl's political legacy, Jabotinsky claimed at least some part of his authentic Jewish charisma and wholeness. "I felt that truly there stands before me a man of destiny, a prophet and leader by the grace of God, deserving to be followed even through errors."[70] If we accept Derek Penslar's conclusion that "every generation invents its own Herzl, from the stern and tragic visionary of classic Zionist ideology to the post-Zionist image of Herzl as the neurasthenic aesthete, a narcissist suffering from unrequited love," then Jabotinsky's Herzl should be afforded a niche of his own—that of a postcolonial political leader who inspired the late imperial generation of his followers to embrace their "true self" and overcome a colonial subject within.[71]

THE TROPE OF "PURE BLOOD"

"The sense of national specificity is in the man's 'blood,' in his physical-racial type, and only there," Jabotinsky wrote in 1904, and continued, "it is not in one's upbringing that we should look for the source of the sense of national."

> That is why we do not believe in spiritual assimilation. For a Jew who is born without any admixtures into generations of Jewish blood to adopt the psyche of a German or a Frenchman is physically as inconceivable as for a Negro to cease being a Negro. It is even more inconceivable, because the nucleus of one's psyche is a much more inseparable and irremovable race feature than the color of skin, facial index, or skull form. A Jew reared among Germans may adopt German traditions, words, and habits, [he can] be soaked to the bone with German fluid [*nemetskoi zhidkostiu*]—but the nucleus of his psyche would remain Jewish because his blood, his body, and his physical-racial type are Jewish.[72]

If such a culturally Germanized yet "pure-blooded" Jew marries a "pure-blooded" Jewess, Jabotinsky continued, "their son again will be incontrovertibly Jewish to the very marrow of his bones."[73] This deterministic statement was articulated by someone with the recent and quite successful experience of participating in the imperial Russian, or indeed in the cosmopolitan European culture and "psyche," if not body. The story of a pure-blooded Jewish couple that was culturally assimilated into another higher culture, producing a *son* who was Jewish only by virtue of his inherited blood, was a version of Jabotinsky's personal family history reduced to its biological essentials. This interpretation made Jabotinsky's belated national awakening resemble something scientifically predetermined and objectively inevitable—a logical and natural life, a "life as a theorem."

Since 1904, the theme of "pure blood" had firmly established itself in his political rhetoric. Obviously, Jewish concerns about assimilation played a role in this developing fixation. However, on a deeper level, cultural hybridity as a false and passing phenomenon that would be washed out along with other debris of the imperial past disturbed Jabotinsky's less than biological hybridity—this almost inevitable imperial legacy with irreversible consequences. Hence, he kept insisting:

> It is not in the power of a human being to assimilate with the people of a different blood. For true assimilation, one has to change the body: to become their kin by blood, that is, through a sequence of mixed marriages, over the course of many dozens of years, to produce such a great-grandson, who would have only a negligible admixture of Jewish blood. . . . There is no other way. As long as we remain Jews by blood, the children of a Jew and a Jewess, we may be subject to threats of persecution, disdain, or degradation, but assimilation in the proper sense of the word, assimilation as the complete disappearance of our psychological specificity—is of no danger to us.[74]

Preserving the purity of blood was thus a national mission, especially in an imperial situation where racial mixing presented a permanent danger. It is obvious that Jabotinsky extrapolated from his experience as an assimilated and urban intellectual, for the "danger" of mixed marriages and blood "contamination" in the Pale was still quite low. He therefore warned integrated Jews like himself that "the prevalence of mixed marriages is the only unmistakably efficient means to exterminate nationality as such."[75] Moreover, Jabotinsky predicted that "wars and customs will disappear, but individual differences will never smooth out; they are reflected in the inborn race and are perpetuated by differences of soil and climate; and they absolutely do not hinder friendly progress and mutual respect between nations."[76] To restrain from blood mixing was, therefore, a nation's contribution to the progress of humanity. Family law was the only legal sphere that Jabotinsky found more preferrable in the old Russian and Ottoman Empires than in more modern and democratic states, precisely because these empires preserved confessional marriage and, unlike France or Italy, did not impose a universal civic or religious (Catholic in Italy) legal norm in this exceptionally important sphere. For Jabotinsky, who regarded marriage and family as key institutions of race reproduction, confessional law, at least in its application to Judaism, was a sure means of protecting these institutions from being appropriated by the post-imperial national democratic regimes. As he explained in 1913 in his two-part programmatic article "Self-Governing of the National Minority," "marriage and family laws are intimately connected to the psychological sphere where national and religious moments are especially pronounced. This is the most national part of any national law, ... and here, proud Europe could learn something from the instinctive state wisdom of Turks."[77] In the sphere of marriage regulation, Jabotinsky was ready to borrow not just from the "Turks," but from the repertoire of the "confessional state," as Robert Crews has defined the Russian imperial mechanism of population governance.[78]

No less original was Jabotinsky's deployment of the "pure blood" trope against the competing versions of Jewish nationalism in the Russian Empire. For example, he applied it to disqualify autonomists, whose political goal was the attainment of cultural-administrative autonomy in a democratized empire. Jabotinsky predicted that such an autonomy—without the radical and comprehensive politics of nationalism, without citizenship being exercised exclusively through belonging to a nation, and without turning the empire into a real Nationalitätenstaat— would lead "absolutely naturally and absolutely inevitably" to the proliferation of mixed marriages: "Being myself a brunet, who has nothing against blonds, and living in a city with a population of 15 percent dark-haired people and 85 percent light-haired people, I would encounter and befriend blonds at least three times more often than brunets. And if a Jew socialized among non-Jews three times more intensively than among Jews, it would be only natural (taking into consideration their complete mutual agreement and respect) that in seventy-five out of one hundred cases he would feel attracted not to a Jewish woman, but to a woman of another kin [*inoplemennoi*]."[79]

All the fixations and phobias of Jabotinsky's nationalism reveal themselves in this passage: the male as the main actor on the marriage market and, hence, the one responsible for reproduction of the nation with pure blood (the proverbial "son"); the danger stemming from the urban imperial "mating pot"; the menace of hybridity; the meaningless and even counterproductiveness of the struggle for collective Jewish rights within the old imperial setting; and a belief in the biological foundation of social phenomena. He denied the right to identify as nationalists those who disagreed with his biological arguments: "But do not call yourselves nationalists. Nationalists are those who aspire to preserve racial particularity [*plemennuiu samobytnost'*] forever and by any means."[80] When measured by this criterion, autonomism was not nationalist enough. Jabotinsky wondered how politically and nationally conscious people who were familiar with modern science could disregard the danger of blood mixing. How autonomists could accept that in the future "someone from Kamchatka could develop a racial psyche and a racial type identical to that of someone from Tunis,"[81] or that marriages were possible between "the Portuguese and Samoyeds, or Albanians and Chinese. One cannot speak seriously about such things."[82]

Jabotinsky even more harshly exposed the false logic of Jewish socialists who either did not grasp the primacy of race and the progressive nature of nationalism or put universalist socialist goals ahead of national interests, producing yet another erroneous compromise. In the 1900s he dealt with this problem in dozens of newspaper columns, journal essays, and public presentations. But Jabotinsky delivered his most powerful condemnation of Jewish socialism in a different and unexpected genre— in his play in verse, *A Strange Land* (*Chuzhbina*), published in Petersburg in 1910. The play exposed the moral bankruptcy of all sorts of Russian Jewish socialists, whose ideological schemas could not compete with the elementary forces of history and human nature. Of Jabotinky's literary work, *A Strange Land* is the one least known to scholars but one that deserves serious attention.[83] Omri Ronen prized it as "the best poetic play in the Russian language since [Alexander Griboyedov's] *Woe from Wit*."[84] As a historical document, it is no less remarkable: at every level, from composition to meter and from articulated ideologies to the dramatis personae section (where protagonists are divided into two distinct groups, [1] Russians, and [2] Jews), it employs a consistent, elaborate politics of difference.[85] Ronen has noted that many of the play's protagonists "speak in their national meter: ordinary Jews—in folklore accentual verse, Ukrainians—in *Kolomyika* verse. The intelligentsia use iambic pentameter, and a Jewish schoolboy proves a theorem in iambic hexameter."[86] Older religious Jews in a synagogue speak differently from their assimilated and politicized children; and the play ends with their prayer and their voice. As one reviewer in 1910 summarized the lesson of the play: "When a new scum of strange land sweeps over [*kogda pronositsia novaia nakip' chuzhbiny*], the Jew, the root of the Jewish people, continues doing what he was doing before he was interrupted." Only a "hardly audible chorale of grief" rises over the half-darkened synagogue.[87] The reviewer was referring to the final dramatic scene in which "children" interrupted the prayer of their "fathers" in view of the approaching pogrom and staged a political rally in the synagogue. The "children" had been invested in the politics of class liberation of the "strange land" and strange people, who were now betraying them. As it turns out, "proletarians" were among the pogromists, and the non-Jewish socialist intelligentsia were not immune to antisemitism. And the Jewish "children" proved predictably incapable of protecting their "fathers."[88]

Jabotinsky did not spare any of the young Jewish socialists in the play, including the one who came closest to abandoning Marxism and embracing nationalism (Gonta). But even he, or especially he, is stained by the attachment to the "strange land" and strange race. Gonta is in love with a Russian girl, Natasha, from whom he conceals his Jewishness because Natasha feels an intuitive disgust regarding Jews. Gonta does not reject blood mixing, whereas Natasha rejects him the moment his identity is disclosed. For Jabotinsky, Gonta's willingness to risk the purity of Jewish blood undervalues and undermines his ideological nationalism, and hence he is assigned, together with the rest of Jewish socialists, to the "scum of the strange land." Gonta's love story thus extends the limits of personal drama and personal moral failure. Gonta, the only nationally thinking protagonist among the Jewish socialists in the play, appears to be willing to commit a crime against his race, a political crime. He remained a hybrid and corrupt product of the empire, spoiled by socialist universalism. The play powerfully exposed such universalism in a "strange land" as a grave political mistake and a personal failure. Under colonial conditions, Jewish nationalism and the politics of purity of blood were the only possible political choices for Jabotinsky.

That Jabotinsky's struggle with imperial hybridity for national/racial purity and the politics based on it were so profoundly gendered and permeated with concerns over marriage regulation and sexual selection is not in the least surprising. As the historian Mirna Sheldon has aphoristically put it, "during the nineteenth century sexuality became a secular theory of race,"[89] and Jabotinsky's search for the appropriate idiom of authentic and modern Jewishness shows that it remained so in the twentieth century too, especially in the underregulated and underrationalized imperial milieus. More interestingly, the case of Jabotinsky and his Zionist followers does not neatly fit the Foucault-inspired notions of biopolitics and biopower as techniques of population management and control deployed by modern states. Biopolitics, even when it ceases to be a politics of sovereignty and becomes a politics of society, is still associated with governmentality, with the mechanism of state power "that endeavors to administer, optimize, and multiply it [life], subjecting it to precise controls and comprehensive regulations."[90] But Jabotinsky's conscious embrace of the subaltern position places these same mechanisms within a powerless, colonized nation that has neither its own state nor territory or an institutionalized power machine capable of deploying biopolitical technics.[91] Jabotinsky's anti-imperial racialized Zionism was a vision of subaltern biopolitics of the powerless that lacked institutional foundations as well as conceptual coherency. As we have seen, it combined Eastern and Western, scientific and religious ("confessional marriage") concepts and approaches. This inward-looking biopolitics appealed to race as the source of national consciousness—the essence of nationality—that alone could mobilize the nation to perform as a biopolitical state.

FOUR

JEWISH RACE VERSUS RUSSIAN RACE

> When two parties are struggling among themselves, they try to convince each other; when two nations are competing, they try to force each other out.
>
> Vladimir Jabotinsky, "Samoupravlenie natsional'nogo men'shinstva," 1913

> Among Arians, Russians make up one of the most homogeneous groups.... Jews do not have a national life but remain a race. Race is basic, the most elemental form of life of a nation.
>
> Ivan Sikorsky, *Chto takoe natsiia i drugie formy etnicheskoi zhizni?* 1915

THE IDEAL OF PURE BLOOD and the complete nationalization of politics were hardly attainable in the Russian imperial situation, and not just for the Jews. Modern Russian nationalists of the early twentieth century struggled especially hard to reframe complex imperial Russianness in such restrictive normative categories. Lacking a coherent Russian national body or at least unable to ensure its uncontested purity, and struggling with the overlap between the contiguous imperial territorial possessions and what could have been imagined as the Russian national "heartland," they too felt that the empire in many ways had distorted the natural order of things.¹

One of the most outspoken among these modern Russian nationalists, the psychiatry and neurology professor of Kiev St. Vladimir University Ivan Sikorsky (1842–1919), was in some sense an evil doppelgänger of Jabotinsky.² He actively participated in nationalist politics, denounced hybridity, and tried to educate his readers about the phenomena of race and nationality. Sikorsky advanced a national project that had more reasons and more resources to claim its hegemonic status vis-à-vis other nationalisms, and his goal was a Russian nation-state rather than *Nationalitätenstaat*. Nonetheless, he and Jabotinsky shared the same rhetorical repertoire in their criticism of the old empire, and a similar understanding of scientific politics. Like Jabotinsky, Sikorsky argued that the time had come to do away with archaic imperial life— only in the name of the "Russian people and the state created by this people."³ He also acknowledged the fact of "racial mixing" in antiquity that had led to the formation of modern races, including the Russian race. Both of them understood human history as progressing from the racial to the national stage, with race always functioning as the basis for "national individualism" (Jabotinsky's term). Sikorsky speculated that a genuinely fruitful racial mixture, one enhancing the qualities of races, was achievable only through the voluntary convergence of mutually complementary races.⁴ Apparently, this was the case with the prehistoric Slavic and Finnish races: the latter had voluntarily dissolved itself in the Slavic race, changed its religion, and adopted a better "instrument for expressing thoughts," that is, a Slavic language.⁵ Similarly to Jabotinsky's interpretation of the racial history of Jews in Canaan, Sikorsky imagined a race-colonizer absorbing complementary, though inferior, races. The resulting stable formula of the Russian race ensured the durability of the modern Russian nation.⁶

Directly extrapolating from this conclusion, Sikorsky argued that the superior Russian-Aryan race was capable of absorbing lower races without compromising its initial racial composition and that this was a natural mechanism of nationalizing the empire. To prove his point, Sikorsky had to manipulate Russia's imperial map of human diversity. For example, he tried to ignore the presence of Muslims in Russia's geographic heartland (the Volga and Kama basins), with their developed cultural tradition and religion. The civilizational status of Muslims undermined their placement among the primitive lower races that could easily have been absorbed by the superior Russian Aryan race. Only with internal Muslims disappearing from view could Russians be imagined as racially colonizing smaller non-Russian peoples in their midst, thus producing a Russian racial core that would be surrounded by the non-Russian peripheries. This was Sikorsky's biopolitical blueprint for turning the Russian Empire into a modern Western-type empire with the Russian nation-state as its core and with distinct colonial peripheries.[7]

Jews constituted an obstacle for the implementation of this brilliant plan because they were spread all over the core territory and did not have their own territorial periphery. In addition, Jews as a race were not complementary to the Russian race and hence could not be assimilated without inflicting harm on it. In Sikorsky's language, the "life-program" of the Semitic race constituted a complete opposite to that of the Russian Aryan race. Interestingly, contrary to his stated intentions, this perspective on the empire endowed only Russians and Jews with independent subjectivities, expressed in their incompatible "life-programs." For the rest, only two options remained: to be absorbed into the Russian racial and national body, or to be openly reduced to colonial status. In his own way, Jabotinsky also stressed the paradoxical symmetry between the imagined nationalized Russians and Russian Jews: "I consider Russia an amazing country: the best Slavs and the best Jews live there. Best in the sense that they are entirely whole, entirely devoid of that superficiality that Ahad Ha'am decried in western 'Israelites' as 'Slavery in freedom.'"[8]

Sikorsky and Jabotinsky were partners in the postimperial dialogue and, regardless of their strong political differences, stood together in the attempt to nationalize—although in different ways—the empire and its political sphere.

In 1911, Jabotinsky literally played out their uneasy dialogue in the feuilleton "Exchange of Compliments: Conversation," in which two interlocutors, a Russian and a Jew, discussed the issue of race.[9] The Jew opened the conversation by asserting that humanity was divided into distinct races that were nonetheless "approximately equivalent." To a skeptical remark from the Russian, "How come? Are Chukchees and Hellenes equals?" the Jew replied that under the same conditions Chukchees would have done as well as Hellenes did.[10]

The opposition of Chukchees and Hellenes was symptomatic of the Russian political and intellectual debates of the 1910s. In the discourse of new Russian nationalism, Russians stood for a nation that belonged to Western civilization rooted in the ancient Greek and Roman heritage. The mysticism of the pagan, prehistoric Slavic past played little role in this science-oriented, rational discourse. Chukchees, on the other hand, exemplified a primitive stage of evolutionary development and even a civilizational and historical deadlock. But in the broader fin-de-siècle political and cultural context, they could rhyme with Jews, as both were described through the fashionable trope of primitivism.[11] Russian Jewish nationalist intellectuals also deployed it as an equalizing comparative framework in the imperial context. Whereas the leading imperial anthropologists of the "primitive" Siberian *inorodtsy* and the activist of Jewish liberal politics and racial anthropology, Lev Shternberg, personally did not like parallels between the subjects of his Siberian ethnography and his "militant" Jewish science, members of his immediate circle, such as the former Russian populist, exile, and ethnographer of Siberian natives Vladimir Bogoraz or another former populist-turned-Jewish ethnographer, S. An-sky (Shloyme Zanvl Rappoport), did embrace this approach. Shternberg's refusal to consider Jews as "primitives" (i.e., preserving authentic forms of social organization and culture and living a protocommunist communal life) was motivated by his understanding of race and nation. He argued that Jews had developed an autonomous and sophisticated cultural sphere and located race in their national psyche, whereas Siberian natives' social, economic, and cultural spheres were not yet clearly differentiated. The latter still needed to progress toward the stage when their "racial psyche" would be able to generate complex forms of national consciousness.[12] However scholastic and at times cumbersome, this and similar interpretations of primitivism exemplified the politics of intra-imperial comparison present in every project of imperial modernization or revolutionary transformation. The Jabotinsky's feuilleton Russian and Jewish protagonists clearly operated within this comparative semantic field. The fictional Russian, for example, demonstrated solid familiarity with the Russian Jewish situation and scholarly theories of Jewish race: "I cannot say that I completely agree with [Houston Stewart] Chamberlain, although he is a very intelligent and very thoughtful thinker. I also cannot completely agree with your own [Otto] Weininger, although he cites many striking, profound arguments that prove that the Jewish race is defective, so to speak. Then, I read something written from your side as well—by [Heinrich] Graetz, who discards race altogether, or by a new author [Ignaz] Zollschan, who thinks that the Jewish race is superb."[13]

Finally, in addition to academic literature, both Jabotinsky's protagonists were well-informed about the politics of race in the United States, and in this they mirrored an interest common to Russian political elites, from socialists to liberals and from regionalists to modern nationalists. Jabotinsky often referred to the United States to illustrate his view of racial hatred as being endemic to any political regime, from autocracy to democracy. In a 1910 newspaper column, "Homo Homini Lupus," he observed: "A Russian Jew, if he cannot bear it anymore, after all, can convert. American Negroes were Christians long ago, and they have no further recourse. Race cannot be washed out."[14] The message of this essay was twofold: it denounced racism, but at the same time posited the objective nature of racial differences, grounded in human nature, and the need to deal with them politically.

Unlike Jabotinsky, his Russian protagonist identified with the racism of white Americans.[15] In comparing the black race in the United States and the Jewish race in the Russian Empire he closely followed the blueprint offered by Professor Sikorsky, who most probably served as a prototype for this erudite modern Russian nationalist. Sikorsky usually referred to American "negroes" when he wanted to justify segregation and violence against Jews: "There, the predatory sensuality and erotic boldness of Negro elements present a danger for each white woman who finds herself near a colored fellow. Separate coaches in railway trains, special halls in restaurants, and the very fact of a profound segregation of whites from blacks cannot be explained only by the Negro's odor or his skin color. To an even greater degree, this segregation is caused by the danger of the wild instinct. Defending against it, a cultured American cannot restrain himself from pogroms and lynch law."[16]

The word *pogrom*, unlike *lynching*, clearly belonged to Russian realities, and its appearance in the previous quote (coming from Sikorsky's study of the racial type of Russia's greatest poet, Alexander Pushkin) was not accidental. Sikorsky stressed parallelism between "Negros" and "Jews" who both exhibited wild racial instincts. Civilized citizens—white Americans and Russians—had no other choice but to protect themselves by resorting to "pogroms and lynch law." Like Jabotinsky, who proudly called himself a nationalist, Sikorsky never felt ashamed to expose his antisemitism and never restrained himself from acting according to his views. In addition to publishing and lecturing on the topic, in 1913 he testified as an expert scholarly witness in court, supporting the blood libel accusation against the Kyiv Jew Mendel Beilis, and by extension, the entire Jewish people. In the courtroom he claimed, "The psychological basis of crimes of that type is sought in racial revenge" and reminded the court that the Jewish race was dangerously "interspersed among other nationalities, where it carries the traits of its racial psychology."[17] Sikorsky applied his ideas in medical practice, too. At the Kiev University clinic for nervous disorders, he treated individual Jewish patients as bearers of collective traits of their race and performed painful experiments on them. He never asked for their consent and rarely refrained from disclosing their names in the articles published in the journal *Problems of Neuropsychiatric Medicine and Psychology*, which he edited.[18]

Sikorsky's provocative frankness about his views, especially in academic and legal settings, and his readiness to act on them, was not very typical even in his ideological and political milieu, not to mention among those who did not share his version of Russian nationalism. Beilis's experienced defense attorney, Oskar Osipovich Gruzenberg, who held no illusions regarding the antisemitism of those who supported the accusation, was still troubled by Sikorsky's racism. Soon after the trial he confessed to the interviewer of *Razsvet*: "Just imagine this nightmare: the Jewry, the three-thousand-year-old [Jewish] culture, which Jews have been lavishly scattering around the world to all peoples, now have to defend themselves against the accusation of cannibalism!"[19] This was Gruzenberg's reaction to the "wild instincts" talk. But Sikorsky's rhetorical strategy had a lot in common with Jabotinsky's (of which more examples to follow). Both of them considered the available political language of monarchism or socialism to be unsuitable for conveying the essence of their nationalisms and they looked to science as a resource for new political idioms and arguments (Sikorsky: "The duty of Russian nationalists consists in all-embracing study of the Russian people and all the other peoples, races, and tribes that belong to the state"[20]). Both Sikorsky and Jabotinsky insisted on constructing rigid binary oppositions and on sharpening the wording and conclusions in nationalist political statements; both aspired to eliminate obstacles between discourse and action; and both tried to eradicate ambiguity and hybridity from their political speech.

The Russian and Jew of the Jabotinsky's feuilleton were advertisements of these principles. They believed in the reality of race and agreed on the usefulness of racial separation, although differently understood. For the Jew, separation would secure the freedom of development to diverse but equal races. For the Russian, it meant separation from the inferior, "undeniably defective" race. He articulated a laundry list of the usual anti-Jewish racist stereotypes: Jews were incapable of original creativity—they only borrowed and popularized, including the very idea of monotheism; the Jewish "gamut of sensations is very small and does not have chromatic shades," Jewish religion is pragmatic and lacking in abstract qualities, the Jewish race is incapable of loyalty and patriotism, and so on. In real life, Sikorsky was among those who readily supplied such lists for both the academic and political markets. His programmatic work, *What Is a Nation and Other Forms of Ethnic Life?* (1915), a synthesis of the expert discourse of modern Russian nationalism, featured the most extended version of the list.[21] The title unmistakably evoked the famous Sorbonne lecture by Ernest Renan, "What Is a Nation?" (1882), suggesting that Sikorsky saw himself as a Russian heir to the famous scholar. Trying to imitate Renan, he fashioned himself as a specialist on Jewish civilization. Thirty out of fifty-six pages of his nationalist synthesis were dedicated to Jews—a strikingly disproportionate number, unless he viewed Jews as an integral part of the project of modern Russian nationalism, its indispensable negative pole compensating for the absence of a proper positive scenario of self-sufficient Russianness. The list of stereotypes, organized as binary oppositions, had to illustrate the antagonistic nature of the two races. The binaries included: idealism (Russian Aryans) versus rationalism (Jews);

developed moral and emotional spheres versus insolence, cynicism, and emotional primitivism ("elementary and vulgar nature" of Jews)[22]; patriotism and superior collectivity versus propensity for treachery, primitive groupness, and the underdeveloped idea of fatherland (Jews "do not cherish the territory where they live and do not regard it as a fatherland")[23]; a settled way of life versus nomadism (Jews were not a Diaspora; they were never expelled—they led a nomadic life in accordance with their racial instinct; by introducing the Jewish Pale of Settlement, Russia wanted to help the Jews to become sedentary yet failed to stop this "racial stream")[24]; perfection of the nation's spiritual world versus numerical growth of the race and the accumulation of wealth for it; and original creativity versus the nonexistence of a proper Jewish art. The conclusion demanded racial segregation—a policy that under the old regime had never been implemented on the scale and with the ideological consistency desired by Sikorsky. Even during World War I, when the Russian military authorities assumed full control over the borderland territories adjacent to the eastern front, the official empire did not make a de facto institutionalized racism toward Jews (and also Germans and Catholic and Uniate peasants of the Western Borderlands) an official state policy.[25]

In the world of the feuilleton, Jabotinsky prevented the realization of Sikorsky's racist utopia by making the Jew a winner in the rhetorical competition. For this, however, the Jew had to give up his inconsistent racial egalitarianism (all races are different but equal). In the actual ideological context in which Jabotinsky operated, the line between the two positions was indeed quite thin. *Razsvet*, the official periodical of the Russian Zionist organization in which Jabotinsky played a leading role, had an especially hard time balancing racial egalitarianism. For example, one of *Razsvet*'s premier publicists, Daniil Pasmanik, propagated the view that all races were mixed in their composition and creative and equal in terms of their abilities. He opened the article "Racial

Anti-Semitism" (October 1911) with the claim that the Jewish race was no different from others, was mixed (a "mixture of Bedouins, Hittites, and Amorites, of which all three, probably, were Semites"), but from "the time of Ezra" it has closed itself to further mixing and remained pure. Throughout history, Pasmanik asserted, Jews have contributed to the progress of Western civilization by participating in all spheres of the life of Western societies. The normalizing tone, however, had changed abruptly by the end of the article: "We, Jews, should remember that we are not just a religious congregation but a distinct race.... To other nations we can say only this: 'Yes, we differ from you, but we are not a bit inferior to you. To the contrary, you were still savages when we generated timeless values for humanity. And until nowadays you continue to consume our values.'"[26] This defensive-aggressive ending closely resembled the final exchange between Jabotinsky's fictional protagonists.

The same issue of *Razsvet* featured another article focused on race, "The Aryan Knights." Like Jabotinsky's feuilleton, it was structured as a rhetorical competition between the author and his friend, on the one side, and Russian nationalists treating Jews as a lower race, on the other. Prime Minister Petr Stolypin and the leading columnist of the Russian nationalist newspaper, *Novoe Vremia* (New Times), Mikhail Men'shikov, personified the latter group. The Jewish "party" identified them as fake "Slavs-Aryans," themselves belonging to an inferior race:

> Once my friend and I enjoyed a chance to observe Mr. Men'shikov. We saw him with our own eyes and at a close distance. We saw Mr. Men'shikov in his bodily incarnation, independently from his moral "spirit." And suddenly, we felt so joyful.
>
> Look! my friend exclaimed! Look at his face: This man! This is the man who distributes certificates to races and divides them into higher and lower! This man! Is he a Slav? He looks either like a Buryat, or a Mongol, or God knows who; his eyes are hardly visible and his carnivorous mouth hangs on the spike of his face....

Oh, this is beautiful! . . . A representative of the higher race! . . . A Blond Aryan![27]

Jabotinsky's version of transition from racial egalitarianism to overt racial competition was more sophisticated. His Jewish protagonist did not comment on the "degenerative" physical appearance of the Russian. Instead, he replicated his polemical strategy, based on tendentious reading of the authoritative course of Jewish history by the German Jewish historian Heinrich Graetz.[28] Jabotinsky's fictional Jew, in turn, chose the empire's most popular history textbook by Dmitry Ilovaiskii.[29] He interpreted the foundational story of the "invitation of the Varangians" to rule over the "Russian" tribes, or the subsequent submission of the Rus' princes to Mongol rule as evidence of the weakly developed national self-consciousness. The latter reflected the weakness of the race.

> Should we begin measuring one against the other, all will depend on the yardstick, and I . . . will insist then on a yardstick of my own: someone is superior who is more adamant, who can be exterminated but cannot be "taught a lesson"; those who never, even when oppressed, would give away their internal independence. Our history begins with the words "you are a *stiff-necked people.*" And today, after so many centuries, we are still struggling, still rebelling, we have not given up. We are an indomitable race forever and ever. I do not know a higher aristocratism than this one.[30]

"Aristocratism"—a favorite word in Jabotinsky's vocabulary of nationalism—connoted dignity, but like any aristocratism it had to be based on the exclusivity of origins (as in his portrait of Herzl). The Jews may have been colonized externally, but they preserved their aristocratic purity of blood and dignified perception of the self. This uncompromising stance brought the opinions of Jabotinsky closer to that of the ideologues of Russian racial nationalism and antisemitism such as Sikorsky, who advocated national isolationism and the complete exclusion of Jews from Russia's life.

"ON MIMICRY AND MAN" AND INSTINCTS

Jabotinsky loudly declared his position on Jewish self-exclusion in the discussion triggered by the 1908 article "Jews and Russian Literature," penned by his close friend and fellow Odessan Kornei Chukovsky (born Nikolai Korneichukov). Chukovsky's article instigated a huge scandal in intelligentsia circles by openly articulating what had already been in the air—the idea of Jewish organic otherness.[31] "The midwife is not the same as the birth-giving mother," Chukovsky wrote. Jews' contribution to Russian culture could not conceal the fact that they were "barren and fatally unable to give birth" (Chukovsky's organicist language and his gendered bodily metaphors speak volumes about this social discourse).[32] Having formed "on a different national soil," the Jewish race could not organically express itself through Russian culture. Regardless of his own blurred ethnic origin, cosmopolitan Odessa upbringing, and profound embeddedness in the Russian culture, Chukovsky denied the existence of the imperial cultural canon in Russian. To him and Jabotinsky, this was an ethnic culture of ethnic Russians in their Russian language, the product of a shared biological and historical experience of the Great Russian people. Chukovsky had publicly promoted such views since 1904—under Jabotinsky's influence and following his friend's Zionist evolution—in local Odessa periodicals and in the Zionist press associated with Jabotinsky. But now, being presented for the broader intelligentsia readership, the same views acquired a new, scandalous resonance. It not only became apparent that they closely mirrored the antisemitic discourse. Chukovsky's views challenged the intelligentsia's universalism and cosmopolitanism as false and hypocritical feelings.

Jabotinsky did his best to publicize his friend's message. He reiterated the "sad conclusion" that Jewish participation in Russian literature had yielded no useful fruits and that Russia should be left for Russians.[33] At the same time, Jabotinsky did not stop at juxtaposing Jews to Russians, but used Chukovsky's article to advance a more basic colonial dilemma common to all non-Russian intellectuals in the Russian Empire—whether Ukrainian, German, or Georgian—the dilemma of provincialism, nature, and purity versus metropolitan position, urbanity, and hybridity. In his text, the Jewish and other non-Russian cultures in the empire stood for a "village," a remote provincial nook, and the act of abandoning this village was described as migration to a big colonial urban metropolis symbolically designated as Rome: "Every mediocre man prefers Rome to a village."[34] Rome as the archetypal empire and the pre-Zionist Jabotinsky's favorite European destination connected his personal and impersonal anti-imperial iconoclasm on an existential level.

His new discourse of coloniality, in turn, generated responses that went far beyond the conventional intelligentsia's ideological repertoire. A commentator in *Razsvet* insightfully highlighted the sense of mimicry embedded in Jabotinsky's critique of Jewish self-betrayal: "You [the Jews] are very able, but any village boy can dance the *Kamarinskaya* [Russian folk dance] better than you. Hence, here is my advice for you: *Do not grimace, stay true to yourself the way nature and your long history created you.*"[35]

The dancing Russian village boy was an apt metaphor that summed it all up: non-Russians' participation in Russian culture was no more than superficial mimicry (grimacing, aping); Russianness itself was an ethnonational rather than an imperial complex identity; being a natural product of his racial base and national soil, the dancing Russian village boy embodied original cultural creativity—unlike the most sophisticated Jewish "mimic man." That at least Zionist intellectuals could understand and support a conversation in this language was one of Jabotinsky's accomplishments, proof that the work he initiated in 1903 with the language of identity yielded real fruits. Jabotinsky kept addressing his readers—both followers and opponents—with statements that were far from self-evident, that sounded challenging, and required intellectual and emotional investments to be properly understood. "From the days of Bar Kokhba we have not actively participated in our history," Jabotinsky wrote in 1904. The modern Jew was "no self" (*ne ia*), and "one has to wash out the alien layer of him to get to his 'self.'"[36]

People like the aforementioned Vladimir (Waldemar in the English equivalent) Bogoraz (Tan), a Jew and a Russian writer, a well-known populist, exile, and ethnographer, were intellectually paralyzed by this language: "I cannot reject my double nature. To what extent I am Jewish, and to what extent I am Russian—I myself do not know. If you want to find out, carve out my heart and weigh it."[37] Amazingly, Bogoraz (Tan) had already had a similar conversation earlier, in 1904, during his tenure as a reporter for the liberal newspaper *Russkie Vedomosti* (Russian News) at the trial that followed the 1903 anti-Jewish pogrom in Gomel (a city in present-day Belarus).[38] He then interviewed Ivan Kotliarevskii, the chair of the special tribunal, who explained that Jews could never integrate with Russians and into the texture of Russian life, and hence there could not be a Russian Jew:

> Jewish assimilation does not exist. Anthropology denies it; it teaches that in the course of four thousand years, the Jewish type has remained unchanged.
> "I also read Renan," Kotliarevskii remarked with modesty. Nothing has changed from ancient times. Jews were always an alien element amid other peoples. Neither schools, nor Russian language and literature, nor aspirations of Jewish youth for higher education can help this. Jewish nationality [lies] deeper than the language.
> "But you are a Zionist!" I responded involuntarily.[39]

Apparently, Bogoraz felt much more confident, at least morally, polemicizing with a non-Jewish "Zionist" and an antisemite rather than with a Jewish Zionist like Jabotinsky. He believed that the pogrom resulted from the hateful propaganda and isolated existence of Gomel's Jewish and Christian communities.

They simply did not know each other well enough to realize how interconnected their lives were. Bogoraz pointed to friendships that he observed among the thirty Jewish and thirty Christian defendants who had spent a few months together in prison awaiting the trial: "In prison and during the trial, they could observe each other closely. They could see that the so-called racial hatred to which the indictment refers so often and which it directly ascribed to Jews and attributed to Russians only in the form of a 'profound indignation and antagonism,' that all this national discord presumably based on differences in hair color, or accents, or rituals—is not an obstacle to universal harmony."[40]

This was an example of the populist intelligentsia rhetoric that had lost its moral and intellectual prowess after the revolution of 1905. In the postrevolutionary situation of disappointment in the radical intelligentsia's politics and ethos,[41] and with empire being scientifically denaturalized as a passing stage of human evolution and race objectified as the basis for national self-consciousness, it became progressively difficult to find a conclusive response even to the enlightened racial antisemite Kotliarevskii, not to mention Jabotinsky's Manichaean "science of Jewish politics." The power of Jabotinsky's discourse rested in its simplicity and transparency, its postcolonial radicalism and new sincerity. It laid in the "claim by the colonized that their world is fundamentally different. The colonial world is a Manichaean world" (Fanon).[42] Discursively, Jabotinsky already lived in such a Manichaean world and demanded the same from others, especially from the Jewish fellow travelers who embodied for him what Jodi Byrd has called "colonial cacophony."[43] Bogoraz's response to this pressure was very telling:

> Bogoraz: "You want to set up a new closet [for us]" [in response to Jabotinsky's opposition between central/Russian ("a wide and bright hall") and provincial/Jewish ("dark Jewish corner")].
>
> Bogoraz: "I do not feel the desire to take revenge on the Odessa tramps [*bosiaki*] and Volynia *soiuzniki* [members of the nationalist

Union of the Russian People]. They are not to blame; the demons inside them are to blame. . . . 'Father, forgive them, for they know not what they do'" [in response to Jabotinsky's argument that racial hatred is natural and inevitable if nations cannot pursue normal national life].

All Bogoraz's reactions were revealingly centered on the issue of agency. Jabotinsky insisted that all racial/national groups that he imagined as acting in the agonistic imperial political field had to embrace agency and responsibility. This was a precondition for political citizenship, exercised only through belonging to a nation. But the language of Bogoraz was characteristically vague on this very issue. To Jabotinsky's "science of politics" he opposed Christian metaphors of spiritual unity, filtered through Russian populism: "We will not change our old slogans to please Jabotinsky and his neighbors. Our banner is one for all of Russia. One freedom for all, one fraternity for all, and one love for all. We do not dream of turning Russia into many dark closets. We have always wanted and still want to turn Russia into a bright and spacious temple for all."[44]

Besides Marxists, who also advanced a scientific politics and considered nationalism a problem secondary to that of class liberation, very few participants in the 1908 debate about Jews in Russian literature and culture could find an adequate answer to Jabotinsky's challenge. Only irony seemed to work against the Manichaean seriousness of his discourse:

> Ah! Stick to your race!
> Ah! A Jew only for the Jews!
> A Papuan only for the Papuans! . . .
> But where are Kornei's [Chukovsky's] own roots?[45]

Ritualized reminders coming from representatives of the Russian intelligentsia about the danger of racism for the Russian Empire were much less effective: "Sharp-toothed kids are already gape-jawed and are preparing to squabble in the Macedonian style."[46] The collapse of the imperial order and the return to the natural—racial, national—foundations of social life, were precisely the goals of Jabotinsky's politics. Purging political language from the imperial debris was the first step toward this goal. Jabotinsky's provocations directed at the Russian intelligentsia might seem counterproductive and senseless only if one forgets that he became a politician in the context of rising mass politics and never participated in the underground politics of the pre-1905 period. He joined the political field in which leaders of grassroots movements and political parties, along with leaders of public opinion, competed for influence over the masses, and he fully appreciated the power of political speech. Much later, Fanon explicated this practical wisdom from inside his own colonial situation: "In their speeches, the political leaders 'name' the nation. . . . The politicians who make the speeches, who write in the national press, raise the people's hopes. . . . Often the national or ethnic language is used. Here again, expectations are raised and the imagination is allowed to roam outside the colonial order. Sometimes these politicians even declare: 'We black, we Arabs,' and these terms charged with ambivalence during the colonial period take on a sacred connotation."[47]

—⚜—

Jabotinsky led the efforts to "'name' the nation" for Jewish nationalism: he exposed the problematic nature of imperial hybridity and the analytical fuzziness of less radical versions of nationalism. He called a Russian writer of Jewish origin a traitor and conceptualized a Jew as a colonized subject who did not know his true self. "Even my friends told me," admitted Jabotinsky in *Story of My Life*: "You sharpen the edges, exaggerate the points."[48] His intentionally provocative linguistic policy—in fact, stopping short of a full-scale war over language—makes sense only if analyzed in terms of the postcolonial strategy of liberating language as the main instrument of political and cultural expression from domination by the colonial episteme. The same can be said about Sikorsky and other modern Russian nationalists who struggled for liberation of the Russian language from imperial domination and appropriation and advocated its reinstallation as their exclusive national language, the product and instrument of Russian national culture. In his works, Sikorsky explicitly named Russian the national language of the Russian race-nation. His linguistic theory recognized the decisive contribution of "Southern Russians" (he denied the reality of Ukrainians on scientific grounds) to formation of the Russian national linguistic norm in the eighteenth century. This, however, only confirmed the "objective law" recognizing only one national language for one national community that developed from a common racial background: "Southern Russians did not prioritize their own tribal language but joined their Great Russian comrades in thought and speech [*prisoedinilis' k Velikorusskim tovarishcham mysli i slova*]."[49] Naturally, any act of appropriation of a national language and national-cultural production in that language by those belonging to other races/nations amounted to nothing but mimicry. This constituted a sphere of consensus among modern anti-imperial nationalists, although they could derive different conclusions regarding the biological and political limits of Russianness. And another major sphere of consensus had formed around the inadequacy of the empire's political and legal language, which did not reflect the new science of politics—Jewish or Russian, or any other. Sikorsky agreed with Jabotinsky that "the Russian official terminology in this sphere [of nationality] is only in the process of elaboration." Ideally, the new administrative and political language of empire had to reflect the complexity of linguistic and cultural imperialism, Jabotinsky insisted, and he suggested starting with a reinterpretation of the language question in the Russian imperial census of 1897. From a nationalized perspective, the notion of "native" (*rodnoi*) or "natural" (*prirodnyi*) language in the census had to connote not the language spoken at home (for example, Jabotinsky's own home of Russian speakers), which could be a result of accommodation or mimicry, but the language of race—"the language of my nature, my national essence."[50] All that was needed in order to clearly "name the nation," scientifically differentiate Jewishness from Russianness, Ukrainianness and other nations in the imperial polity, and look "outside of the colonial order."

FIVE

NATIONALIZING POLITICS IN THE EMPIRE

> National essence exposes itself not solely in firmly fixed, precisely designated spheres of human activity. Rather it permeates human activity in its totality, and influences every aspect of it, either explicitly or implicitly. The individual's entire psychological apparatus is national in the most profound sense. And because it determines all our conscious or even subconscious functions, there is no such sphere in our active life that would not, one way or another, reflect national differences, attractions, and repulsions.
>
> Vladimir Jabotinsky, "Samoupravlenie natsional'nogo men'shinstva," 1913

THE POLITICS OF NATIONAL REPULSION

The provocative debate about Jews in Russian literature was followed by a literary provocation: in June 1912, the newspaper *Odesskie Novosti* published Jabotinsky's most controversial story "Edmee," about the platonic love of a fifty-year-old German Jewish doctor for a twelve-year-old girl.[1] On the surface, this much less famous predecessor of Vladimir Nabokov's *Lolita* had nothing to do with the Russian Empire and Russian Jews. Rather, it belonged to the decadent European literary canon and reflected turn-of-the-century European fears and sensibilities. Michael Stanislawski has noted that today "Edmee" can be read as a vivid illustration of Edward Said's *Orientalism*. As it opens, the main protagonist remarks: "The Orient! It is entirely foreign to my soul. Here you have a living refutation of your theories about race and the call of blood. I was born a westerner regardless of the treacherous form of my nose."[2] (In *Story of My Life*, Jabotinsky writes in his own voice, "Western civilization... in my view there exists no other—civilization and the Occident are one thing."[3]) The hero of "Edmee" travels to the East, having been upset in the West, where he, a distinguished scholar and successful doctor, was denied a university chair. He rejects conversion as a way of obtaining the position solely out of aesthetic rather than religious considerations. His escape to the East is motivated by an "unconscious protest of [his] sense of race. You offended me, so in turn, to spite you I am going to the native land [*rodnuiu storonu*] of my race."[4]

Stanislawski has also shown how deeply the doctor in "Edmee" depended on European mental geography: the East for him begins in Constantinople, at this imagined border of European civilization. His "native land" is not directly associated with Palestine but coincides with everything that European civilization rejected as tasteless, uncultured, lacking individuality and sophistication. On the island of Prinkipo in the Sea of Marmara, close to Istanbul, the doctor meets the daughter of the French consul, twelve-year-old Edmee. Although she grew up in Constantinople and has no recollections of her early European childhood, Edmee bears "the stamp of the West" and symbolizes "refined Western culture in *partibus infidelium*."[5] For the doctor, she embodies the pure western body and beautiful, delicate western soul. As Edmee's family is preparing to leave the island, she confesses to the doctor that she would miss her "only friend in Prinkipo." The doctor is flattered and puzzled: "Am I indeed your only friend in Prinkipo, Edmee? What about girls with whom you play? Say,

Cleo?" And with Edmee's reply the story ends: "Oh, Cleo... You know, she is a Jewess and this tells it all. In general, what I hate about Prinkipo is that there are always many Jews around. They are so vulgar, I cannot stand them. Can you?"[6] The final "cannot stand" was not a product of Edmee's European upbringing, which she never had; the repulsion of Jews was dissolved in her delicate European body, literally in her blood. Jabotinsky's most decadent story appeared reducible to one simple argument about the instinctive antisemitism of the West.

However, this would be a highly reductionist reading of the story. The real richness of connotations and political message of "Edmee" becomes clear only if it is read in the context of yet another paradigmatic debate in which Jabotinsky took part a few years prior to the story's publication. It began in 1909 as a private event in the home of the Petersburg actor Nikolai Khodotov. The young Jewish writer Sholem Asch was invited to read his new play *White Bone* for a group of Khodotov's guests. To a critical comment on the play's main female protagonist Rosa, Asch responded that only a Jew, with the intimate knowledge of Jewish everyday life, could understand her. The writer Evgenii Chirikov, who happened to be in the audience, turned Asch's words around and suggested that if this were so, Jews were equally incapable of understanding Russian life and psychology. This, however, never prevented them from actively participating in Russian literature and literary criticism. The exchange touched a nerve in some guests, who expressed their indignation in the St. Petersburg Yiddish-language newspaper *Der Fraynd*, known for its collaboration with Yiddish writers such as Mendele Moykher-Sforim, Y. L. Peretz, Sholem Aleichem, Yankev Dinezon, and some representatives of the younger generation, including Sholem Asch, whose first major work, the prose poem *A Shtetle*, was serialized in the paper in 1904.[7] Because this was a newspaper in Yiddish, its readership was necessarily limited. However, the next day, two popular Russian-language Moscow newspapers, *Russkoe Slovo*

(Russian word, no. 47, 1909) and *Utro Rossii* (Russian morning, no. 48, 1909), reproduced the exchange. *Razsvet* and other newspapers followed suit. *Russkoe Slovo* contacted some of Khodotov's Jewish guests from that evening (Sholem Asch, Osip Dymov, and Akim Volynsky) and asked them to confirm *Der Fraynd*'s initial report, which they did.

At this point, Chirikov felt compelled to come out in public with a long article titled "Thanks, It Was Unexpected!" in which he refused to be considered an antisemite and presented his own version of the event. From the outset, Chirikov framed the conflict as having occurred between the Jewish and Russian members of the audience, thus assigning a clear one-dimensional national identity to every participant in the story. He quoted Sholem Asch as saying that his protagonist Rosa "is painted as a fanatic-type heroine who is protecting the aristocratic Jewish blood," and to understand her "one needs to be a Jew or spend five thousand years with them." "None of the Jews present, either writers or journalists, challenged him," Chirikov complained. This silent agreement inspired Chirikov to react on behalf of the non-Jewish part of the audience: "If we Russians appear to be incapable of understanding a play about Jewish life, this means that you Jewish writers and journalists cannot fully understand and feel our Russian life." Why, Chirikov asked, can they say "we, the Jews," and I cannot say that I am a Russian? He called the entire story "a family incident" that has acquired exaggerated proportions due to the "hypertrophy of nationality."[8]

A new wave of articles and protests followed; they, in turn, were reprinted in multiple venues that served audiences usually unconcerned with the family feuds of the intelligentsia. The story gradually acquired broad circulation. Naturally, Jabotinsky could not stay away from it. He asserted that Chirikov was being honest when "protesting the arrival of kosher meals on Russian literature's table."[9] As a mediocre writer, he simply articulated the views and emotions common to his social milieu. The real villain for Jabotinsky was not Chirikov but Sholem Asch, and this seemingly bizarre substitution was, in fact, very logical for someone who prioritized Jewish subjectivity in any situation and context. Jabotinsky accused Asch of inviting "reviewers from all the Russian newspapers but not one from the Jewish press" to his reading,—"this tells you everything you need to know about the psychology of our poet embraced by the Russian market."[10] The Zionist press agreed. Why did Sholem Asch invite Russian writers to judge his play and then "deny their ability to understand it because of racial otherness?" the Warsaw Hebrew daily *Ha-Boker* (Morning) asked. If a Jewish writer wanted approval from Russian critics, it would have been better had he listened to them without evoking a "racial question."[11] The title of Jabotinsky's article, "Defectors and Masters," framed Asch as a national traitor, who had abandoned a small Jewish village having been seduced by the big, bright hall of colonial culture.[12] Asch was deeply offended. He responded publicly in the pages of *Razsvet*, returning the accusation against those "who publish journals for the Jews in all possible languages except in Jewish."[13] His response was immediately propagated by many central and local periodicals, which escalated the scandal.

Everything about this story signaled the coming of "new times": the Yiddish writer Sholem Asch, one of the most notable representatives of Jewish modernism, was targeted as a traitor by the national Jewish press, whereas the Russian litterateur Evgenii Chirikov, known as an attentive and benevolent observer of Jewish life, came to embody Russian nationalism, antisemitism, and the crisis of the old intelligentsia ethos of inclusivity.[14] Chirikov might have been a mediocre writer, as Jabotinsky insisted, but he was the author of the play *Evrei* (The Jews), earlier hailed by the Zionist press for "artistic objectivity" and for telling "real truth" about Jewish life in the Russian Empire. A review of *Evrei* in *Evreiskaia Zhizn'* (1904) predictably cautioned that Chirikov's "truth" had to be taken with a grain of salt because he was not a Jew writing from his own experience, but even this reviewer admitted that Leiser, the play's main protagonist, was "depicted truthfully."[15] Another article in a Zionist periodical introduced Chirikov's *Evrei* as a rare example of the "unusual—for a gentile writer—knowledge of Jewish everyday life, Jewish thought, and Jewish characters." Chirikov grasped "the inner sense of Jewish life," the soul of the modern Jew.[16] The review pointed out that during the days of October 1905, Chirikov's *Evrei* was staged as an antipogrom propaganda play. "There were even instances when theater directors invited real pogromists onstage in the fourth act, for the sake of utter realism, thus diverting them from their lively 'activity' [*kipuchei 'deiatel'nosti'*] in those October days.... Almost every staging of *The Jews* is still accompanied by cases of hysteria and fainting in the audience. Those terrible days are still too close!"[17]

Additional evidence supports this seemingly improbable testimony. According to one recollection, on November 23, 1905, when *Evrei* premiered at the New Theater in St. Petersburg, the theater "resembled a political club," in which the audience held "improvised political rallies" after every show. "Sometimes, these rallies would erupt in the middle of a performance as, for example, during the performance of the play *Evrei*, which was popular at the time."[18] Another reporter emphasized the impact on the New Theater's audience of the pogrom scene in *Evrei*: "At the beginning of the last act, when a distressed Jewish family collects its miserable belongings in anticipation of the pogrom, the entire auditorium becomes one continuous moan [*zritel'nyi zal prevratilsia v odin sploshnoi ston*]. When threatening shouts of the approaching crowd begin to resonate from afar, the mood of the public reaches its apogee; many, especially ladies, rush away from the theater."[19]

In 1906–1908, *Evrei* was performed by traveling theater groups in more than forty towns across the empire, including Tiflis, Warsaw, Vilna, Riazan, Smolensk, Minsk, Orenburg, Tobol'sk,

Khar'kiv, Barnaul, and Ekaterinoslav. In 1906 in Odessa, the city theater's production of the play generated record-high profits.[20] By the end of the revolution (1907), the play had been published in Ukrainian translation, and its title read *Evrei* rather than the region's more traditional and widespread Polish *Żidy*, which sounded derogative in Russian and, apparently, offended sensibilities of some educated Ukrainian, too. Jabotinsky's fellow anti-imperial nationalist, Symon Petliura—at the time, the editor of Ukrainian nationalist periodicals (the Kyiv newspaper *Slovo* (Word) and, a bit later, the journal *Ukrainskaia Zhizn'*, the "twin" of *Evreiskaia Zhizn'*)—authored the introduction to this Ukrainian translation. Like many other Ukrainian nationalists at the time, he considered the Ukrainian theater, which had only recently been legalized by the authorities, one of the most important public venues for national work. Hence Petliura's insistence on staging *Evrei* in these theaters for the Ukrainian-language public was all the more significant.[21] This episode is particularly remarkable, because in his capacity as the chief of military forces and head of the government of independent Ukraine (1918–1919) during the turbulent years of the Ukrainian revolution and Civil War, Petliura became associated in Jewish memory and historiography with pogroms and antisemitism. Collaboration with Petliura through this period became a highly problematic episode in Jabotinsky's biography.[22] But before 1914, they both believed in a strategic alliance between Jewish, Ukrainian, and all other non-Russian national movements, none of whom had its own nation-state yet. In his introduction to Chirikov's play, Petliura referred to Judeophilism and humanism as common features of all the nationalisms of the oppressed: "The suffering of Nachman in Chirikov's *Evrei* will evoke profound sympathy in everyone even if they do not belong to this nationality, whose historical destiny has been to carry the heavy cross of oppression and violence.... And even if not everyone agrees with Nachman's idea that the medicine he wants to use to heal the wounds of his people will produce the desired results, the necessity to pour healing balm on these wounds is nevertheless obvious."²³

These responses to Chirikov's *Evrei* suggest that, to contemporaries, it was more than just a play about Jewish life. It was a symbol of the Russian intelligentsia's humanism and universalism; one of the rare examples of "truthful" representation of the Jews in Russian literature; a condemnation of antisemitism and pogromist nationalism; and, for some, a confirmation of humanism embedded in nationalisms of the oppressed. That the author of such an exemplary play became the center of the scandal over the acceptance of Jews by the humanist and universalist Russian culture and intelligentsia, meant that the familiar sociocultural and political landscape had changed and new ideological divisions had surfaced. Given this symbolism, no wonder the scandal became known as the "Chirikov incident."

EMBRACING A "NATIONAL FACE" AND THE POLITICS OF ASEMITISM

The scandal culminated in March 1909, when the leading Russian liberal politician and intellectual Peter Struve published an article, "Intelligentsia and the National Face," in the newspaper *Slovo*.²⁴ By that time Struve had completed his personal journey from legal Marxism to the criticism of intelligentsia revolutionarism and then to liberal imperialism of the "Greater Russia" and new Russian nationalism.²⁵ He subscribed to the liberal agenda of providing equal rights to individual citizens of the empire but demanded that the Russian intelligentsia become self-consciously "nationally Russian," defending its right to feel and publicly express elementary and natural "repulsions" of non-Russians, Jews in particular. Struve revised the old thesis that "nationality is race" understood as external physical appearance: "Once they thought that nationality meant race, that is, the skin color, the width of the nose ('nasal index'), etc. But nationality is something much more apparent and at the same time delicate. It is spiritual attractions and repulsions. To become aware of them, one does not have to use anthropological instruments or genealogical studies. They [i.e., attractions and repulsions] live and tremble in our soul."²⁶

And he continued:

> The Russian intelligentsia has always regarded Jews as their own, as Russians, and this was not something accidental, something granted for nothing or as a "misunderstanding." A conscious initiative to reject Russian culture and establish Jewish "national" specificity belongs not to the Russian intelligentsia, but to that Jewish movement known under the name of Zionism. . . . I do not sympathize with Zionism, but I understand that the problem of Jewish nationality exists, and that at the moment this is probably even a growing problem. And at the same time, in Russia there are no other aliens [*inorodtsy*] playing the same role in Russian culture as the Jews. And another complication: they play this role while remaining Jewish.²⁷

Jabotinsky, who was implicitly addressed in this passage, called Struve's ambivalent position vis-à-vis Jews "a-Semitism," which was not yet antisemitism but a transitional stage in the Russian intelligentsia's transformation.²⁸ He wrote that the Judenrein slogan was gradually penetrating progressive Russian journalism, literature, and theater, and this was happening independently of conscious antisemites. "The Russian progressive intelligentsia will not turn anytime soon to anti-Semitism in its crude sense. They will simply express the desire to be left alone, without constantly having a Jewish witness around, [a witness] who has acclimatized too well, feels too much at home, interjects himself into everything, and speaks out on every occasion."²⁹ For Jabotinsky, there was nothing new per se in this prognosis, but he had never before had a chance to present his views at such a high political podium and engage the leading members of Russia's oppositional political elites in a public conversation. Paul Miliukov, the leader of the Constitutional Democrats and the party's most outspoken Duma deputy, joined the debate. He did this in the pages of his party's central organ, the newspaper *Rech'* (Speech, March 11, 1909), thus further broadening Jabotinsky's potential audience. "Mr. Jabotinsky can now rejoice," Miliukov asserted bitterly, "he has lured the bear from the lair," that is, forced the intelligentsia to openly acknowledge the problem of nationalism. Miliukov hoped that this was a temporary nuisance but acknowledged that "the beginning of the new political life in Russia put an end to the old Russian intelligentsia, which was holy and pure in its ignorance." Although the intelligentsia's naive universalism had become a thing of the past, Miliukov saw nationalism as neither a desirable nor an inevitable option and warned his followers against adopting the politics of pitching "[one] nationalism against [another] nationalism."[30] Jabotinsky, to the contrary, welcomed this type of politics, although he also believed in the peaceful cooperation of nationalisms once "natural forms of life" were reestablished. He therefore welcomed the arrival of the mature Great Russian nationalism of Struve as opposed to the pogromist Black Hundred type of nationalism. In Jabotinsky's view, this was a positive development that could speed up the nationalization of all other peoples in the empire and bring it closer to the Nationalitätenstaat ideal.[31]

The debate about nationalism with the leaders of Russian liberalism evidenced how unprepared they were to articulate any convincing alternative to the old-type empireness and new nationalism. In addition, it exposed the split within the elite of the Constitutional Democrats (CD) over the program of liberalization and modernization of the empire. Petr Struve stood on one side of the divide, supported by moderate liberals and some conservatives who believed that empire had impeded the proper development of the Russian nation. Vasily Maklakov, a leading member of the CD party, in his speeches upheld Struve's distinction between a liberal and lawful state that could not embrace antisemitism as an official policy, and Russians in this state who, as individuals and a nation, were fully entitled to ignore Russia's Jews, "to ostracize them socially and boycott them in their business dealings, to avoid looking at works of art they had produced or listening to music they had written."[32] Many left-leaning liberals who aligned themselves with non-Russian national causes also shared this assessment. For example, Maksim Slavinsky seconded Struve's call to "embrace a national face" on behalf of Ukrainian nationalism. Like Jabotinsky, Slavinsky hoped that the development of a "Russian national face" would legitimize other national projects (help "other national faces in the empire to become healthier").[33]

The other side of the broadening divide was represented by Miliukov and many Jewish liberals, including a member of the party's Central Committee Maxim Vinaver and the economist and Jewish activist Ber Brutzkus. Like Miliukov, they waited for "the intelligentsia's reactionary mood to dissipate."[34] As Vinaver wrote in *Rech'*, "despite the pogroms and oppression," it was wrong to place "the problem of 'repulsions'" at the center of the Jewish cause or any other national cause.[35] It was expected that the elimination of all forms of political oppression and inequality in the empire by the liberation movement would automatically resolve the issue of interethnic "repulsions."

Jabotinsky remained largely immune to this criticism because he was outlining an agenda for the politics of the future rather than discussing the realities of the past. Instrumentalization of the "Chirikov incident" was his great victory, as he had succeeded in promoting the issue of nationalism from the margins of intelligentsia discourse to the very center of political debate. By directly engaging the country's leading political and intellectual figures, such as Struve and Miliukov, along with a broad range of Duma deputies, party activists, and influential publicists from both the liberal center and the right, Jabotinsky contributed to nationalizing the mainstream political discourse in the empire. This was his goal since the introduction of the State Duma in 1905.

In 1910 Jabotinsky explained asemitism by analogy with American racism, which, in his view, was based on "something elemental, like the 'national repulsions' of Mr. Struve. That is why they, the white people, in fact cannot bear the presence of a Negro."[36] In 1911 Jabotinsky called "repulsions" the "abnormal life expressions of a nation," which was still a positive sign revealing the presence of "national instincts," much valued by Jabotinsky. He explained that instincts prevailed over reason only when the nation in question was denied legitimate means of self-expression.[37] Written during this time and published in 1912, "Edmee" marked the next stage in Jabotinsky's "psychoanalysis" of the national subconsciousness. Now he questioned the localization of "attractions and repulsions." Instead of connecting them to some ephemeral national soul, he located them in a more tangible substance—in the nation's blood and the nation's psyche. Born with an instinctive repulsion toward Jews, Edmee felt it before she even had a chance to socialize in European society and culture.

Jabotinsky and Struve obviously disagreed on how to normalize the political expressions of "repulsions and attractions"— in the form of a nationally Russian state (Struve) or Nationalitätenstaat (Jabotinsky). At the same time, they both considered attempts to reform the Russian Empire into a democratized supranational or anational polity a nonstarter. This was not only a theoretical debate about the future political arrangement; the two shared a sense of urgency regarding the need to disentangle the imperial mix as a necessary precondition for modern politics. That is why both Struve and Jabotinsky found themselves deeply invested in the fate of Ukrainian nationalism. Jews, Poles, and Ukrainians lived together in the Western Borderlands of the empire and had had a long history of mutual "repulsions and attractions" that were now acquiring new political significance. Struve, like Sikorsky and the majority of modern Russian nationalists, denied the reality of existence of East Slavic nations other than the Russians. He insisted that Ukrainians and Belarusians belonged to one big Russian nation and were mutually "attracted" due to racial, linguistic, cultural, and historical kinship. Dreaming about transforming the empire into the Russian nation-state, Struve worried about inflating the share of Russians. Admitting the persisting cultural differences within the hypothetical big Russian nation, he called it "nation in the making"—using this English phrase in the Russian text and introducing the term as a direct borrowing from the American political language.[38] He translated "nation in the making" into Russian literally, as *tvorimaia natsiia*, but ignored the open-ended and inclusive connotation of the American concept. Struve's version of the Russian *natsiia* was restricted solely to the three East Slavic peoples defined by their racial and cultural proximity. He also recognized only "one Russian culture in a sense that can be applied to national cultures," the high culture of the Russian Empire proclaimed as reflecting the greatest spiritual achievements of the organic big Russian nation. Appropriating and nationalizing this imperial culture as the Russian national culture meant that no comparable Ukrainian culture was objectively possible or needed. Struve maintained that no other people of the empire, except for Finns and Poles, had a national culture comparable to the Russian one, and hence the hegemony of the Russian national culture was an "absolutely natural fact."[39] The nation in the making did not imply the possibility of the progressive integration and amalgamation of willing individuals into a common cultural sphere and citizenship. What Struve meant was the objectively existing Russian nation's arrival at a true understating of self.[40] He estimated that the tripartite big Russian "nation in the making" constituted 65 percent of the empire's population, which was a strong argument in favor of its hegemonic role in an empire that would be then reconstituted in the form of a Russian national core with non-Russian peripheries.

Jabotinsky was quick to identify this political interest behind Struve's calculations: "If, as P. B. Struve wants, all Little Russians and Belarusians will be assigned to a single Russian nation, this nation will rise to 65 percent of the entire population of the empire, thus making a huge majority of two-thirds [of the population]; then the picture will probably indeed be close to the 'nation-state' [model] (1911)."[41] If, however, one considered Little Russians and Belarusians as separate nations, Great Russians were left with only 43 percent of the population and could not claim the status of a titular nation. Jabotinsky therefore urged the Jews of the Pale not to feed the Ukrainian "repulsion" of their race by serving as agents of Russification in a region with a mostly non-Russian-speaking population. As long as the Ukrainian national movement rejected the ideology of the "big Russian nation" and was ready to recognize Jewish national rights in the Diaspora, Jews had no justification for acting as agents of Russian assimilation. At the same time, Jabotinsky released Jews from any moral obligations toward Polish nationalism that did not recognize the right of Jewish nationality to cultivate its cultural and political forms. Here, the situation was abnormal and the Jewish national "repulsions" were given free flow.[42]

There were always many colleagues around Jabotinsky who pointed to antisemitic tendencies in Ukrainian nationalism and recalled the reality of pogroms in the Pale. But like liberal Jewish activists who believed in the democratization of the imperial regime as the universal answer to the Jewish problem, Jabotinsky believed in ultimate conflict resolution through national mobilization and separation. Jews had to separate from Ukrainians, Poles, Russians, and all the others; Ukrainians—from all their neighboring nationalities; Great Russians—from Belarusians, Ukrainians, Jews, and all others. Separate coexistence—based on the recognition of each other's strict boundaries and subjectivities, the rejection of any fluidity and hybridity of identities, and the elimination of any complexity of political formations—was the best and only scientifically sound political remedy against national and racial "repulsions."

Jabotinsky favored Ukrainian nationalism not because he saw manifestations of racial attractions between the two peoples but because he foresaw the possibility of taming national repulsions between them. The colonial situation of the two nations, in his view, was structurally similar. They both experienced oppression by Russian and Polish nationalists; both were unable to conduct cultural policy in their native languages; and both had to deal with the intelligentsia assimilated into the colonial Russian culture and refusing to serve their national "provincial" causes. In 1911, going against the Russian and Jewish nationalist mainstreams, Jabotinsky promoted the celebration of the fiftieth anniversary of the Ukrainian poet Taras Shevchenko's death.[43] Because of his Odessa upbringing and linguistic talent, Jabotinsky could read Shevchenko in the original Ukrainian, which he recognized as a language separate from Russian. He valued Shevchenko as an iconic Ukrainian poet who overcame the almost inevitable subalternity and successfully resisted Russian epistemological and political domination.[44] For someone like Jabotinsky it was not hard to imagine Shevchenko as a fellow postcolonial intellectual, a Manichaean fighter for national culture and racial purity: "O lovely maidens, fall in love, / But not with Muscovites, / For Muscovites are foreign folk, / They do not treat you right" (Taras Shevchenko, "Kateryna," translated by John Weir).[45] Shevchenko's "repulsion" of the Muscovites was a strong argument against the "big Russian nation" project, whereas his greatness, his being living proof of the existence of Ukrainian culture, confirmed Jabotinsky's deepest belief: only those who remain true to their national/racial self could produce a work of real genius. Jabotinsky assumed that the Ukrainian postimperial nation of Taras Shevchenko and the Jewish postimperial nation of Theodor Herzl would be able to mutually separate in such a way as to neutralize "repulsions" and make "attractions" and the structural parallelism of their experiences a basis for rational politics. This could be possible only as long as both nationalisms recognized the primacy of national principle in all spheres of life and with regard to every group, territorial or not, that could show a developed sense of national self-consciousness.[46]

SACRIFICIAL POSTCOLONIALITY

In his last and probably most accomplished novel, *The Five*, published in Paris in Russian in 1936, Jabotinsky offered a postfactum reflection on the entire experience of his generation of Jews in the Russian Empire.[47] Scholars who have studied *The Five* believe that it is "best classified as an autobiographical novel, with its fictional overlay giving Jabotinsky the freedom not just to indulge in nostalgia for a lost past, but also to offer a deeply felt commentary on the telling matters of the day that came to determine his future direction."[48] Stanislawski has even argued that the book provides a more nuanced account of Jabotinsky's spiritual and ideological development than the *Story of My Life*.[49] If so, *The Five* is the most tragic personalized account of the transition from imperial complexity to postimperial simplicity and purity. The novel is set in an imperial city—a topos very central to Jabotinsky's crusade against hybridity, interracial marriage, and cultural assimilation. The city is of course the beautiful and vibrant Odessa. The narrator, often identified with Jabotinsky, tells the very sad story of five members of the Russian Jewish Milgrom family who either died or choose suicide. The family follows the hopeless path of assimilation and, along the way, lose their organic connection with the Jewish collective body and soul, while gaining nothing in exchange. The Milgrom children either die literally (Marusia and Marko), or turn into helpless invalids (Serezha), or become baptized (Torik), or disappear in the revolutionary underground (Lika). Jabotinsky equated the last two choices to death.

The Five was not a Jewish bildungsroman echoing Jabotinsky's formal memoirs, nor did it simply reflect Jabotinsky's political views of the 1930s, coded as a parable from the past. This novel about the decline and degeneration of assimilated Russian Jewish youth did not resonate with the militant and optimistic tone of Jabotinsky's revisionist Zionism. Rather, it picked up an old theme that Jabotinsky had articulated back in 1903 when he complained for the first time that modern Russian literature was dominated by a peculiar protagonist: the young neurasthenic, libertine man with no cultural roots and life goals.[50] Serezha in *The Five* embodied this decadent and uprooted type. Writing in the 1930s, Jabotinsky was already able to confidently oppose to him a new type of Jewish hero who would resemble his Beytar nationalist militant youth. The fact that no such hero appears in *The Five* suggests that its plot and characters belong to the period of Jabotinsky's Russian Zionism. *The Five* is not just a more "truthful" memoir by Jabotinsky. It is an important political testimony connecting the imperial and postimperial parts of his life, and it thus deserves special scrutiny.

―⁂―

On January 15, 1903, the *Odessa News* published Jabotinsky's regular column under his pen name, Altalena, about the Odessa schoolteacher Milgrom.[51] This name was not particularly Jewish-sounding (it can be taken for a German name and was in fact of German origin) or famously Odessan, and the actual teacher in the article, a graduate of the Zhitomir rabbinical seminary, had little in common with the Milgrom father from *The Five*.[52] But for some reason this name stuck in Jabotinsky's memory, as did many other things from that fateful year of 1903.

Later the same year, before departing for the Basel Zionist Congress, Jabotinsky wrote the words that he repeated thirty-three years later in *The Five* as a nostalgic farewell to the beloved Odessa that now ceased to be his "real motherland": "I was born and raised in Odessa. The place where we are born is not always our motherland. My genuine motherland is not on these shores, but I have always loved Odessa very much and even when I leave her, I will never stop loving her."[53] "I'm indifferent only to Russia," wrote Jabotinsky in *The Five*, "I'm not really 'attached' to any country; at one time I was in love with Rome, and it lasted a long time, but even that passed. Odessa's a different matter: it hasn't ever passed and it won't."[54]

Michael Weiskopf has located the prototypes of the young Milgroms in Jabotinsky's play *Chuzhbina*, discussed earlier.[55] I would more cautiously say that these were not direct prototypes but social types (and themes connected to them) that helped Jabotinsky to substantiate his Manichaean worldview. The protagonists of *The Five* did have direct prototypes but not among the *Chuzhbina*'s Jewish socialists.

In June 1910, in *Odesskie Novosti*, Jabotinsky published two feuilletons under the common title "The Five." This text was already a more or less complete synopsis of the future novel.[56] It mentioned five children born to an Odessa intelligentsia family, representatives of a generation that matured "without anxieties, tragedies, and aspirations."[57] Some psychological types are already fully developed in these feuilletons (for example, Marusia and Serezha of the novel), and others are only sketched (the novel's Marko and Lika). Only Marusia, the oldest Milgrom daughter, would retain her original name in the final text of the 1936 novel. One of the Milgrom siblings in the 1910 text, Max (Marko in the novel), contemplates a typical intelligentsia life scenario for himself. He questions the author, Altalena (Jabotinsky): Why does he "insist so strongly on the separation of nations? Isn't this chauvinism? Aren't there some broader ideals? And why does he have to love one group of people more than all humanity in general?"[58] Writing in 1910, Jabotinsky dated this conversation to 1904—the eve of the 1905 Revolution, for which Max/Marko was preparing himself.[59]

The second feuilleton starts in 1906, with Altalena meeting one of the Milgrom sisters, Nadia (Lika in the novel). The timing is clearly marked politically by "the elections to the first Duma." Writing in 1910, Jabotinsky characterized this high revolutionary moment as one of senseless hopes and disappointments, a "puppet comedy" (this description did not make it into the novel): "No doubt, this was historical time, big time; if people had not committed stupid things, this time could be called great. But, excuse me, there was little nice about it."[60] Nadia/Lika—a radical revolutionary—embodies all that was "bad" about that time and the revolutionary choice of so many Russian Jews of her generation. She has no real emotional attachments or personal loyalties, only abstract ideas, and her political fight is driven by hatred, not love. She does not care about her family and, by extension, her nation, or any human life at all. Even her hatred of the bourgeoisie is devoid of true emotional intensity: "This is not hatred, this is nothing," she admits to Altalena.[61]

The fourth Milgrom child, Sasha (Serezha in the novel), crosses paths with Altalena in 1908, at the time of the postrevolutionary apathy, when only nationalists like Jabotinsky retained a direct and clear political vision. Sasha/Serezha symbolizes extreme decadence and moral degradation. He reports on his fellow students to the police and is financially supported by his older female lover. Still worse, he forges his father's signature on a check and attempts to cash it (all these episodes were later developed in the novel). When the father, who "almost lost his mind from grief and shame," confronts him, Sasha/Serezha responds: nonsense. In 1910, Jabotinsky's attitude toward this protagonist was univocally negative, much less ambivalent than in 1936: "And for a moment it appeared to me that indeed, in his [Sasha/Serezha's] persona, I was facing something of a higher nature—the sharp-cut, dry mentality of a generation that has grown on bare soil, without an everyday life routine [*bez byta*], without traditions, that has survived the collapse of great pipedreams."[62]

The fifth Milgrom, Zigfrid (Torik in the novel), completes the family's tragic journey of alienation. Unlike his older siblings, Marko and Lika, he is apolitical, and unlike Marusia and Serezha, he is not immoral. But he takes the last step toward ceasing to be Jewish even in the formal sense upheld by the empire—by converting to Christianity.

Such was Jabotinsky's pessimistic vision of the collective Jewish fate in the Russian Empire, which could be altered only by a true national revival. Remarkably, neither in 1910 nor in 1936 did this narrative even mention the Pale of Settlement and its Jewish population or the pogroms. For Jabotinsky, the most essential Russian Jewish experience had been that of the assimilated, urban Russian Jewish intelligentsia—their politics and their sexual and moral choices. It was *their* self-denial and self-destruction that proved the futility of imperial universalism and justified Jabotinsky's own radical reinvention and his Manichaean nationalism. Urban, modern, educated Jewish hybrids like himself were Jabotinsky's main fixation. Among the most striking examples of this is his 1909 feuilleton dedicated to a police double agent, Evno Azef, who happened to be a Jew and whose double betrayal triggered one of the loudest "scandals of empire" in the proper Dirksian sense of exposing the immoral structure of imperial politics and making it a public event leading to the empire's ideological realignment.[63] The head of the terrorist branch of the Party of Socialist Revolutionaries, Azef was exposed as an informant for the Russian secret police (*okhranka*) in 1909. Outraged commentators on both the right and left of the political spectrum unanimously described the phenomenon of *Azefovshchina* as an expression of systemic parallelism between the idealized revolutionary underground and the immoral and illegitimate regime's secretive methods of political policing.[64] But Jabotinsky did not consider these parallels important. He saw in Azef one of those demoralized and assimilated urban Jews, who did not differ in principle from the uprooted Milgroms (the feuilleton's title was "Yet Another One"): "In big cities, among the Jewish middle class, one can encounter people 'without prejudices' and without traditions, whose upbringing... was not connected to any higher principle—of religion, patriotism, or national feeling."[65] The exact same explanation was offered in *The Five* for Sasha/Serezha's moral bankruptcy. Between 1910 and 1936, Serezha had evolved into a complicated character, who can be described in Jabotinsky's terms as talented but obviously not a genius. In addition to having multiple talents, he was spontaneous, smart, artistic, free, and immoral to the extreme.[66] But while Serezha's personality was acquiring new and more sophisticated traits, the key to it remained unchanged: the propensity to ask the relativizing and hence demoralizing question, "Why is it forbidden?" Jabotinsky has his protagonist articulate this question in the 1910 feuilleton, and then repeats it in his own voice in an essay addressed to young Jewish converts to Christianity ("An Ordinary Occurrence," published first in *Razsvet* in 1910 and then separately in 1911): "Those who wandered in the last years on the so-called 'Jewish street' are well familiar with this fatal question: 'Why is it forbidden?'... And you feel confused, and suddenly understand that, essentially, you do not have an answer. For there are things that cannot be proved."[67]

In *The Five*, this line is developed in a lawyer's monologue:

> "But why is it forbidden?" Let me assure you that no power of agitation can be compared to this question in its devastating impact. From time immemorial the moral equilibrium of humanity has rested on the fact that we hold certain axioms: some closed doors bear the inscription "Forbidden." Simply "forbidden," with no explanation; these axioms stand firm, doors are locked... But if only once you pose the question: "But why is it forbidden?" these axioms come crashing down.... There's no more "forbidden" and everything becomes "permitted." Not only the rules of conventional morality, such as "don't steal" or "don't lie," but even the most instinctive, most innate (as in this matter) reactions of human nature—shame, physical squeamishness, the voice of blood—everything dissolves into dust.[68]

Moral rules turn out to be products of national instincts, of "the voice of blood," immanent to a healthy national organism. Moral relativism becomes a reflection of the crisis of the natural conditions of life that ensure harmony between individual and collective choices.

In the same 1910 essay, "An Ordinary Occurrence," Jabotinsky tells the story of a young man from Odessa, "once my protégé," who in 1907 approached the author with a plan: to send a letter of extortion to a banker, and if the banker refuses to pay the ransom, shoot him. "I became outraged, agitated, I started talking him out of this, but he cut me short with the question: 'Why is it forbidden? Prove it!'"[69] The story transitioned to the novel with a few alterations: Sasha became Serezha; instead of an extortion letter he sent his friends to the banker, who turned out also to be Jewish and even a close friend of the Milgrom family. But the principal element of the story remained unchanged: when confronted by the narrator, Serezha responded with the "Why is it forbidden?"

Jabotinsky's feuilletons of the early 1910s were written with indignation and contempt for those who did not know "why it was forbidden," and who were thus lost for the national cause. In the 1930s, he spoke about them with compassion, sadness, and even love. Now Jabotinsky was not simply rejecting his imperial hybrid past but viewed it as a necessary sacrifice for the postimperial rebirth of the nation. Victims of assimilation paved the way for the new generation of self-conscious Jews who reunited with their racial and national selves. The Milgroms' graves were important milestones on the way toward national rejuvenation: "Torik had said, 'Disintegration.' Maybe he's even right; the lawyer defending Rovensky also talked about disintegration, but he added [that] periods of decline are sometimes the most fascinating. Who knows: perhaps not only fascinating but even sublime in their own way? Of course, I'm in the camp that struggles against disintegration; I don't want neighbors; I want all people living on their own islands; but—who knows? One historical truth has already been well demonstrated: one has to pass through disintegration in order to achieve regeneration."[70]

It seems that in *The Five*, Jabotinsky finally reconciled the two parts of his life, and possibly two parts of his self. But not only that: he also incorporated the imperial epoch of Jewish modernity—with its main themes of assimilation, hybridity, cultural dependence on hegemonic discourses, and the absence of any specific Jewish subjectivity—into the postcolonial vision of the heroic and integral Jewish nation. *The Five* recognizes the immense sacrifice made on the altar of postimperial nationalism by modern, urban, imperial Jews like the Milgroms and Jabotinsky himself. Although *The Five* was never interpreted in scholarship as a postcolonial novel, it resonates with similar works of postcolonial intellectuals. One can see, for example, obvious parallels between Jabotinsky's love of Odessa as an old imperial/colonial city and Edward Said's love of colonial Cairo. Gyan Prakash finds in Said's recollections the same recognition of consciously committed sacrifice in the name of the postcolonial ideal:

> My eyes leapt to the essay on the remembered Cairo of his youth.[71] It is a wonderful evocation of Cairo as a cosmopolitan city. The European influence was plentiful and dominant. The most prominent European presence was, understandably, the British Cairo, visible, among other places.... There were, in addition, other cultural enclaves—French, Italian, Greek, Belgian, American, Jewish, and Syrian. Said writes about growing up in this Cairo of an annual opera and ballet season, recitals, concerts, tennis, golf, regular performances by the Comédie Française and the Old Vic.... It was Cairo that was immensely malleable to European cultural influences but only fitfully open to its Arab and Islamic lives. Deeply aware of this division between the European world and Arab world, Said speaks of his fleeting encounters with native Cairenes on the street and in public places. He describes these encounters as a "contact with nature."... Said evokes these brief encounters to speak about the traffic between Europe and Cairo, about a time when Cairo was "cosmopolitan, free, full of wonderful privileges."[72]

Prakash goes on to observe that what Said remembers is not the "'imported mythology' of European superiority, not the protocols of colonial order" but a Polish-Jewish pianist living in Cairo and his veiled female student—"figures made possible by colonialism and also exceeding its logic of separation and segregation."[73] Jabotinsky remembered Odessa—the old empire—in the same way and, like Said, he decidedly left it behind in the past. In the last paragraph of *The Five* he dreams about settling peoples on islands ("I don't want neighbors; I want all people living on their own islands"). When working on the novel, he was already living in the postimperial world. The collapse of the Russian, Austro-Hungarian, and Ottoman Empires as well as Jabotinsky's experience in rapidly nationalizing Poland and in Palestine, where the British exposed the worst aspects of the camouflaged colonial politics and the Arab-Jewish confrontation intensified, confirmed his deep belief that the road toward "recovery" should lead through disintegration. In 1925, in a letter to Oscar Gruzenberg, the Russian Jewish lawyer and liberal, Jabotinsky shared his view of the future political arrangement of the world as "a federation generally," where small states and nations will live separately and secure.[74] The island utopia may thus be the most extreme expression of this vision.[75]

However, from the vantage point of *The Five*—a novel about the disintegration of modern empires (the metaphorical multifaceted "Odessas")—the appearance of the "national island" on the ruins of the former mainland was not a moment of postcolonial triumph, but rather a social catastrophe and personal tragedy, a sacrifice to the future nation. Culture was sacrificed to nature ("race"), and complexity—to simplicity. Hybridity was replaced with purity, and irresponsible, even immoral yet wonderful freedom—with the grim determinism of race. Instead of the seductions of glamorous megalopolises came self-isolation on small, provincial, national islands. Jabotinsky's anti-imperial nationalism turned out to be a sacrificial postcoloniality that dwelled on "race" as the strongest positivist explanation and the impersonal, objective justification of the painful self-reductionism that he and many intellectuals like him had agreed to endure in the name of their postcolonial nationalism.

CONCLUSION

I SEE THE MOST OBVIOUS conclusion of this book in the idea that racialized Jewish politics in the Russian Empire was a form of the anti-imperial and postcolonial politics proliferating at the time. The degree of a political discourse's racialization is correlated with the extent and intensity of the rejection of the old imperial order by its politically mobilized subjects. Race functioned as a fairly open-ended language that was capable of conveying a variety of political dispositions. And here we come to the second, no less important, conclusion that conditions the first one. As a social language, race remained a flexible and polyvalent trope only within the imperial society. At least in Russian Jewish politics, race started to lose its ambiguity and emancipatory potential once the nationalizing empire no longer provided a context that elucidated the meaning and function of race.

It is worth noting here again that nationalism did not come *after* empires. It was a product of empires and a constant factor of their realignment and readaptation. Many prominent Zionists, like Jabotinsky, whose paradigmatic case has structured the discussion in this book, could tolerate imperial polities, especially if these were evolving into Nationalitätenstaat. They could even be sentimental about the old hybrid, morally contaminated, and irregular imperial societies. But to conduct their new antiimperial national politics in empires, they needed race. Jabotinsky in particular, while tolerating empire as a kind of empty exoskeleton, resolutely placed modern political sovereignty exclusively within a nation understood as a living racial organism. This postimperial nonterritorial nation, which, however, aspired to territorialization at some point in the future, was constructed through Manichaean oppositions to the old imperial principles. A return to the natural pre- and postimperial condition of social and political being was possible only as a return to race—the purest and most authentic source of national evolution that was resistant to colonial domination.

Jabotinsky and many of those who shared his generational experience imagined the collective Jewish body and the racial psyche within it as the only spaces controlled by Jews themselves, regardless of their political and cultural subalternity. The resulting vision of a new, modern, strong, self-conscious Jewish nation emerging on the organic and timeless basis of race received solid scientific backing from race science as well as modern sociology and political theory. As we have seen, Jabotinsky's discourse of race featured implicit and explicit references to physical anthropology, racial demographics and medical statistics, and theories of nationalism. But he also attempted a personal "scientific" experiment in 1903, when he initiated his own postcolonial transformation. Jabotinsky reemerged from his anational imperial past as a Jew and a Zionist and explained this as the implementation of the objectively predetermined racial scenario (the life theorem). The scientific politics of race that he pursued afterward heavily exploited direct analogies between personal and collective decolonization, individual and national bodies, and intimate and public Jewishness. Likewise, his subaltern biopolitics posited the self-conscious reproduction of race through sexual selection as the greatest duty of each individual member of the nation.

Jabotinsky's family-centered imagery, his scientific delegitimization of mixed marriages, and the discourse of pure blood were shared, often selectively, by proponents of modern Jewish or Russian nationalism or any other modern nationalism. The parallelisms between these national projects expose race as the basic code of the self and groupness in the transitional context of the modernizing and nationalizing empire. Anti-imperial national movements could rely on the race argument as a source of self-control and self-mobilization, which was important in the absence of a nation-state biopolitical machine that reproduced gender, class, and racial order, as envisioned by Foucauldian normative theory. While helping to strictly delimit nations in a messy imperial society, race was a powerful homogenizing instrument that leveled class differences within the organic community of subalterns and secured the old patriarchal gender regime. As one can clearly see in the case of Vladimir Jabotinsky, projects of racialized anti-imperial national modernity, similar to his own, were riddled with contradictions, and their very coherence depended on an external factor—the empire. Retaining the empire as a negative political pole and an epistemological framework allowed the anti-imperial nationalists to construct and embrace a subaltern positionality and square its internal inconsistencies.

Jabotinsky's racialized Zionism was thus as much an imperial phenomenon as it was an expression of modern Jewish nationalism. It highlights some crucial aspects of the Russian late imperial situation that are not visible otherwise. For example, it exposes the Russian public sphere's high degree of autonomy from the political regime, especially when it comes to elaborating and debating ideologies and policies of race and nationalism. Relative to a state- or even Duma-centered perspective on the early twentieth-century political process in the empire, the case of Vladimir Jabotinsky offers a much broader view on it. Jabotinsky's interiorized position as a colonized subject, who speaks from his colonial situation in a purified political language marked by an unprecedented degree of sincerity and frankness bordering on cynicism, endowed him with the moral authority to challenge the leading players on the imperial political field. Anti-imperial nationalists like Jabotinsky facilitated profound divisions within the contemporary socialist and liberal movements. They forced the Russian intelligentsia to see and recognize the fact of imperial diversity and the existence of hierarchical relationships of domination and subjugation reflected in the intelligentsia's own "national indifference" and national biases.

At the same time, the epistemological embrace of race thinking that was quite ubiquitous at the turn of the century did not necessarily lead to the political instrumentalization of race. The Viennese philosopher Martin Buber is the best example of this. Like many of his contemporaries, he believed in race and urged young Zionists in the Habsburg Empire to become "aware of the significance of this blood within us." But Buber refrained from taking the next logical step and politicizing his philosophical vision. Instead of calling for national self-purification and political mobilization around the idea of the purity of blood and the nationalization of culture and civic life, Buber suggested embracing cultural hybridity and belonging to composite polities through an act of conscious choice: "choice does not mean that one must expel, relinquish, or overcome the one or the other; it would be senseless, for instance, to try to shed the culture of the world about us, a culture that, in the final analysis, has been assimilated by the innermost forces of our blood, and has become an integral part of ourselves. We need to be conscious of the fact *that we are a cultural admixture,* in a more poignant sense than any other people. We do not, however, want to be slaves of this admixture, but its masters."[1]

Facing a similar choice, Jabotinsky decided in favor of pure blood. He declared a war on "cultural admixture" and tirelessly worked to spread race thinking into all spheres of Jewish individual and collective existence. Instead of embracing "admixture" through a conscious act of recognition and thus acquiring control over it, Jabotinsky rejected hybridity as a reflection and a consequence of colonialism. His case shows that the racialization of politics was a willful, rational act that required an elaborated critique of empire as an unnatural political formation. Pursuing the politics of race involved a strong, conscious effort to disentangle personal and social bodies from the imperial mix. It necessitated a new political language and a new political positionality.

As I have argued in this book, Jewish nationalists championed the cause of the racialization of politics in the Russian Empire. They were the best prepared and best motivated for the task. The older idioms of Jewishness available to them did not suit the needs of mass political mobilization and modern nationalism. In addition, this traditional Jewishness did not satisfy the criteria of scientific politics embraced by many politically active Jewish intellectuals who were well familiar with modern sciences and Western culture, with which they often identified. The nonterritoriality and internal cultural heterogeneity of Jews of the Russian Empire provided additional stimuli for turning to race as a unifying category of political practice. Antisemitism, especially racial antisemitism, served as a strong incentive to use arguments about racial exclusion to substantiate self-exclusion. But the main motivation for the racialization of politics resulted from the gradual erosion of the old principle of imperial hybridity that formerly provided a workable framework for various Jewish identifications as simultaneously Jewish, Russian (in a nonethnic sense), regional, and modern. The nationalization of the social and political imagination and the nationalist scenario of power, embraced by the dynastic imperial regime, produced a crisis that had at least three potential resolutions. First, it was possible to embrace a different model of national belonging—for example, to the global "nation" of the proletariat. Second, there was a possibility of redefining the old hybridity on new foundations, as Buber suggested to his fellow Zionists. A third scenario implied reinventing Jewishness as a modern groupness on the basis of race or a new secular cultural canon (that would still inevitably exclude some Jewish groups). Jabotinsky's case was an example of the latter strategy turned into political ideology and practical politics.

As this study suggests, in turn-of-the-century Russian Jewish politics, even when it assumed the most consistent postcolonial stance, race was deployed contextually and rarely for racist purposes. Internally, race helped safeguard authenticity and purity and establish clear boundaries of the national, while in a broader transnational context it could confirm Jews' legitimate belonging to the European societies in which they lived. The Mediterranean race concept performed this work particularly well. As we have seen, discursively, Jews as a Mediterranean race remained "pure" and retained their distinct racial composition. At the same time, the Mediterranean race, reconsidered through Jewish inclusion, decentered and hybridized the normative idea of Europe from within. Naturally and finally, the race concept was evoked to substantiate Jewish rights to Palestine, but it was no less useful as hard proof of nationality in the internal imperial politics.

The evocation of race also helped elaborate the concept of minority (a minoritarian people), which was new for particularistic empires that did not categorize populations in terms of majority-minority. Jabotinsky took on this task in his two-part article "Self-Governance of the National Minority" (1913). Based on exhaustive comparative statistical and political analysis, primarily of cases of population distribution and population politics in the Habsburg and Ottoman Empires, Jabotinsky defined "minority" as "only such a group that cannot even theoretically be imagined as having a designated and separate territorial region."[2] He further admitted that neither language nor sheer numbers qualify a group as a national minority. Only self-consciousness, which was supposed to have some deeper objective basis, made such a group a minoritarian *nation* deserving political and administrative recognition and self-governance. Jews were thus an archetypal minority, an "abnormal" nation in an empire or in a postimperial nation-state, whose reality and legitimacy depended on establishing an objective racial basis on which the sense of nationhood develops.

As these and many other examples considered in these pages show, Russian Jewish political activists had many reasons to see in race a useful concept for their subaltern anti-imperial nationalism. It served them well as a language of social critique of the "archaic" empire, framing the calls for both the empire's modernization (along the liberal empire-of-knowledge or empire-of-nations model) and anticolonial resistance through collective self-racializing. Moreover, the story told in this book suggests that race can be a weapon of the weak or an instrument of oppression and exclusion, or both at the same time, because race is a language and narrative in need of deciphering. The language of race is always essentializing, but what is being essentialized, when, and why, as well as how and by whom, remains historically and situationally conditioned. Race reflects processes of renegotiations of power, of inclusion and exclusion (the case of Jabotinsky entitles us to safely add the prefix *self-* here), at all levels of social and political hierarchies. But these negotiations are especially complex in imperial situations, which are always defined by the coexistence and overlap of multiple, often incongruent contexts and chronotopes. Hence, reading race as a language and keeping empire as a context inevitably complicates simplistic and linear genealogies of nationalism and colonialism.

Reflecting on this complexity, in his seminal essay "Is Zionism a Colonial Movement?" Derek Penslar calls for a historical conceptualization of the "relationship between colonialism and nationalism" and for a narrative that would embrace categories of postcolonial theory alongside theories of colonization, nationalism, and modernity.[3] The story of Jews, race, and the politics of difference in the Russian Empire as told in this book can be regarded as such an experiment. The final cautionary conclusion derived from it consists of the admission that such a historical methodology helps us understand the past but does not automatically explain the present and the connection between the two. Understanding the racialized politics of today requires similarly careful contextualization and deciphering in a radically different historical context.

NOTES

INTRODUCTION

1. Schechtman, *Rebel and Statesman*; Schechtman, *Fighter and Prophet*; Katz, *Lone Wolf*; Halkin, *Jabotinsky: A Life*; Horowitz, *Vladimir Jabotinsky's Russian Years*.

2. Heller, *Jabotinsky's Children*.

3. On the early stages of Jewish "discovery" of race concept, see Mogilner, *A Race for the Future*, chap. 1, "The Dawn of the Jewish Race in the Late Nineteenth-Century Russian Empire."

4. Vucinich, *Darwin in Russian Thought*, 2.

5. Rabinovich, "Fel'eton," 31.

6. Here the historiography is abundant. Selected examples include Poliakov, *Arian Myth*; Low, *Jews in the Eyes of the Germans*; Chamberlain and Gilman, *Degeneration: The Dark Side of Progress*; Gilman, *Jewish Self-Hatred*; Gilman, *Jew's Body*; Weindling, *Health, Race and German Politics*; Kleebatt, *Too Jewish?*; Hart, "Racial Science, Social Science, and the Politics of Jewish Assimilation," 268–97; Zimmermann, *Anthropology and Antihumanism in Germany*; Turda and Weindling, *Blood and Homeland*; Jahoda, "Intra-European Racism in Nineteenth-Century Anthropology," 37–56; and others.

7. Efron, *Defenders of the Race*; Efron, *Medicine and the German Jews*; Efron, *German Jewry and the Allure of the Sephardic*; Hart, *Jews and Race*; Hart, *Social Science and the Politics of Modern Jewish Identity*; Abu El-Haj, *Genealogical Science*.

8. El'kind, "Evrei (Sravnitel'no-antropologicheskoe issledovanie, preimushchestvenno po nabliudeniiam nad pol'skimi evreiami)," 1–458; El'kind, "Antropologicheskoe izuchenie evreev i disput A. D. El'kinda," 230.

9. On El'kind, see Mogilner, *A Race for the Future*, chap. 3: "Arkadii Danilovich El'kind (1868–1921): Constructing a Jewish 'Cultured Nation.'"

10. For more on the Russian school of liberal anthropology, see Mogilner, *Homo Imperii*.

11. On Weissenberg, see Mogilner, *A Race for the Future*, chap. 2: "Samuel Abramovich Weissenberg (1867–1928): 'Provincializing Europe' through Jewish Racial Self-Description." On Weissenberg in a German context, see Efron, *Defenders of the Race*. For a brief discussion of El'kind's and Weissenberg's Jewish anthropology, see Mogilner, "Between Scientific and Political," 45–63.

12. For more on this classification, see Mogilner, *Homo Imperii*; Mogilner, "Classifying Imperial Russianness," 205–40.

13. Although the historiography of the Russian Empire is immense, race and racism still remain largely underexplored. Whereas those studying the Soviet period are now debating the applicability of race to the history of the USSR, the imperial period remains an exception. On the pre-1917 period, see Avrutin, "Racial Categories and the Politics of (Jewish) Difference in Late Imperial Russia," 13–40; Avrutin, *Jews and the Imperial State*; Avrutin, *Racism in Modern Russia*; Blakely, *Russia and the Negro*; Tolz, "Discourses of Race in Imperial Russia, 1830–1914," 133–44; Tolz, *Russia's Own Orient*; Lemon, "'What Are They Writing about Us Blacks?' Roma and 'Race' in Russia," 34–40; Rainbow, *Ideologies of Race*; Bojanowska, *World of Empires*; Mogilner, *Homo Imperii*; Mogilner, "Racial Psychiatry and the Russian Imperial Dilemma of the 'Savage Within,'" 99–133; Glebov, "Race and Politics," 93–110.

14. Dolbilov, "Emancipation Reform of 1861 in Russia and the Nationalism of the Imperial Bureaucracy"; Sunderland, "Greatest Emancipator."

15. Wortman, *Myth and Ceremony in Russian Monarchy*.

16. The described complex political dynamics of the early twentieth century is considered in detail and from the perspective of new imperial history in Gerasimov, Mogilner, and Glebov, *Novaia imperskaia istoriia Severnoi Evrazii*.

17. Głębocki, *Fatalna Sprawa*; Dolbilov, "Stereotype of the Pole in Imperial Policy," 44–88; Becker, "Toward a Genealogy of the Nationalizing Empire," 185–234.

18. L. Sh-g [Shternberg], "Besedy s chitateliami," 1911a, 6. On Shternberg, see Kan, *Lev Shternberg*; Mogilner, *A Race for the Future*, chap. 4, "Lev Iakovlevich Shternberg (1861–1927): The Political Science of Jewish Race."
19. L. Sh-g [Shternberg], "Besedy s chitateliami," 1911b, 5.
20. Zangwill, "Jewish Race," 268–79, 270–71, 277, 279.
21. L. Sh-g [Shternberg], "Besedy s chitateliami," 1911a, 7.
22. Frankel, *Prophecy and Politics*.
23. [Zamenhof] Gomo Sum, *Gillelizm*, quoted and analyzed in O'Keeffe, *Esperanto and Languages of Internationalism*, esp. 30–34.
24. O'Keeffe, *Esperanto and Languages of Internationalism*, 33.
25. Chakrabarty, "Postcoloniality and the Artifice of History," 1–26.
26. For a discussion of Russian Jewish biopolitics based on the outlined reading of race, see Mogilner, *A Race for the Future*, part 2, "The Biopolitics of Race."
27. The pamphlet "Tragediia shestimillionnogo naroda" was first published in April 1905 in the newspaper *Syn otechestva*. Later it was reprinted four times in different editions.
28. Ratner, "Sovremennaia postanovka evreiskogo voprosa," 130–31.
29. Ibid., 147.
30. See Struve, "'Sovremennost' i 'elementarnost' russkoi revolutsii," 23.
31. Krutikov, *Yiddish Fiction and the Crisis of Modernity*, 74.
32. Ibid.
33. Uri, *Barricades and Banners*, 1.
34. Ibid., 16.
35. Veidlinger, *Jewish Public Culture in the Late Russian Empire*, 11.
36. Krutikov, *Yiddish Fiction and the Crisis of Modernity*, 216.
37. Slezkine, *Jewish Century*, 1.
38. The Birobidzhan story is a special case of Soviet "affirmative action" nation-building that failed to produce a modern Soviet Jewish nation (Weinberg, *Stalin's Forgotten Zion*).
39. On "realism of the group," see Brubaker and Cooper, "Beyond Identity," 1–47.
40. "Critical Discussion: Forum on Race and Bias (Introduction and 14 Contributions)," 203–340. The discussion here is a brief summary of my contribution to this forum (Ibid., 207–15).
41. Engelstein, *Keys to Happiness*; Engelstein, "Combined Underdevelopment," 338–53.
42. Praskov'ia Tarnovskaia, *Zhenshchiny-ubiitsy: Antropologicheskoe issledovanie*; Praskov'ia Tarnovskaia, "Antropometricheskie issledovaniia

prostitutok, vorovok i zdorovykh krest'ianok-polevykh rabotnits"; Praskov'ia Tarnovskaia, *Vorovki (antropologicheskoe issledovanie)*; Pauline Tarnowsky, *Etude anthropométrique sur les prostituées et les voleuses*. For more on Russian criminal anthropology, Tarnovskaia, race, and so on, see Mogilner, *Homo Imperii*, 328–46.

43. See, for example, Hoffmann and Kotsonis, *Russian Modernity*.

44. Beer, *Renovating Russia*.

45. Stoler, *Race and the Education of Desire*, 8.

46. The term *strategic relativism* is coined as an opposite to Gayatri Chakravorty Spivak's characterization of the modern episteme of groupness as *strategic essentialism* (*In Other Worlds*, 205). Correspondingly, strategic relativism should be understood as a discourse and stance that relativizes the bounded and internally homogeneous nature of the constituent elements of the sociopolitical space and governance and produces a situation of uncertainty, incommensurability, and indistinction. For more, see Gerasimov et al., "New Imperial History and the Challenges of Empire," 20.

47. Stoler, *Race and the Education of Desire*, 15; Clifford, *Predicament of Culture*, 265.

48. The contemporary consensus is well summarized by Etienne Balibar: "Culture can also function like a nature, and it can in particular function as a way of locking individuals and groups a priori into a genealogy, into a determination that is immutable and intangible in origin" ("Is There a 'Neo-Racism?,'" 22).

49. For the most consistent articulation of the Sonderweg discourse on race, see Knight, "Ethnicity, Nationality and the Masses," 41–64; Knight, "Vocabularies of Difference," 667–83. For a refutation of such an approach from a history of science and ideology perspective and with emphasis on Eurasia and Eastern and Central Europe, see McMahon, *National Races*.

50. Stoler, "Racial Regimes of Truth," 251.

1. RACE, ZIONISM, AND THE QUEST FOR JEWISH AUTHENTICITY

1. Gordon, *Toward Nationalism's End*, 14.

2. Ibid., 39.

3. Bialik, "Present Hour," 6–7. Quoted in Falk, "Zionism, Race and Eugenics," 144.

4. Falk, "Zionism, Race and Eugenics," 142.

5. Hart, "Jews and Race: An Introductory Essay," in *Jews and Race*, xxiii–xxix.

6. Shumsky, *Beyond the Nation-State*. Earlier historical works that reached a similar conclusion focused on relatively marginal figures in the history of Zionism, such as Simon Rawidowicz, Mordecai Kaplan, Oscar Janowsky, or, indeed, Hanse Kohn. See Stanislawski, *Zionism and the Fin de Siècle*; Myers, *Between Jew and Arab*; Pianko, *Zionism and the Roads Not Taken*; Naor and Jacobson, *Oriental Neighbors*; and Gordon, *Toward Nationalism's End*. Unlike these authors, Shumsky examines ideologies of the key figures of political Zionism such as Leon Pinsker, Theodor Herzl, and Vladimir Jabotinsky.

7. Tsurumi, "Was the East Less Rational Than the West?" 375.

8. Taro Tsurumi has articulated a similar agenda in his studies of Zionism. His goal is to reconstruct the original imperial context of "ethnicization," as he calls it, of Jewish identity in "Eastern Zionism." He is also interested in the "imagined contexts" of those who had accomplished such "ethnicization." See, for example, Tsurumi, "Was the East Less Rational Than the West?" 361–94. Imperial contexts of Zionism are considered in Mintz, "Jewish Nationalism in the Context of Multi-National States," 201–24 [in Hebrew]; Bartal, *Jews of Eastern Europe, 1772–1881*; Goldstein, *Russian Zionism* [in Hebrew]; and others. Joshua Shanes, who embraced a similar optics in his study of Jewish nationalism in Habsburg Galicia, was able to show that Zionism there developed in "conversation and cross-fertilization" with other East European nationalisms and with imperial ideology (*Diaspora Nationalism and Jewish Identity in Habsburg Galicia*, 2).

9. Penslar, "Is Zionism a Colonial Movement?," 276. In this respect, my study can contribute to what has recently been dubbed the "Jewish imperial turn" in historiography (Katz et al., *Colonialism and the Jews*, 14, among others).

10. In early twentieth-century Russian Zionism, which is the focus of my analysis here, there were two major trends—socialist, mainly represented by Poale Zion, and what can be called liberal, primarily represented by the Russian Zionist Organization. Taro Tsurumi calls the latter simply "Russian Zionism," "because its primary language for publication was Russian, whereas others more often used Hebrew or Yiddish, and its ideologists envisioned a *reformed* Russia, rather than revolution" ("Imagined Context of a Nation," 78).

11. On Zionism in the Russian Empire, see: Maor, *Zionist Movement in Russia* [in Hebrew]; Slutsky, *Russian-Jewish Press in the Twentieth Century*,

1900–1918 [in Hebrew]; Frankel, *Prophesy and Politics*; Goldstein, "Zionist Movement in Russia (1897–1904)"; Goldstein, "Attitude of the Jewish and the Russian Intelligentsia to Zionism in the Initial Period (1897–1904)," 546–56; Zipperstein, *Elusive Prophet*; Levin, "Jewish Politics in the Russian Empire during the Period of Reaction, 1907–1914"; Tsurumi, "Was the East Less Rational Than the West?"; Tsurumi, "Neither Angels, nor Demons, but Humans," 531–50; Horowitz, "What Is Russian in Russian Zionism?," 61–76.

12. Zeev Jabotinsky to Ahad Ha'am, March 16, 1905, Jabotinsky Institute in Israel, Archive, Letter # 98, Ref. no. A1-2/1, pp. 1, 3.

13. Ibid.

14. The text of the program appeared in *Evreiskii narod* 7 (1906): 52, a weekly that existed for a year. It replaced *Khronika evreiskoi zhizni* [*Chronicle of Jewish Life*, 1905–1906], a supplement of the monthly Petersburg Zionist journal, *Evreiskaia zhizn'* [*Jewish Life*]. *Evreiskii narod* was replaced in 1907 by the weekly *Razsvet* [*Dawn*].

15. Veidlinger, *Jewish Public Culture in the Late Russian Empire*.

16. For the Zionist turn to imperial politics, see Orbach, "Zionism and the Russian Revolution of 1905," 7–23.

17. Lohr, *Russian Citizenship*; Kotsonis, *States of Obligation*.

18. Burbank, "Imperial Rights Regime," 397–431.

19. Brutzkus, "Evreiskii Vopros v Russkoi Pechati," 203.

20. For details, see Fishman, "Bund and Modern Yiddish Culture," 107–19.

21. Veidlinger, "Emancipation: See Anti-Semitism," 407.

22. For more on Lenin's view of the Jewish question, see Gitelman, *Jewish Nationality and Soviet Politics*, 43–44, and elsewhere in the same book.

23. Stalin, "Marxism and the National Question," 301.

24. Ibid., 307.

25. Otto Bauer was a prominent Austrian Social Democrat and someone who exemplified the connection between modern science and socialist politics. He received a doctorate in law in 1906 from the University of Vienna and published his first book, which developed a theory of nationalism and modern citizenship in 1907: *Die Sozialdemokratie und die Nationalitätenfrage*. Bauer posited that instead of annihilating national cultures, capitalism resulted in promoting a differentiation of human personalities and that nations were "communities of character that grows out of a community of destiny" ("Nation," 52).

26. Stalin, "Marxism and the National Question," 310. Some historians believe that such a view explains Stalin's insistence on Jewish

territorialization and resistance to their assimilation under the Soviet regime. See Shumsky, "Stalin's Nationalities Policies and Jewish Assimilation."

27. Stalin, "Marxism and the National Question," 312–13.
28. Rabinovitch, *Jewish Rights, National Rights*, 3.
29. Ibid.
30. Ibid., 59.
31. Kautsky, *Are the Jews a Race?* 244.
32. Goldstein, "Jabotinsky and Jewish Autonomy in the Diaspora," 224–36; Gechtman, "Conceptualizing National-Cultural Autonomy," 17–49; Tsurumi, "Imagined Context of a Nation," 77–96, esp. 82–89.
33. On Ruppin and his statistical work, see Hart, *Social Science and the Politics of Modern Jewish Identity*, esp. 1–95. Amos Morris-Reich has shown that race remained central for Ruppin from his first published work in 1903 to his last one in 1940 ("Arthur Ruppin's Concept of Race," 1–30). In fact, Ruppin "remained true to his anthropologist's view of the Jews as a race even in 1938 when he corresponded with the racial anthropologist Hans F. K. Günter, an enthusiastic supporter of the Nazi regime." See Falk, "Zionism, Race and Eugenics," 146.
34. Hart, *Social Science and the Politics of Modern Jewish Identity*, 91.
35. Jabotinsky, "Partiisnost' ili zhizn'?" 374. Obviously, such a perception was common to many Jews, including ideological opponents of Zionism. According to Jonathan Frenkel, in the 1880s, the Bundist model of workers' education began with the basics of Russian language, natural history, and political economy. The next stage included some arithmetic and anatomy. At the highest stage, workers advanced to lessons on Darwinism and Marxism (*Prophecy and Politics*, 186).
36. On Vermel', see Mogilner, *A Race for the Future*, part 1, "A Necessary Introduction." Ruppin's essay "Darwinismus und Sozialwissenschaft" was awarded the second prize. On Ruppin and his statistical work, see Hart, *Social Science and the Politics of Modern Jewish Identity*, esp. 1–95. On the dependence of Ruppin's social imagination on sciences such as anthropology and statistics, see Penslar, *Zionism and Technocracy*, 80–109. On Ruppin's anthropological work, see Falk, "Zionism, Race and Eugenics," 146; Morris-Reich, "Arthur Ruppin's Concept of Race," 1–30.
37. Nordau, "V. Kongressrede," 113. Nordau's twelve-volume collected works were published in Russian translation in 1902. His views continued to be publicized in multiple formats, including such marginalia as his speeches on the usefulness of gymnastics for the Jews. For example,

"'Znachanie Gimnastiki dlia Evreev' Maksa Norday," *Budushchnost'* 4 (January 30, 1904): 77–81.

38. *Stenographisches Protokoll der Verhandlungen des IV Zionisten-Congresses*, 4:117–31. See also his speech translated into English, in Mandelstamm, *How Jews Live*.

39. Veidlinger, *Jewish Public Culture in the Late Russian Empire*, 109.

40. Hart, *Social Science and the Politics of Modern Jewish Identity*, 29–73. On the formation of the medicalized social movement in the Russian Empire, see Mogilner, "Toward a History of Russian-Jewish 'Medical Materialism,'" 70–106.

41. Horowitz, *Vladimir Jabotinsky's Russian Years*, 48.

42. An excellent collective portrait of this social cohort of Russian Zionists is offered in Horowitz, "What Is 'Russian' in Russian Zionism?," 54–70.

43. Avraami, "Osnovy i factory natsional'nogo kharaktera," 63, 64. Zvi Avrahami was the pen name of Grigorii Abramovich. On his Zionist and socialist views, see Frenkel, *Prophecy and Politics*, 248–251, 64.

44. Avraami, "Osnovy i factory natsional'nogo kharaktera," 65.

45. Taro Tsurumi, for example, interprets Zionism as such a constructivist ideology, pointing to its political "anti-essentialism" ("Neither Angels, nor Demons., but Humans," 361–94). He bases this conclusion on the analysis of polemical arguments advanced by Zionists against Bundists and other advocates of Yiddish culture as the basis for Jewish national autonomy in the Russian Empire. Tsurumi's argument, however, does not seem convincing in this particular case, simply because the critique of Yiddishism never precluded other types of cultural or biological essentialisms. See also Tsurumi, "Imagined Context of a Nation," 91–92.

46. Avraami, "Osnovy i factory natsional'nogo kharaktera," 69.

47. See also his definition of nationalism as a "collective individualism," in Abramovich, "Genezis natsional'noi idei i sushchnost' natsionalizma," 82–100.

48. Pasmanik, "Natsiia li evrei?," 26–49.

49. Ben-Samuel [D. Pasmanik], "Pis'ma k evreiskoi molodezhi: Pis'mo tret'e," 125.

50. Natkovich, "A Land of Harsh Ways," 31.

51. Borokhov, "O Kharaktere Evreiskogo Uma: I," 317.

52. Ibid., 337. Borokhov's "Nasha platforma" (Our Platform) became the manifesto of the Po'ale Tsiyon Party in 1906, and he was one of the creators who made this organization a distinct movement within international Zionism. Not only did constructivism and essentialism not exclude

each other in Borokhov's concept of Jewishness, but he also combined socialism and Zionism and Zionism with Yiddishism.

53. Tolz, "Re-negotiating Cultural Diversity."

54. On the trope of "class instinct" and the rise of racial psychiatry, see Mogilner, "Racial Psychiatry and the Russian Imperial Dilemma of the 'Savage Within,'" 99–133.

55. Brown, "Revolution and Psychosis," 283–302; Beer, *Renovating Russia*; McReynolds, "P. I. Kovalevskii," 63–84.

56. Gorny, *Science Embattled*, 284.

57. Jabotinsky, "O Russkom liberalizme," 54–55.

58. Chukovsky, "Sluchainye zametki," 177–78.

59. Ibid., 179.

60. Zhitomirskii, "Prakticheskie tseli evreiskoi shkoly," 4–5.

61. Chukovsky, "Sluchainye zametki," 181.

62. One typical example is Abramovich, "Genezis natsional'noi idei i sushchnost' natsionalizma." He starts with the Reformation as the "epoch of the birth of the national idea," traces the evolution of the absolutist state into a national state, discusses the influence of the French Revolution and revolutions of the 1840s, criticizes economic determinism in explaining the origin of the nation-state idea, and so on.

63. "Programma po izucheniiu natsional'nogo voprosa," 126–47.

64. See, especially, Kareev, *Rasy i natsional'nosti s psikhologicheskoi tochki zrenia.*

65. "Programma po izucheniiu natsional'nogo voprosa," 130.

66. Ibid., 145.

67. The original is Judt, *Żydzi jako rasa fizyczna*; German translation: Judt, *Die Juden als Rasse*. Among Zionist race scientists, Judt remains the less studied. He is mentioned by Efron and Hart but is never sufficiently analyzed and thoroughly read. Hence, his name appears in passing, and he always stands for a typical Zionist anthropologist who stressed Jews' non-European origin and racial purity (Hart, *Social Science and the Politics of Modern Jewish Identity*, 89–90; Efron, *German Jewry and the Allure of the Sephardic*, 72, 96).

68. "Programma po izucheniu natsional'nogo voprosa," 145.

69. Judt, "Evrei kak fizicheskaia rasa (Antropologicheskoe issledovanie)," 1904a, 1904b, 1904c, 1904d, 1904e. English-language readers can get a feel of the text thanks to the translation project by Mitchell Hart: "J. M. Judt, *The Jews as a Race* (Preface and Part 1 of *Die Juden als Rasse* [Berlin: Jüdische, 1903])," in Hart, *Jews and Race*.

2. MEDITERRANEAN AS NEW EUROPEAN

1. Beddoe, "On the Physical Characteristics of the Jews," 222–37; Blechmann, *Ein Beitrag zur Anthropologie der Juden*.
2. Judt, "Evrei kak fizicheskaia rasa," 1904b, 121. Józef Mejer and Izydor Kopernicki were two leading Kraków anthropologists in the second part of the nineteenth century. About them, their role in establishing the Kraków school of physical anthropology and their views on the Jewish race, see Rhode, "Matter of Place, Space, and People," 105–40.
3. Judt, "Evrei kak fizicheskaia rasa," 1904a, 138.
4. Ibid., 127.
5. Judt, "Evrei kak fizicheskaia rasa," 1904b, 133.
6. Shumsky, *Beyond the Nation-State*, 50–89 (chap. 2, "Theodor Herzl: A Non-Jewish State of Jews").
7. El'kind, "Kritika i bibliografiia," 105–7.
8. Judt, "Evrei kak fizicheskaia rasa," 1904a, 142.
9. Judt, "Evrei kak fizicheskaia rasa," 1904e, 132.
10. For a discussion of El'kind's dissertation and his branding of the Jews of the Russian Caucasus as "allotypical," see Mogilner, *A Race for the Future*, chap. 3: "Arkadii Danilovich El'kind (1868–1921): Constructing a Jewish 'Cultured Nation.'"
11. Ikow, "Neue Beiträge zur Anthropologie der Juden," 369–89.
12. Lagneau, "Sur la race juive et sa pathologie," 539–49, 556–57.
13. As an example of such reasoning, see the work by the Zionist anthropologist Auerbach, "Die Jüdische Rassenfrage," 332–61. To maintain that Jews were Semites, he was ready to contest the view that Semites were originally dolichocephalic. Another obvious example is Ignaz Zollschan, who insisted that the tribes encountered by the ancient Hebrews in Canaan belonged to "one race" with the Jews (*Jewish Questions*, 42). For more on Zionist anthropology, see "Zionism and Racial Anthropology" in Efron, *Defenders of the Race*, 123–74.
14. Judt, "Evrei kak fizicheskaia rasa," 1904c, 127.
15. Ibid., 106.
16. Ibid., 128.
17. Ibid., 118.
18. Judt, "Evrei kak fizicheskaia rasa," 1904e, 149, 150.
19. McMahon, *Races of Europe*, 209.
20. Ripley, *Races of Europe*, 1899, 205.
21. Judt, "Evrei kak fizicheskaia rasa," 1904d, 152.

22. Ripley, "The Racial Cartography of Europe," 1898, 1899; Ripley, *Races of Europe*, 1900, 368–400 (chap. 14, "The Jews and Semites").

23. Sergi, *Specie e Varietà Umane*. Lombroso's student and Sergi's younger contemporary, the physical anthropologist Alfredo Niceforo, who reached prominence under Mussolini, borrowed the idea of the Mediterranean race but rejected Sergi's negative view of Aryans. Without denying the national unity of Italians, he objectified the superiority of northern Italians over southernness. According to Niceforo, Mediterranean traits proved better in antiquity but had to be modified for modernity, which required more discipline and control. On this, see Caglioti, "Race, Statistics, and Italian Eugenics," 465–66.

24. McMahon, *Races of Europe*, 213.

25. Ibid.

26. Sergi, *Mediterranean Race*, 30, 31.

27. This illustrates the pattern discussed in Chakrabarty, *Provincializing Europe*.

28. The concept of "American Mediterranean" was introduced in Humboldt's thirty-volume *Voyage to the Equinoctial Regions of the New Continent*, which was published between 1805 and 1839. Today it is available in numerous abridged editions. See, for example, von Humboldt, *Personal Narrative of a Journey*; Gillman, "Humboldt's American Mediterranean," 505.

29. von Humboldt, *Cosmos*, 1:119.

30. Sergi, *Mediterranean Race*, v–vi.

31. On how they actually worked to justify nationalism and colonialism, see Taylor, "Anthropology and the 'Racial Doctrine' in Italy before 1940," 45–58; Quine, "Making Italians," 127–52.

32. Sergi, *Origine e diffusione della stirpe mediterranea*, 123.

33. Sergi, *Mediterranean Race*, 70–71.

34. Ibid., vi.

35. Du Bois, "African Origin of the Grecian Civilization," 336.

36. Gilroy, *Black Atlantic*, 127.

37. Du Bois, "African Origin of the Grecian Civilization," 341–42.

38. Ibid., 344.

39. Bernal, *Black Athena*, 34.

40. Jabotinsky, *Samson Nazorei*.

41. As far as I can tell, no one has ever paid attention to this source of Jabotinsky's literary imagination, although literary scholars have composed an impressive catalog of the literary and philosophical influences reflected in *Samson*. The list includes, besides the obvious biblical Judges,

Titus Flavius Josephus's *Antiquities of the Jews*, Alexander Pushkin's *Gavriliada*, Raffaello Giovagnoli's *Spartacus* (which Jabotinsky translated into Hebrew), and even a scene from Camille Saint-Saëns's opera *Samson and Delilah*. See Fridman and Shwatzband, "K voprosu ob istochnikakh povesti Vl. Jabotinskogo 'Samson Nazorei,'" 210–25. Michael Weiskopf adds to the list the first part ("Julian the Outcast") of Dmitry Merezhkovskii's trilogy *The Christ and Antichrist*, Friedrich Nietzsche's *Thus Spoke Zarathustra* (directly and, possibly, via his Russian followers such as Akim Volynskii and Viacheslav Ivanov), and even Rudyard Kipling's *Kim* and *The Jungle Book* ("Mezhdu Bibliei i avangardon," 131–44).

42. For the English translation I am using: Jabotinsky [Zeev, pseud.], *Samson*, 146–47. This is a republication of the book originally published in 1930: [Jabotinsky, Vladimir] Altalena, *Judge and Fool: The Story of Samson and Delilah* and then reissued in 1945 as [Jabotinsky, Vladimir] Altalena, *Prelude to Delilah*.

43. Jabotinsky [Zeev, pseud.], *Samson*, 307.

44. The translation is mine from the Russian original, as I want to avoid omissions and inaccuracies that traveled from the German to the English-language edition. The Russian text that I use comes from a reprint: Jabotinsky, *Samson Nazorei*, 9.

45. This part is also translated by me from Russian: Ibid., 39.

46. Jabotinsky [Zeev, pseud.], *Samson*, 52.

47. Svetlana Natkovich has written about Jabotinsky's love for English literature, in which he saw a healthy fusion of fiction as entertainment and literature as an expression of the national spirit. In 1914 he "described the English literary corpus as the one closest in spirit to primordial myth." *Samson* apparently was Jabotinsky's own version of the fictionalized primordial myth, with all the appropriate structural elements for a narrative of the primordial, including the mythical connection between race and place (Natkovich, "Land of Harsh Ways," 27).

48. Jabotinsky (Zeev), "'Race and Nationality' handwritten article (in English; 1939)," in Jabotinsky Institute in Israel, A1–7/2, p. 1, http://en.jabotinsky.org/archive/search-archive/item/?itemId=114713. This is the English-language translation of the original Russian-language article published in 1911 in the newspaper *Odesskie Novosti* (Odessa news) under a different title: Jabotinsky, "Vne ocheredi," 2. In 1939 Jabotinsky gave the article a new and very precise title—"Race and Nationality." The translation was edited and published in the English-language collection in 1961: Jabotinsky Ze'ev, *Nation and Society*.

49. Jabotinsky [Zeev, pseud.], "'Race and Nationality' handwritten article (in English; 1939)."
50. Ibid.
51. For 1939 translations: Ibid.
52. Jabotinsky, "Vne ocheredi," 2.
53. On the role of racialized Jewishness in Jabotinsky's Zionism, see Mogilner, "Racial Purity vs. Imperial Hybridity," 103–31.
54. A beautiful analysis of Jabotinsky as a man of fin-de-siècle Europe is offered in Stanislawski, *Zionism and the Fin de Siècle*, 116–238.
55. Jabotinsky, *Slovo o Polku*, 122.
56. Jabotinsky [Zeev, pseud.], "*Hebrew Accent.*" The first publication of this text was in Hebrew: Vladimir Jabotinsky, *ha-Mivta' ha-'Ivri* (Hotza'at ha-Sefer, 1930). The same year, in September 1930, it came out in Russian translation in the Zionist weekly *Razsvet* published in Paris: V. Jabotinsky, "Evrei i Araby s tochki zreniia fonetiki."
57. Jabotinsky, "Evrei i Araby s tochki zreniia fonetiki."
58. Ibid.
59. Ibid.
60. Jabotinsky's novella *Tristan de Runha*, originally written in English and published in 1925 in the English-language anthology of his novellas, still poorly known to students of Jabotinsky, specifically mentions Ferri, Cesare Lombroso, and Rafaele Garofalo. The novella reveals that Jabotinsky shared the concept of the criminal as a primordial type, clearly borrowed from Lombrosian criminal anthropology. For an analysis of this novella and the "Italian connections" behind it, see Natkovich, "Land of Harsh Ways," 34–35. Natkovich also quotes from Jabotinsky's curriculum vitae written for the *Lexicon of Russian Writers* in 1913: "From 1902 on, I tried to appeal to the [broader] echelons of Jewish society. One catalyst was my seven-week stay at the Odessa prison in 1902, where for the first time I met the younger Jewish masses" and identified in them "pride, audacity, and unapologetic national consciousness"—qualities that Jabotinsky came to regard as primordial traits of the Jewish race (Ibid., 47n46, 35).
61. Kaplan, *Jewish Radical Right*, 43.
62. Falk, "Zionism, Race and Eugenics," 143.
63. For example, see his feuilletons published consecutively in a single month: Altalena, "Vskol'z'," 1902a, 3 (a feuilleton that discusses the introduction of free labor in prisons); Altalena, "Vskol'z'," 1902b, 3 (a feuilleton that illustrates syndicalist economic ideas by referring to Italian

cooperatives); Altalena, "Vskol'z'," 1902c, 3 (on degeneration as reflected in the reduction of "really beautiful" female faces), and so on.

64. Natkovich, "Rise and Downfall of Cassandra," 4.

65. Natkovich and Cohen Skalli, "Vladimir Jabotinsky's Perception of Mediterranean Culture and Italian *Mediterranismo*," unpublished paper. I am very grateful to the authors for sharing their work with me.

66. Cassata and O'Loughlin, *Building the New Man*, 43; Finaldi, "Italy, Liberalism, and the Age of Empire," 47–66, esp. 63; Gillette, *Racial Theories in Fascist Italy*, esp. chaps. 1–3.

67. Some students of Jewish history believe that the initial Eurocentrism of the leaders of Zionism led to the "Aryanization of the Jewish state" (to use the title of Michael Selzer's book, in which he pursues a direct line between German antisemitism, the orientalization of Eastern European Jews by German Jews, and the orientalization of the Arab Jews by immigrants from Eastern Europe in Palestine) (*Aryanization of the Jewish State*). I would argue that Jabotinsky's perpetual return to anthropological justifications and Mediterranean race theory exposes a much more conscious engagement with Jewish Europeanness than a simple reproduction of the inferiority/superiority complex implied by Selzer. One can approach this problem either by diving deeper into the specific turn-of-the-century historical context, as I do here, or from a structuralist perspective, as Joseph Massad does in his exploration of the Zionist discourse toward Palestinian Arabs (and which I find to be rather schematic). As he writes, "This is not simply a superstructural neurosis that has afflicted Zionism; it is rather the epistemological foundation on which it rests" (Massad, *Persistence of the Palestinian Question*, 175).

68. On Zollschan, see Efron, *Defenders of the Race*, esp. 153–66.

69. For a nuanced discussion of Jabotinsky's inconsistent views of Nationalitätenrecht and nation-state, see Shumsky, *Beyond the Nation-State*, 124–71 (chap. 4, "Vladimir Jabotinsky: A Jewish State of Nationalities").

70. "Strategic relativism" is used as an opposite to Chakravorty Spivak's characterization of modern episteme of groupness as "strategic essentialism" (*In Other Worlds*, 205). Correspondingly, "strategic relativism" should be understood as a discourse and stance that relativizes the bounded and internally homogeneous nature of the constituent elements of the sociopolitical space and governance and produces a situation of uncertainty, incommensurability, and indistinction. For more, see Gerasimov et al., "New Imperial History and the Challenges of Empire," 20.

3. RACIAL PURITY VERSUS IMPERIAL HYBRIDITY

1. Altalena, "Vskol'z: O natsionalizme," 4.
2. Jabotinsky, "Sionizm i Turtsiia (Nakanune IX Sionistskogo kongressa)," 4. Jabotinsky wrote an introduction to the Russian translation of Karl Renner: Jabotinsky, "Predislovie." Rudolph Springer is Karl Renner's pseudonym.
3. Jabotniskly, "Nabroski bez zaglaviia: VIII. Rol' oppozitsii v III Dume," 2.
4. Fanon, *Wretched of the Earth*, 22.
5. Shumsky, *Beyond the Nation-State*, 119.
6. Jabotinsky, "Novaia Turtsiia i nashi perspektivy," 1909f, 5.
7. Jabotinsky, "Nashi zadachi: III," 3.
8. For an exhaustive and nuanced discussion of Jabotinsky's views of the Habsburg and the Ottoman Empires in transition and his understanding of the composite statehood and national citizenship, see Shumsky, *Beyond the Nation State*, esp. chapter 4, "Vladimir Jabotinsky: A Jewish State of Nationalities," 124–71. For examples of Jabotinsky's positive evaluation of the prospects of the Ottoman Empire, see Jabotinsky, "Novaia Turtsiia i nashi perspektivy," 1909a, 1909b, 1909c, 1909d, 1909e, 1909f, and others.
9. As Shumsky explains, this had changed after World War I and the collapse of the continental empires. In a new geopolitical situation, Jabotinsky envisioned the fulfillment of Jewish self-determination "only in the form of a state—a Jewish state with a Jewish majority in all of Palestine, including the east bank of the Jordan River" (*Beyond the Nation State*, 153). However, he accepted that the Jewish state in Palestine would be multinational and would be structured on the model of a federalist empire-state. Shumsky notes that at this stage too, for Jabotinsky, the state remained a "mechanical and somewhat abstract" instrument of mediation between collective personalities of nations (153).
10. Jabotinsky, "O federatsii," 2.
11. Fanon, *Wretched of the Earth*, 10.
12. On Jabotinsky's activities at the beginning of the first revolution of 1905–1907, see Horowitz, "Vladimir Jabotinsky," 105–24.
13. Jabotinsky, "Nabroski bez zaglaviia," 1906a, 15. Quoted in Horowitz, *Vladimir Jabotinsky's Russian Years, 1900–1925*, 58–59.
14. Gassenschmidt, *Jewish Liberal Politics in Tsarist Russia*.

15. His magisterial work was Ostrogorsky, *La démocratie et l'organisation des partis politiques*; also see Ostrogorsky, *Democracy and the Organization of Political Parties*.

16. Semyonov, "Imperial Parliament for a Hybrid Empire," 8.

17. Ostrogorsky, *Democracy and the Organization of Political Parties*.

18. Semyonov, "Imperial Parliament for a Hybrid Empire," 8; On Ostrogorsky in the Duma, see *Deiatel'nost' M. Ia. Ostrogorskogo v Pervoi Gosudarstvennoi Dume*.

19. Semyonov, "Imperial Parliament for a Hybrid Empire," 8.

20. Horowitz and Katsis, *Vladimir Jabotinsky's "Story of My Life*," 85.

21. One can get a good idea of Jabotinsky's thesis by reading his long two-part article "Selfgoverning of a National Minority," published in 1913 in one of the most influential Russian intelligentsia "thick journals," *Vestnik Evropy* (Messenger of Europe): Jabotinsky, "Samoupravlenie natsional'nogo men'shinstva," 1913a, 1913b.

22. Jabotinsky, "Samoupravleniie natsional'nogo men'shinstva," 1913a, 119.

23. Altalena, "Vskol'z: O natsionalizme," 4.

24. Jabotinsky, "Rasa," in Jabotinsky, *Fel'etony*, 167. Jabotinsky added this essay to the original *Fel'etony* published in St. Petersburg in 1913.

25. Ibid., 172.

26. Ibid., 173.

27. Ibid. Therefore, to reduce Jabotinsky's views to a response to anti-semitism, as some historians do, is rather simplistic. For the most recent example of such a rather narrow interpretation, see Goldstein, *Zionism and Anti-Semitism in the Thoughts and Actions of Ze'ev Jabotinsky*.

28. On the history of Odessa, see Zipperstein, *Jews of Odessa*; Herlihy, *Odessa: A History*; Makolkin, *History of Odessa*; Richardson, *Kaleidoscopic Odessa*; King, *Odessa*; and Gerasimov, "Subaltern Speaks Out," 147–70.

29. Jabotinsky's father, Evgenii, was originally from Novorossiia (New Russia). He worked as a commercial agent for a Russian sea-trade company. He was not an observant Jew and did not speak Yiddish. Jabotinsky's mother, Chava (Eva) Zak, grew up in a well-to-do family in Berdichev. She knew Yiddish but was assimilated and culturally oriented toward German and Russian cultures. Among the best-known biographies of Jabotinsky are Schechtman, *Rebel and Statesman*, and Schechtman, *Fighter and Prophet* (Schechtman was Jabotinsky's comrade-in-arms and wrote his biography as hagiography) as well as Katz, *Lone Wolf*, and Halkin, *Jabotinsky*, which faithfully follows Jabotinsky's autobiography.

30. Shindler, *Triumph of Military Zionism*, 64–65.

31. The *Story of My Life* roughly covers the period until the end of World War I, and the early biographical text, *Story of the Jewish Legion*, picks up from there. The very first English translation of the *Story of My Life*, with commentary and an extended introduction, came out only in 2016: Horowitz and Katsis, *Vladimir Jabotinsky's "Story of My Life."* As Brian Horowitz states in the introduction, Jabotinsky wrote his autobiography with a "political purpose: to provide the reader with a portrait of a charismatic leader who has acquired his right to lead by virtue of his biography—his family, spiritual origins, and practical experiences" ("Introduction: Muse and Muscle," 1). On the constructed nature of this version of the Jewish Bildung, see Stanislawski, *Autobiographical Jews*.

32. Jabotinsky, "Slovo o Polku," 267. In 1926 and 1927, fragments of *Slovo* appeared in Yiddish ("Di Geschichte fun Yidischer Legion" in New York's *Der Morgen Zshurnal*) and in Hebrew in the newspaper *Ha Tzofe*. For more, see the bibliography of Jabotinsky's works: Grauer, *Writings of Ze'ev Jabotinsky 1897–1940*. The first complete edition of *Story of the Jewish Legion* was in Russian: Jabotinsky (Zeev), *Slovo o Polku*. The English translation was published in 1945 (Jabotinsky, *Story of the Jewish Legion*), but it omits some lines from the Russian original, including the passage cited in this text.

33. Horowitz and Katsis, *Vladimir Jabotinsky's "Story of My Life,"* 42. Yehoshua Ravnitzky, one of the greatest Hebrew writers of the day, was Jabotinsky's neighbor and, according to Jabotinsky, his first teacher of Hebrew (although Jabotinsky had to learn the language from scratch as a young adult).

34. Pil'skii, "Jabotinsky," 7.

35. "V. Jabotinsky: Pis'ma russkim pisateliam," 200–221. For the analysis most sensitive to the circumstances of Jabotinsky's upbringing, family background, linguistic situation, and aesthetic preferences, see Stanislawski, *Zionism and the Fin de Siècle*, esp. 121–27.

36. "V. Jabotinsky: Pis'ma russkim pisateliam," 205.

37. Stanislawski, *Zionism and the Fin de Siècle*, 116–49.

38. For the social analysis of this milieu (on the basis of questionnaires distributed among Jewish students in the early twentieth century), see Ivanov, *Evreiskoe studenchestvo v Rossiiskoi imperii*, 77–164.

39. Gordon, *Toward Nationalism's End*, 27, 28.

40. Horowitz and Katsis, *Vladimir Jabotinsky's "Story of My Life,"* 43.

41. On the formation of this intelligentsia's ethos, see Mogilner, *Mifologiia "podpol'nogo cheloveka."*

42. Horowitz, "Introduction: Muse and Muscle," 8.

43. For an analysis of the gendered construction of male Jewishness, see Natkovich, *Among Radiant Clouds*. See especially chap. 3, "The Writer as a National Activist: Between Materialism and Transcendentalism (1904–1922)," 95–150.

44. Altalena, "Vskol'z': Apokrif," 7.

45. Altalena, "Vskol'z'," 1903b, 4.

46. Altalena, "Vskol'z': O natsionalizme," 4.

47. In 1904 Jabotinsky translated a famous poem by Hayyim Nahman Bialik from Hebrew into Russian, "In the City of Slaughter," thus reacting to this tragic event as a Jew, a poet, and an intellectual who still addressed the entire Russian society rather than Jews only.

48. Horowitz and Katsis, *Vladimir Jabotinsky's "Story of My Life,"* 50.

49. Altalena, "Vskol'z: Getto," 5.

50. Stanislawski, *Zionism and the Fin de Siècle*, 176.

51. Altalena, "Vskol'z: Getto," 5.

52. Altelena, "Vskol'z: Eshche o getto," 1903a, 4.

53. Altelena, "Vskol'z: Eshche o getto," 1903b, 4.

54. Fanon, *Wretched of the Earth*, 40.

55. Jabotinsky, "Nakanune kongressa," 2–3; Jabotinsky, "Bazel'skie vpechatleniia," 2; Jabotinsky, "Bazel'skie vpechatleniia: Mizrakhi," 1; Jabotinsky, "Bazel'skie vpechatleniia, III," 3; Jabotinsky, "Iz Bazel'skikh vpechatlenii (Ot nashego korrespondenta)," 2. For an excellent analysis of Jabotinsky's reports from Basel, see Stanislawski, *Zionism and the Fin de Siècle*, 163–72.

56. Jabotinsky, "Bazel'skie vpechatleniia," 2.

57. Jabotinsky, "Hesped," 8–10. The Russian original was translated into Yiddish by Aaron Zeitlin and then into English by Joseph Leftwich (see Jabotinsky Zeev, "'Hesped' (Eulogy)—Poem," in Jabotinsky Institute in Israel Archive, Ref. Code A1-10/2, p. 3, http://en.jabotinsky.org/archive/search-archive/item/?itemId=115645).

58. "Hesped (On the Death of Theodor Herzl): Translated from the Russian by M. Boyarsky," 5.

59. Mogilner, *Homo Imperii*, chap. "'Jewish Physiognomy,' the 'Jewish Question,' and Russian Race Science between Inclusion and Exclusion," 217–50; Mogilner, "Toward a History of Russian-Jewish 'Medical Materialism,'" 70–106.

60. El'kind, "Evrei (Sravnitel'no-antropologicheskii ocherk)," 4.

61. Stanislawski, *Zionism and the Fin de Siècle*, 98.

62. Jabotinsky, "Bazel'skie vpechatleniia," 3.
63. Horowitz and Katsis, *Vladimir Jabotinsky's "Story of My Life,"* 75.
64. Ibid., 82.
65. Elena Tolstaya identified this protagonist as Akim Volynskii. See Tolstaya, *Mir posle kontsa*, 65–68.
66. Jabotinsky, *Five*, 109–10.
67. Horowitz, *Vladimir Jabotinsky's Russian Years*, 41.
68. Jabotinsky, "Sidia na polu...," 22.
69. Jabotinsky, "Sidia na polu...," 27.
70. Horowitz and Katsis, *Vladimir Jabotinsky's "Story of My Life,"* 69–70.
71. Penslar, "Foundations of the Twentieth Century: Herzlian Zionism," 118–19.
72. Jabotinsky, "Pis'mo ob avtonomizme," 117.
73. Ibid.
74. Ibid., 118.
75. Ibid.
76. Jabotinsky, *Kritiki Sionizma*, 12.
77. Jabotinsky, "Samoupravlenie natsional'nogo men'shinstva," 144.
78. Crews, "Empire and the Confessional State," 50–83; Crews, *For Prophet and Tsar*.
79. Jabotinsky, "Pis'mo ob avtonomizme," 119.
80. Ibid., 122.
81. Jabotinsky, "Pis'mo ob avtonomizme, II," 83.
82. Jabotinsky, "Rasa," 174.
83. Scholars continue to reproduce the misleading information that *Chuzhbina* was written in 1908 but never published before 1917 due to censorship restrictions. The year of its first publication is usually indicated as 1922, although this should be 1910. For an example of this mistake, see Katsis, "Vladimir (Zeev) Jabotinsky and His Recently Discovered Works," 434.
84. Ronen, "Chuzheliubie."
85. Jabotinsky, *Chuzhbina: komediia v piati deistviaikh*, 3–4 ("Destvuiushchie Litsa"), 1910.
86. Ronen, "Chuzheliubie."
87. Noemi, "Chuzhbina," 34.
88. Jabotinsky, *Chuzhbina*, 1910. For the 1922 edition, see Jabotinsky, *Chuzhbina*, 1922. Later the play was translated into Hebrew.
89. Perez Sheldon, "Race and Sexuality," 149.

90. Foucault, *Will to Knowledge*, 137.

91. Foucault, *History of Sexuality*; Foucault, "Society Must Be Defended"; Stoler, Race and the Education of Desire.

4. JEWISH RACE VERSUS RUSSIAN RACE

1. Studies of modern Russian nationalism are not particularly numerous. The problem was reopened and reconceptualized by historians only in the late 1990s: Hosking, *Empire and Nation in Russian History*; Hosking and Service, *Russian Nationalism Past and Present*; Wortman, *Scenarios of Power*, vol. 2; Tolz, *Inventing the Nation*; Podbolotov, "Tsar i narod: populistskii natsionalizm Nikolaia II," 199–223; Lohr, *Nationalizing the Russian Empire*; Miller, *Ukrainian Question*; Miller, *Romanov Empire and Nationalism*; Staliūnas, *Making Russians*; Remnev and Suvorova, "'Russian Cause' on the Asiatic Borderlands," 157–222; Maiorova, *From the Shadow of Empire*; Dolbilov, "Russian Nationalism and the Nineteenth-Century Policy of Russification," 141–58; Dolbilov, *Russkii krai, chuzhaia vera*; Brüggemann, "Representing Empire, Performing Nation?," 231–66; Lohr et al., *Empire and Nationalism at War*; Zorin, *By Fables Alone*; Shevelenko, *Modernism kak arkhaizm*; Fedevich and Fedevich, *Za Viru, Tsaria i Kobzaria*; and Savino, "Reactionary Utopia," 31–46.

2. Ivan Sikorsky was quite successful in his academic and public pursuits. In Kyiv he founded and edited the journal *Voprosy nervno-psikhiatricheskoi meditsiny i psikhologii* [Problems of neuropsychiatric medicine and psychology] (1886–1910) and was among the founders of modern experimental child psychology; he set up the Kyiv University Clinic for Nervous Disorders and the Medical-Pedagogical Institute for Mentally Challenged Children. In 1912 Sikorsky opened the world's first institute for child psychopathology. He broadly published in the fields of pathological anatomy, clinical psychiatry and pedagogy, ethnic psychology, and anthropology. Sikorsky was the father of the famous aircraft designer Igor Sikorsky, and hence, I transliterate his family name according to the accepted spelling of Sikorsky (and not Sikorskii). For the best critical biography of Sikorsky as a psychiatrist, see Menzhulin, *Drugoi Sikorsky*. Sikorsky as a race scientist is discussed in Mogilner, *Homo Imperii*, 167–200, and Mogilner, "Racial Psychiatry and the Russian Imperial Dilemma of the 'Savage Within,'" 1–35.

3. Sikorsky, *Chto takoe natsiia i drugie formy etnicheskoi zhizni?*, 52.

4. Ibid., 2–8.

5. Ibid., 7.
6. Ibid., 9.
7. Ibid., 21, 20.
8. Jabotinsky, "Bazel'skie vpechatleniia: Gertzl' i Neinsager'y," 3.
9. Jabotinsky, "Obmen komplimentov: Razgovor," 181–94. First published as Jabotinskii, "Obmen komplimentov," *Odesskie Novosti*, 2.
10. Jabotinsky, "Obmen komplimentov: Razgovor," 182.
11. Safran, "Jews as Siberian Natives," 635–55.
12. For a detailed discussion, see Mogilner, *A Race for the Future*, chap. 4: "Lev Iakovlevich Shternberg (1861–1927): The Political Science of Jewish Race."
13. Jabotinsky, "Obmen komplimentov: Razgovor," 183.
14. Jabotinsky, "Homo Homini Lupus," 103.
15. Jabotinsky, "Obmen komplimentov: Razgovor," 182.
16. Sikorsky, *Antropologicheskaia i psikhologicheskaia genealogia Pushkina*. Quotations are from the reproduction of this text in *Russkaia rasovaia teoriia do 1917 goda*, 309.
17. Sikorsky's expert testimony is published in translation as "Document 22" in Weinberg, *Blood Libel in Late Imperial Russia*, 99–100.
18. For an analysis of these experiments based on the medical reports published by Sikorsky in *Voprosy nervno-psikhiatricheskoi meditsiny i psykhologii*, see Menzhulin, *Drugoi Sikorsky*, 204–11.
19. D. S., "Beseda s O. O. Gruzenbergom," 5.
20. Sikorsky, *Chto takoe natsiia i drugie formy etnicheskoi zhizni?*, 19.
21. Ibid.
22. Ibid., 32.
23. Ibid., 28.
24. Ibid., 27.
25. Gatrell, *Whole Empire Walking*; Lohr, *Nationalizing the Russian Empire*; Sanborn, *Drafting the Russian Nation*; von Hagen, *War in a European Borderland*.
26. Pasmanik, "Rasovyi antisemitism," 7, 8, 9.
27. Poliakov, "Ariiskie Rytsari," 5.
28. Graetz, *Geschichte der Juden von den ältesten Zeiten bis auf die Gegenwart*.
29. Ilovaiskii, *Kratkie ocherki russkoi istorii*; Ilovaiskii, *Rukovodstvo k russkoi istorii*.
30. Jabotinsky, "Obmen komplimentov: Razgovor," 194.
31. Chukovsky, "Evrei i russkaia literatura," 3.

32. Ibid.
33. Jabotinsky, "Pis'mo (O 'Evreiakh i russkoi literature')," 3.
34. Ibid.
35. Emes, "Evrei i russkaia literatura," 8–10 (emphasis added); see especially, Ibn-Daud, "Zametki," 16.
36. Jabotinsky, "Gertsl," 21.
37. Tan, "Evrei i literatura," 3; see also D'Or, "Lichnye nastroeniia: Otvet Vl. Jabotinskomu," 3. For the most recent scholarship on Bogoraz (Tan), see Kasten, *Jochelson, Bogoras and Shternberg*.
38. The pogrom took place in August 1903, and the trial lasted from October 1904 until January 1905. The Gomel pogrom was the first in which Jewish self-defense units acted against the pogromists, so Jews were accused of staging violence and were tried together with the Christian pogromists. Vladimir Bogoraz went to Gomel to document the trial. He later wrote a series of newspaper essays called "Impressions from Gomel," which he published in his collected works in 1911 under the title "Gomel Silhouettes." See Tan (V. G. Bogoraz), *Sobranie sochinenii V. G. Tana*, 5:293–452.
39. Tan, "Posle pogroma (iz gomelskikh vpechatlenii)," 1904b, 3. The first report: Tan, "Posle pogroma (iz gomelskikh vpechatlenii)," 1904a, 4–5.
40. Tan, "Posle pogroma (iz gomelskikh vpechatlenii)," 1904a, 4.
41. On this see Mogilner, *Mifologiia "podpol'nogo cheloveka."*
42. Fanon, *Wretched of the Earth*, 6.
43. Byrd, *Transit of Empire*, 75.
44. Tan, "Evrei i literatura," 3–4. For more on various contemporary reactions to Tan's polemics with Jabotinsky, see Emes, "Iz russkoi pechati," 8–11.
45. Teffi, "Evrei i russkaia literatura," 10.
46. Gornfel'd, "Literaturnye besedy," 4; Tan, "K voprosu o natsional-izme," 3.
47. Fanon, *Wretched of the Earth*, 29.
48. Horowitz and Katsis, *Vladimir Jabotinsky's "Story of My Life,"* 57.
49. Sikorsky, *Chto takoe natsiia i drugie formy etnicheskoi zhizni?*, 11.
50. Jabotinsky, "Samoupravlenie natsional'nogo men'shinstva," 1913a, 136.

5. NATIONALIZING POLITICS IN THE EMPIRE

1. I am using the following edition: Jabotinsky, "Edmee: Rasskaz pozhilogo doktora," in Jabotinsky, *Piatero*, 254–64.
2. Jabotinsky, "Edmee: Rasskaz pozhilogo doktora," 255.

3. Horowitz and Katsis, *Vladimir Jabotinsky's "Story of My Life,"* 98.
4. Jabotinsky, "Edmee: Rasskaz pozhilogo doktora," 255.
5. Ibid.
6. Ibid., 264.
7. Asch, *Shtetl*, 7. For an English translation (slightly altered), see Asch, "Little Town." On Asch, see Krutikov, *Yiddish Fiction and the Crisis of Modernity*; Madison, *Yiddish Literature*; and Stahl, *Sholem Asch Reconsidered*. *Der Fraynd* had a circulation that could not have been imagined for an earlier Jewish newspaper in any language: initially published in fifteen thousand to nineteen thousand copies, it quickly increased to fifty thousand or more. In his memoirs, Shaul Ginsburg refers to ninety thousand copies, but that was probably an exceptional case. Novershtern, *Der Fraynd*.
8. I am quoting this letter as it was reprinted in Chirikov, "Blagodariu, ne ozhidal! (Pis'mo v redaktsiiu)," 9–10.
9. Jabotinsky, "*Dezertiry i khoziaeva*," 8.
10. Ibid., 9.
11. The article was reprinted in N-m, "Everiskaia pechat'," 12.
12. Jabotinsky, "*Dezertiry i khoziaeva*," 10.
13. "Pis'mo Sh. Ascha," 11. Asch did not use the plural and insisted on "THE" Jewish language, which for him was Yiddish (whereas Jabotinsky and the *Razsvet* group were known as uncompromising fighters for Hebrew).
14. In his original and fascinating study of Yiddish modernist literature between 1905 and 1914, Mikhail Krutikov thus defines Asch's contribution to Jewish modernism: "Asch's endeavor was the use of the European literary model, disguised as authentic Jewish fiction. He successfully developed this trend in his later novels, the most famous of which is *Salvation* (*Der tilim-yid*, 1933). Asch was able to satisfy the increasing demand of Jewish and non-Jewish audiences for an undisturbed rural idyll, which reflected a social reaction to the anxiety of modernization. *A Shtetl* and *Reb Shloyme Noged* were an important new stage in the development of Yiddish literature. They represent the artistic response to the rapidly changing conditions of Eastern Europe at the beginning of the twentieth century" (Krutikov, *Yiddish Fiction*, 38).
15. Eizenbet, "Evrei v drame g. Chirikova i v povesti g. Yushkevicha," 140, 143.
16. "Literaturnye nabroski," 167–68.
17. Ibid., 174.
18. Gorin-Goriainov, *Aktery: iz vospominanii*, 118.
19. Linskii [V. A. Vakulin], "Novyi teatr," 740.

20. Liubimova, "Dramaturgiia Evgeniia Chirikova i russkaia stsena 900-kh gg.," 48.

21. The first permanent Ukrainian theater was permitted to open in Kyiv in 1907 (the Sadovskii Theater). For the 1907 season, Sadovskii was preparing the production of Chirikov's *Evrei* in Ukrainian, with the great actress Mariia Zinkovetska as Leah. Censorship forbade the premiere at the time, but a year later, in 1908, the play, advertised as an answer to the pogroms of 1905, premiered in the theater.

22. For details, see Hunczak, *Symon Petliura and the Jews*, and Engel, introduction to *Assassination of Symon Petliura*, 7–94.

23. Petliura, "Uvagy pro zavdannia ukrains'kogo teatru: Peredmova," in E. M. Chirikov, *Evrei*, xvii.

24. Struve, "Intelligentsiia i natsional'noe litso," 3.

25. Pipes, *Struve: Liberal on the Left*; Pipes, *Struve: Liberal on the Right*; Semyonov, "Russian Liberalism and the Problem of Imperial Diversity," 67–90.

26. Struve, "Intelligentsiia i natsional'noe litso," 3.

27. Ibid.

28. Jabotinsky, "Asemitizm," 28–32.

29. Jabotinsky, "Dezertiry i khoziaeva," 9. For similar arguments, see also Jabotinsky, "Nabroski bez zaglavia," 1909b, 8–13.

30. Miliukov, "Natsionalizm protiv natsionalizma," 2.

31. Jabotinsky, "Nabroski bez zaglavia," 1909c, 6.

32. Vital, *Zionism*, 39–40.

33. Slavinsky, "Russkie, velikorossy i rossiiane," 2.

34. Brutzkus, "O russkom i evreiskom natisonalizme," 59–68.

35. Vinaver, "Otkrytoe pis'mo Struve," 4. See also Emes, "Chirikovskii intsident i russkaia pechat'," 7–11; Jabotinsky, "Medved' iz berlogi," 4–7; N-m, "Evreiskaia pechat'," 23–26.

36. Jabotinsky, "Homo Homini Lupus," 105.

37. Jabotinsky, "Urok iubileia Shevchenki," in *Fel'etony*, 3; originally published in Jabotinsky, "Urok iubileia Shevchenki," *Odesskie Novosti* (February 27, 1911), 2.

38. Struve, "Na raznye temy," 185.

39. Ibid., 186, 187.

40. Ibid., 186n2.

41. Jabotinsky, "O iazukakh i prochem," in Jabotinsky, *Fel'etony*, 219; originally published in *Russkaia Mysl'* 1 (1911): 95–114.

42. Jabotinsky, "Otpor," 1913b, 8–11. See also Jabotinsky, "Otpor," 1913a, 5–9; Jabotinsky, "Otpor," 1913c, 23–27; and *Poliaki i evrei: Materialy o pol'sko-evreiskom spore*.

43. For more on this, see Kleiner, *Vladimir (Zeev) Jabotinsky i ukrains'ke pytannia*, 86–96, and elsewhere.

44. Jabotinsky, "Urok iubileia Shevchenki," *Fel'etony*, 1922, 231–41.

45. In Ukrainian: Кохайтеся, чорноброві, / Та не з москалями, / Бо москалі—чужі люде, Роблять лихо с вами.

46. Jabotinsky, "Samoupravlenie natsional'nogo men'shinstva," 1913a, 132.

47. The very first publication was attempted in the Paris Zionist periodical *Razsvet* in 1933 but was suspended. Now the novel is available in English: Jabotinsky, *The Five*.

48. Scherr, "Odessa Odyssey," 94–115.

49. Stanislawski, *Zionism and the Fin de Siècle*, 228.

50. Altalena, "Vskol'z'," 1903d, 3.

51. Sig, "Okolo zhizni," 3.

52. Not a single Milgrom is mentioned among the thousands of Odessa homeowners and summer-house owners in the 1902 city directory: *Vsia Odessa 1902–3 gody*.

53. Altalena, "Vskol'z': ne o iubilee Peterburga," 4.

54. Jabotinsky, *Five*, 197.

55. According to Weisskopf, "comrade Rachel" predated Lika from *The Five*, the thief Yashka was Serezha's prototype, and a nice-looking and flirtatious Nina was the earlier version of *The Five*'s Marusia ("Predislovie," 14).

56. Copies of both original feuilletons from *Odesskie Novosti* are preserved among Jabotinsky's materials at the Jabotinsky Institute in Israel Archive: "Vskol'z': piatero," F-1910/902/RU.

57. Altalena, "Vskol'z': Piatero," 1910a, 1.

58. Ibid., 2.

59. Ibid., 2.

60. Altalena, "Vskol'z': Piatero," 1910b, 1.

61. Ibid., 3.

62. Ibid., 6.

63. Dirks, *Scandal of Empire*.

64. On the discussion of the phenomenon of *Azefovshchina*, see Mogilner, *Mifologiia "podpol'nogo cheloveka."*

65. Jabotinsky, "Esche odin," 4.

66. Barry Scherr suggests that Serezha "bears certain resemblances to the youthful Jabotinsky." Scherr, "Odessa Odyssey," 106. He also believes that Serezha owed something to Aleksandr (Sasha) Eizengardt who "like Serezha . . . composed short verses (which Jabotinsky published at one point), had frequent problems with authorities, and seemed to recognize few if any moral limits" (106n55). On Aleksandr (Sasha) Eizengardt, see

the memoir by Eizengardt's sister, Liudmila Miklashevskaia: Miklashevskaia and Katerli, *Chemu svideteli my byli*, esp. 71–73.

67. Jabotinsky, "Bytovoe iavlenie," 1910a, 25–28, 1910b, 3–7; Jabotinsky, *Nashe bytovoe iavlenie (Vopros o vykrestakh)*; reprinted in and quoted from Jabotinsky, "Nashe bytovoe iavlenie," in *Fel'etony*, 168, 169.

68. Jabotinsky, *Five*, 166–67.

69. Jabotinsky, "Nashe bytovoe iavlenie," 171.

70. Jabotinsky, *Five*, 199.

71. Said, "Cairo Recalled," 268–75.

72. Prakash, "Edward Said in Bombay," 499–500.

73. Ibid., 501.

74. The letter is quoted in English translation in Horowitz, *Vladimir Jabotinsky's Russian Years*, 169.

75. In 1925, Jabotinsky published his English-language novella "Tristan da Runha," in which the events are also set on an island. According to Svetlana Natkovich, Jabotinsky fantasized an isolated island community of exiled criminals to "investigate the conditions necessary for the creation of an ideal society, one organized in accordance with primal intuition and thus without need of coercive regulatory mechanisms" ("Land of Harsh Ways," 25). Knowing how fundamental the role of primal intuition was in Jabotinsky's construction of the race/nation, we can safely assume that what he investigated on the island was a process of nation-building.

CONCLUSION

1. Gordon, *Toward Nationalism's End*, 48.
2. Jabotinsky, "Samoupravlenie natsional'nogo men'shinstva," 121.
3. Penslar, "Is Zionism a Colonial Movement?," 277.

BIBLIOGRAPHY

Abramovich, Grigorii. "Genezis natsional'noi idei i sushchnost' natsional-izma." *Evreiskaia zhizn'* 11 (1904): 82–100.
Abu El-Haj, Nadia. *The Genealogical Science: The Search for Jewish Origins and the Politics of Epistemology*. Chicago: University of Chicago Press, 2012.
Altalena [Vladimir Jabotinsky]. "Vskol'z'." *Odesskie Novosti*, no. 5580 (March 16, 1902a): 3.
———. "Vskol'z'." *Odesskie Novosti*, no. 5583 (March 19, 1902b): 3.
———. "Vskol'z'." *Odesskie Novosti*, no. 5585 (March 21, 1902c): 3.
———. "Vskol'z'." *Odesskie Novosti*, no. 5949 (April 20, 1903a): 3.
———. "Vskol'z'." *Odesskie Novosti*, no. 5991 (June 7, 1903b): 4.
———. "Vskol'z': Apokrif." *Odesskie Novosti*, no. 5937 (April 6, 1903): 7.
———. "Vskol'z: Eshche o getto." *Odesskie Novosti*, no. 6114 (October 18, 1903a): 4.
———. "Vskol'z: Eshche o getto." *Odesskie Novosti*, no. 6124 (October 29, 1903b): 4.
———. "Vskol'z: Getto." *Odesskie Novosti*, no. 6108 (October 12, 1903): 5.
———. "Vskol'z': Ne o iubilee Peterburga." *Odesskie Novosti*, no. 5972 (May 17, 1903): 4.
———. "Vskol'z: O natsionalizme." *Odesskie Novosti*, no. 5874 (January 30, 1903): 4.
———. "Vskol'z': Piatero." *Odesskie Novosti*, no. 8135 (June 9, 1910a): 1–3.
———. "Vskol'z': Piatero." *Odesskie Novosti*, no. 8136 (June 10, 1910b): 2–6.
Asch, Sholem. "The Little Town." Translated by Meyer Levin. In *Tales of My People*, edited by Meyer Levin, 3–143. New York: G. P. Putnam's, 1948.

———. *A Shtetl*. New York: Forverts, 1911. [In Yiddish].
Auerbach, Elias. "Die Jüdische Rassenfrage." *Archiv für Rassen- und Gesellschaftsbiologie* 4, no. 3 (1907): 332–61.
Avdeev, V. B., ed. *Russkaia rasovaia teoriia do 1917 goda: Sbornik original'nykh rabot russkikh klassikov*. Moscow: FERI-V, 2002.
Avraami, Tsvi [Grigorii Abramovich]. "Osnovy i factory natsional'nogo kharaktera." *Evreiskaia zhizn'* 10 (1904): 64–88.
Avrutin, Eugene M. *Jews and the Imperial State: Identification Politics in Tsarist Russia*. Ithaca, NY: Cornell University Press, 2010.
———. "Racial Categories and the Politics of (Jewish) Difference in Late Imperial Russia." *Kritika: Explorations in Russian and Eurasian History* 8, no. 1 (2007): 13–40.
———. *Racism in Modern Russia: From Romanovs to Putin*. London: Bloomsbury Academic, 2022.
Balibar, Etienne. "Is There a Neo-Racism?" In *Race, Nation, Class: Ambiguous Identities*, edited by Etienne Balibar and Emmanuel Wallerstein, translated by Chris Turner, 17–28. London: Verso, 1991.
Bartal, Israel. *The Jews of Eastern Europe, 1772–1881*. Philadelphia: University of Pennsylvania Press, 2002.
Bauer, Otto. "The Nation." In *Mapping the Nation*, edited by Gopal Balakrishnan, 39–77. London: Verso, 2012.
Becker, Seymour. "Toward a Genealogy of the Nationalizing Empire: Chapter Seven, the Era of the Great Reforms (II): Constitutional Projects; Poland and Finland." *Ab Imperio* 22, no. 1 (2021): 185–234.
Beddoe, John. "On the Physical Characteristics of the Jews." *Transactions of the Ethnological Society of London* 1 (1861): 222–37.
Beer, Daniel. *Renovating Russia: The Human Sciences and the Fate of Liberal Modernity, 1880–1930*. Ithaca, NY: Cornell University Press, 2008.
Ben-Samuel, D. [D. Pasmanik]. "Pis'ma k evreiskoi molodezhi: Pis'mo tret'e." *Evreiskaia zhizn'* 4 (1905): 124–32.
Bernal, Martin. *Black Athena: The Afroasiatic Roots of Classical Civilization*. Vol. 3, *The Linguistic Evidence*. New Brunswick, NJ: Rutgers University Press, 2006.
Bialik, Chaim Nachman. "The Present Hour." *Young Zionist* (London, May 1934): 6–7.
Blakely, Allison. *Russia and the Negro: Blacks in Russian History and Thought*. Washington, DC: Howard University Press, 1986.
Blechmann, Bernhard. *Ein Beitrag zur Anthropologie der Juden*. Dorpat: Wilhelm Just, 1882.

Bojanowska, Edyta. *A World of Empires: The Russian Voyage of the Frigate Pallada*. Cambridge, MA: Harvard University Press, 2018.
Borokhov, Ber. "O Kharaktere Evreiskogo Uma: I." In *Illustrirovannyi Sionistskii Al'manakh: 1902–1903*, edited by A. A. Freidenberg, 316–37. Kiev: Tipo-litografiia S. V. Kul'zhenko, 1902.
Brown, Julie. "Revolution and Psychosis: The Mixing of Science and Politics in Russian Psychiatric Medicine, 1905–13." *Russian Review* 46, no. 3 (1987): 283–302.
Brubaker, Rogers, and Frederick Cooper. "Beyond Identity." *Theory and Society* 29, no. 1 (2000): 1–47.
Brüggemann, Karsten. "Representing Empire, Performing Nation? Russian Officials in the Baltic Provinces (Late Nineteenth/Early Twentieth Centuries)." *Ab Imperio* 15, no. 3 (2014): 231–66.
Brutzkus, B. "O russkom i evreiskom natsionalizme: intelligentskaia reaktsiia i antisemitism." *Evreiskii Mir* 5 (1909): 59–68.
Brutzkus, Julii. "Evreiskii Vopros v Russkoi Pechati." *Evreiskaia zhizn'* 1 (1904): 188–203.
Burbank, Jane. "An Imperial Rights Regime: Law and Citizenship in the Russian Empire." *Kritika: Explorations in Russian and Eurasian History* 7, no. 3 (2006): 397–431.
Byrd, Jodi. *The Transit of Empire: Indigenous Critiques of Colonialism*. Minneapolis: University of Minnesota Press, 2011.
Caglioti, Angelo Matteo. "Race, Statistics, and Italian Eugenics: Alfredo Niceforo's Trajectory from Lombroso to Fascism (1876–1960)." *European History Quarterly* 47, no. 3 (2017): 461–89.
Cassata, Francesco, and Erin O'Loughlin. *Building the New Man: Eugenics, Racial Sciences and Genetics in Twentieth Century Italy*. Budapest: CEU Press, 2010.
Chakrabarty, Dipesh. "Postcoloniality and the Artifice of History: Who Speaks for 'Indian' Pasts?" *Representations* 37 (Winter 1992): 1–26.
———. *Provincializing Europe: Postcolonial Thought and Historical Difference*. Princeton, NJ: Princeton University Press, 2000.
Chakravorty Spivak, Gayatri. *In Other Worlds: Essays in Cultural Politics*. New York: Routledge, 1987.
Chamberlain, Edward, and Sander Gilman, eds. *Degeneration: The Dark Side of Progress*. New York: Columbia University Press, 1985.
Chirikov, E. M. *Evrei: P'esa na 4 dii; pereklad Leonid Pakharevs'kii*. Kyiv: Druk S. A. Borysova, 1907.
Chirikov, Evgenii. "Blagodariu, ne ozhidal! (Pis'mo v redaktsiiu)." *Razsvet* 10 (March 8, 1909): 9–10.

Chukovsky, Kornei. "Evrei i russkaia literatura." *Svobodnye Mysli* (January 14, 1908): 3.

———. "Sluchainye zametki." *Evreiskaia zhizn'* 11 (1904): 177–82.

Clifford, James. *The Predicament of Culture.* Cambridge, MA: Harvard University Press, 1988.

Crews, Robert. "Empire and the Confessional State: Islam and Religious Politics in Nineteenth-Century Russia." *American Historical Review* 108, no. 1 (2003): 50–83.

———. *For Prophet and Tsar: Islam and Empire in Russia and Central Asia.* Boston: Harvard University Press, 2006.

"Critical Discussion: Forum on Race and Bias (Introduction and 14 Contributions)." *Slavic Review* 80, no. 2 (Summer 2021): 203–340.

Deiatel'nost' M. Ia. Ostrogorskogo v Pervoi Gosudarstvennoi Dume. St. Petersburg: Tipo-litografiia R. S. Vol'pina, 1906.

Dirks, Nicholas B. *The Scandal of Empire: India and the Creation of Imperial Britain.* Cambridge, MA: Belknap Press of Harvard University Press, 2006.

Dolbilov, Mikhail. "The Emancipation Reform of 1861 in Russia and the Nationalism of the Imperial Bureaucracy." In *Construction and Deconstruction of National History in Slavic Eurasia,* edited by T. Hayashi, 208–235. Sapporo, Japan: Slavic Research Center, 2003.

———. "Russian Nationalism and the Nineteenth-Century Policy of Russification in the Russian Empire's Western Region." In *Comparative Imperiology,* edited by Kimitaka Matsuzato, 141–58. Sapporo, Japan: Slavic Research Center, Hokaido University, 2010.

———. *Russkii krai, chuzhaia vera: etnokonfessional'naia politika imperii v Litve i Belorussii pri Aleksandre II.* Moscow: NLO, 2012.

———. "The Stereotype of the Pole in Imperial Policy: The 'Depolonization' of the North-Western Region in the 1860s." *Russian Studies in History* 44, no. 2 (2005): 44–88.

D'Or, O. L. "Lichnye nastroeniia: Otvet Vl. Jabotinskomu." *Svobodnye Mysli* (March 31, 1908): 3.

D. S. "Beseda s O. O. Gruzenbergom." *Razsvet* 44 (November 1, 1913): 5–6.

Du Bois, W. E. B. "The African Origin of the Grecian Civilization." *Journal of Negro History* 2, no. 3 (1917): 334–44.

Efron, John M. *Defenders of the Race: Jewish Doctors and Race Science in Fin-de-Siècle Europe.* New Haven, CT: Yale University Press, 1994.

———. *German Jewry and the Allure of the Sephardic.* Princeton, NJ: Princeton University Press, 2016.

———. *Medicine and the German Jews: A History*. New Haven, CT: Yale University Press, 2001.
Eizenbet, I. G. "Evrei v drame g. Chirikova i v povesti g. Yushkevicha." *Evreiskaia Zhizn'* 7 (1904): 138–60.
El'kind, Arkadii Danilovich. "Antropologicheskoe izuchenie evreev i disput A. D. El'kinda." *Zemlevedenie* 1–2 (1913): 230.
———. "Evrei (Sravnitel'no-antropologicheskii ocherk)." *Russkii Antropologicheskii Zhunral* 11, no. 3 (1902): 1–44.
———. "Evrei (Sravnitel'no-antropologicheskoe issledovanie, preimushchestvenno po nabliudeniiam nad pol'skimi evreiami)." *Izvestiia IOLEAE* 104 (1903): 1–458.
———. "Kritika i bibliografiia: Dr. I. M. Judt, *Żydzi jako rasa fizyczna. Analiza s dziedziny antropologii. Z 24 rysunakmi, mapa i tablicami w tekste*. Warszawa, 1902." *Russkii Antropologicheskii Zhurnal* 11, no. 3 (1902): 105–7.
Emes. "Chirikovskii intsident i russkaia pechat.'" *Evreiskaia Zhizn'* 11 (March 15, 1909): 7–11.
———. "Evrei i russkaia literatura." *Razsvet* 3 (1908): 8–10.
———. "Iz russkoi pechati." *Razsvet* 20 (May 24, 1908), 8–11.
Engel, David. Introduction to *The Assassination of Symon Petliura and the Trial of Scholem Schwarzbard 1926–27: A Selection of Documents*, edited by David Engel, 7–94. Gottingen: Vandenhoeck and Ruprecht, 2016.
Engelstein, Laura. "Combined Underdevelopment: Discipline and the Law in Imperial and Soviet Russia." *American Historical Review* 98, no. 2 (1993): 338–53.
———. *The Keys to Happiness: Sex and the Search for Modernity in Fin-de-Siècle Russia*. Ithaca, NY: Cornell University Press, 1992.
Falk, Raphael. "Zionism, Race and Eugenics." In *Jewish Tradition and the Challenge of Darwinism*, edited by Geoffrey Cantor and Marc Swetlitz, 137–62. Chicago: University of Chicago Press, 2006.
Fanon, Frantz. *The Wretched of the Earth*. Translated from the French by Richard Philcox, with commentary by Jean-Paul Sarte and Homi K. Bhabha. New York: Grove Press, 2004. Originally published 1963.
Fedevich, Klimentii I., and Klementii K. Fedevich. *Za Viru, Tsaria i Kobzaria: Malorosiiski monarkhisty i ukrainskii natsional'nyi rukh (1905–1917)*. Kyiv: Krytyka, 2018.
Finaldi, Giuseppi. "Italy, Liberalism, and the Age of Empire." In *Liberal Imperialism in Europe*, edited by Matthew Fitzpatrick, 47–66. New York: Palgrave Macmillan, 2012.

Fishman, David E. "The Bund and Modern Yiddish Culture." In *The Emergence of Modern Jewish Politics: Bundism and Zionism in Eastern Europe*, edited by Zvi Gitelman, 107–19. Pittsburgh: University of Pittsburgh Press, 2003.

Foucault, Michel. *The History of Sexuality*. Vols. 1–3. London: Penguin Books, 1976.

———. *"Society Must Be Defended": Lectures at the College de France, 1975–76*. Edited by Mauro Bertani and Alessandro Fontana. Translated by David Macey. New York: Picador, 2003.

———. *The Will to Knowledge: History of Sexuality*. Vol. 1. Translated by R. Hurley. London: Penguin Books, 1998 (first published in English in 1976).

Frankel, Jonathan. *Prophecy and Politics: Socialism, Nationalism, and the Russian Jews, 1862–1917*. Cambridge: Cambridge University Press, 1981.

Fridman, R., and S. Shwatzband. "K voprosu ob istochnikakh povesti Vl. Jabotinskogo 'Samson Nazorei.'" *Jews and Slavs* 4 (1995): 210–25.

Gassenschmidt, Christoph. *Jewish Liberal Politics in Tsarist Russia, 1900–1914: The Modernization of Russian Jewry*. New York: New York University Press, 1995.

Gatrell, Peter. *A Whole Empire Walking: Refugees in Russia during World War I*. Bloomington: Indiana University Press, 1999.

Gechtman, Roni. "Conceptualizing National-Cultural Autonomy: From the Austro-Marxists to the Jewish Labor Bund." *Jarbuch des Simon-Dubnow-Instituts* 4 (2005): 17–49.

Gerasimov, Ilya. "The Subaltern Speaks Out: Urban Plebeian Society in Late Imperial Russia." In *Spaces of the Poor: Perspectives of Cultural Sciences on Urban Slum Areas and Their Inhabitants*, edited by Hans-Christian Petersen, 147–70. Bielefeld: Transcript, 2013

Gerasimov, Ilya, Sergey Glebov, Jan Kusber, Marina Mogilner, and Alexander Semyonov. "New Imperial History and the Challenges of Empire." In *Empire Speaks Out: Languages of Rationalization and Self-Description in the Russian Empire*, edited by Ilya Gerasimov, Jan Kusber, and Alexander Semyonov, 3–32. Leiden, Netherlands: Brill, 2009.

Gerasimov, Ilya, Marina Mogilner, and Sergey Glebov, eds. *Novaia imperskaia istoriia Severnoi Evrazii*. Vol. 2, *Balansirovaniie imperskoi situatsii: XVIII–XX vv*. Moscow: Ab Imperio, 2017.

Gillette, Aaron. *Racial Theories in Fascist Italy*. New York: Routledge, 2002.

Gillman, Susan. "Humboldt's American Mediterranean." *American Quarterly* 66, no. 3 (2014): 505–28.
Gilman, Sander. *Jewish Self-Hatred: Anti-Semitism and the Hidden Language of the Jews*. Baltimore: Johns Hopkins University Press, 1986.
———. *The Jew's Body*. New York: Routledge, 1991.
Gilroy, Paul. *The Black Atlantic: Modernity and Double Consciousness*. Cambridge, MA: Harvard University Press, 1993.
Gitelman, Zvi Y. *Jewish Nationality and Soviet Politics: The Jewish Section of CPSU, 1917–1930*. Princeton, NJ: Princeton University Press, 1972.
Głębocki, Henryk. *Fatalna sprawa: Kwestia polska w rosyjskiej myśli politycznej w latach 1856–1866*. Krakow: Arkana, 2000.
Glebov, Sergey. "Race and Politics: A History from an Imperial Borderland." In *A Cultural History of Race in the Age of Empire and the Nation State*, edited by Marina Mogilner, 93–110. Vol. 5 of *A Cultural History of Race*, edited by Marius Turda. London: Bloomsbury Academic, 2021.
Goldstein, Amir. *Zionism and Anti-Semitism in the Thought and Action of Ze'ev Jabotinsky*. [In Hebrew]. Sde-Boker, Israel: Ben-Gurion University Press and Jabotinsky Institute, 2015.
Goldstein, Joseph. "The Attitude of the Jewish and the Russian Intelligentsia to Zionism in the Initial Period (1897–1904)." *Slavonic and East European Review* 64, no. 4 (1986): 546–56.
———. "Jabotinsky and Jewish Autonomy in the Diaspora." *Studies in Zionism* 7, no. 2 (1986): 224–36.
———. *The Russian Zionism: The Formative Years*. [In Hebrew]. Jerusalem: Magnes Press, 1991.
———. "The Zionist Movement in Russia (1897–1904)." PhD diss., Hebrew University, Jerusalem, 1989.
Gordon, Adi. *Toward Nationalism's End: An Intellectual Biography of Hans Kohn*. Waltham, MA: Brandeis University Press, 2017.
Gorin-Goriainov, B. A. *Aktery: iz vospominanii*. Leningrad-Moscow: Iskusstvo, 1947.
Gornfel'd, Arkadii. "Literaturnye besedy: Chukovsky." *Stolichnaia Pochta* (February 3, 1908): 4.
Gorny, Macej. *Science Embattled: Eastern European Intellectuals and the Great War*. Leiden, Netherlands: Ferdinand Schöningh, ein Imprint der Brill Gruppe, 2019.
Graetz, Heinrich. *Geschichte der Juden von den ältesten Zeiten bis auf die Gegenwart*. 11 vols. Rev. and exp. ed. Leipzig, Germany: Leiner, 1900.
Grauer, Mina, ed. *Writings of Ze'ev Jabotinsky 1897–1940: Bibliography*. [In Hebrew]. Tel Aviv: Jabotinsky Institute, 2007.

Halkin, Hillel. *Jabotinsky: A Life*. New Haven, CT: Yale University Press, 2014.
Hart, Mitchell B. *Jews and Race: Writing on Identity and Difference, 1880–1940*. Waltham, MA: Brandeis University Press, 2011.
———. "Racial Science, Social Science, and the Politics of Jewish Assimilation." *Isis* 90 (1999): 268–97.
———. *Social Science and the Politics of Modern Jewish Identity*. Stanford, CA: Stanford University Press, 2000.
Heller, Daniel. *Jabotinsky's Children: Polish Jews and the Rise of Right-Wing Zionism*. Princeton, NJ: Princeton University Press, 2017.
Herlihy, Patricia. *Odessa: A History, 1794–1914*. Cambridge, MA: Harvard University Press, 1991.
"Hesped (On the Death of Theodor Herzl): Translated from the Russian by M. Boyarsky." *Jewish Herald*, July 22, 1949, 5.
Hoffmann, David L., and Yanni Kotsonis, eds. *Russian Modernity: Politics, Knowledge, Practices*. New York: St. Martin's Press, 2000.
Horowitz, Brian. "Introduction: Muse and Muscle: *Story of My Life* and the Invention of Vladimir Jabotinsky." In *Vladimir Jabotinsky's "Story of My Life,"* edited by Brian Horowitz and Leonid Katsis, 1–31. Detroit, MI: Wayne State University Press, 2016.
———. "Vladimir Jabotinsky: A Zionist Activist on the Rise, 1905–1906." *Studia Judaica* 20, no. 1 (39) (2017): 105–24.
———. *Vladimir Jabotinsky's Russian Years, 1900–1925*. Bloomington: Indiana University Press, 2020.
———. "What Is Russian in Russian Zionism? Avram Idel'son's Thought and Destiny." In *Bounded Mind and Soul: Russia and Israel, 1880–2010*, edited by Brian Horowitz and Shai Ginsburg, 61–76. Bloomington, IN: Slavica, 2013.
———. "What Is 'Russian' in Russian Zionism? Synthetic Zionism and the Fate of Avram Idel'son." In *Russian Idea—Jewish Presence: Essays on Russian-Jewish Intellectual Life*, 54–70. Boston: Academic Studies Press, 2013.
Horowitz, Brian, and Leonid Katsis, eds. *Vladimir Jabotinsky's "Story of My Life."* Detroit, MI: Wayne State University Press, 2016.
Hosking, Geoffrey. *Empire and Nation in Russian History*. Waco, TX: Baylor University, 1992.
Hosking, Geoffrey, and Robert Service, eds. *Russian Nationalism Past and Present*. Houndmills: Palgrave Macmillan, 1998.
Hunczak, Taras. *Symon Petliura and the Jews: A Reappraisal*. L'viv: Ukrainian Historical Association, 2008.

Ibn-Daud. "Zametki." *Razsvet* 5 (1908): 16–18.
Ikow, Constantine. "Neue Beiträge zur Anthropologie der Juden." *Archiv für Anthropologie* 15, no. 4 (1884): 369–89.
Ilovaiskii, Dmitrii. *Kratkie ocherki russkoi istorii: kurs starshego vozrasta.* 9th ed. Moscow: Grachev and K, 1868.
———. *Rukovodstvo k russkoi istorii: srednii kurs.* 40th ed. Moscow: A. V. Vasil'ev and K, 1901.
Ivanov, A. E. *Evreiskoe studenchestvo v Rossiiskoi imperii nachala XX veka: Kakim ono bylo? Opyt sotsiokul'turnogo portretirovaniia.* Moscow: Novyi khronograf, 2007.
Jabotinsky, Vladimir. "Asemitizm." In *Po vekham ... Sbornik statei ob intelligentsii i "natsional'nom" litse,* edited by F. Muskablit, 28–32. Moscow: Obshchestvennaia Pol'za, 1909.
———. "Bazel'skie vpechatleniia." *Odesskie Novosti,* no. 6058 (August 19, 1903): 2.
———. "Bazel'skie vpechatleniia: Mizrakhi." *Odesskie Novosti,* no. 6059 (August 20, 1903): 1.
———. "Bazel'skie vpechatleniia, III: Gerzl and Neiseger'y." *Odesskie Novosti,* no. 6062 (August 23, 1903): 3.
———. "Bytovoe iavlenie." *Razsvet* 50 (December 12, 1910a): 25–28.
———. "Bytovoe iavlenie." *Razsvet* 51 (December 19, 1910b): 3–7.
———. *Chuzhbina: Komediia v piati deistviaikh.* St. Petersburg: Tipografia Ts. Kraiz, 1910.
———. *Chuzhbina: Komediia v piati deistviaikh.* Berlin: Zal'tsman, 1922.
———. "Dezertiry i khoziaeva." *Razsvet* 9 (March 1, 1909): 8–10.
———. "Edmee: Rasskaz pozhilogo doktora." In *Piatero: Roman, Rasskazy,* with an introduction by E. Golubovskii, 254–64. Moscow: Nezavisimaia Gazeta, 2002.
———. "Esche odin." *Razsvet* 27 (July 5, 1909): 3–5.
———. "Evrei i Araby s tochki zreniia fonetiki (Iz broshury "Evreiskoe proiznoshenie")." In Jabotinsky Institute in Israel, Ref. no. F-1930/905/RU. http://www.infocenters.co.il/jabo/jabo_multimedia/Articles/1930_905.pdf.
———. *The Five: A Novel of Jewish Life in Turn-of-the Century Odessa.* Translated by Michael R. Katz. Ithaca, NY: Cornell University Press, 2005.
———. "Gertsl': Idealy, taktika, lichnost.'" *Evreiskaia zhizn'* 3 (1904): 1–27.
———. *Hebrew Pronunciation.* [In Hebrew]. Tel Aviv: Hotza'at ha-Sefer, 1930.

———. "Hesped." *Evreiskaia Zhizn'* 6 (1904): 8–10.

———. "Homo Homini Lupus." In *Fel'etony*, 3rd ed., 101–14. Berlin: Izdatel'stvo S. D. Zal'tsman, 1922.

———. "Iz Bazel'skikh vpechatlenii (Ot nashego korrespondenta)." *Odesskie Novosti*, no. 6064 (August 25, 1903): 2.

———. *Kritiki Sionizma*. 2nd ed. Odessa: Kadima, 1906.

———. "Medved' iz berlogi." *Evreiskaia Zhizn'* 11 (March 15, 1909): 4–7.

———. "Nabroski bez zaglaviia." *Razsvet* 1 (January 10, 1909a): 15–17.

———. "Nabroski bez zaglaviia." *Razsvet* 13–14 (April 5, 1909b): 8–13.

———. "Nabroski bez zaglaviia." *Razsvet* 23 (June 7, 1909c): 4–7.

———. "Nabroski bez zaglaviia: VIII. Rol' oppozitsii v III Dume." *Odesskie Novosti*, no. 7351 (October 11, 1907): 2.

———. "Nakanune kongressa: Bazel." *Odesskie Novosti*, no. 6055 (March 15, 1903): 2–3.

———. "Nashe bytovoe iavlenie." In *Fel'etony*, 166–80. Berlin, 1922.

———. *Nashe bytovoe iavlenie (Vopros o vykrestakh)*. Odessa: Voskhod, 1911.

———. "Nashi zadachi: III." *Khronika Evreiskoi Zhizni* (July 6, 1906): 3.

———. "Novaia Turtsiia i nashi perspektivy." *Razsvet* 3 (January 18, 1909a): 4–7.

———. "Novaia Turtsiia i nashi perspektivy." *Razsvet* 5 (February 1, 1909b): 1–4.

———. "Novaia Turtsiia i nashi perspektivy." *Razsvet* 7 (February 15, 1909c): 1–5.

———. "Novaia Turtsia i nashi perspektivy." *Razsvet* 8 (February 22, 1909d): 8–12.

———. "Novaia Turtsiia i nashi perspektivy." *Razsvet* 10 (March 8, 1909e): 3–8.

———. "Novaia Turtsiia i nashi perspektivy." *Razsvet* 12 (March 22, 1909f): 4–9.

———. "Obmen komplimentov." *Odesskie Novosti*, no. 8546 (October 16, 1911): 2.

———. "Obmen komplimentov: Razgovor." In *Fel'etony*, 181–94. St. Petersburg: Gerol'd, 1913.

———. "O federatsii." *Radikal* (January 15, 1906): 2–4.

———. "O iazukakh i prochem." In *Fel'etony*, 218–30. Berlin, 1922.

———. "O iazukakh i prochem." *Russkaia Mysl'* 1 (1911): 95–114.

———. "O Russkom liberalizme." *Ukrainskaia zhizn'* 7–8 (1912): 54–55.

———. "Otpor." *Razsvet* 11 (March 15, 1913a): 5–9.

———. "Otpor." *Razsvet* 12 (March 22, 1913b): 8–11.

———. "Otpor." *Razsvet* 15 (April 5, 1913c): 23–27.

———. "Partiinost' ili zhizn'?" *Budushchnost'* 20 (May 21, 1904): 373–76.

———. "Pis'mo (O 'Evreiakh i russkoi literature')." *Svobodnye Mysli* (March 24, 1908): 3.

———. "Pis'mo ob avtonomizme." *Evreiskaia Zhizn'* 6 (1904): 113–124.

———. "Pis'mo ob avtonomizme, II." *Evreiskaia Zhizn'* 7 (1904): 81–90.

———. "Predislovie." In *Gosudarstvo i Natsiia*, by Rudolph Springer (Synoptikus), 2–7. Odessa: Kadima, 1906.

———. "Rasa." In *Fel'etony*, 67–76. Berlin, 1922.

———. "Samoupravlenie natsional'nogo men'shinstva." *Vestnik Evropy* 48, no. 9 (September 1913a): 117–38.

———. "Samoupravlenie natsional'nogo men'shinstva: Okonachanie." *Vestnik Evropy* 48, no. 10 (October 1913b): 131–60.

———. *Samson Nazorei*. Moscow: Tekst, 2006.

———. "Sidia na polu . . ." *Evreiskaia Zhizn'* 14 (April 10, 1905): 22–27.

———. "Sionizm i Turtsiia (Nakanune IX Sionistskogo kongressa)." *Odesskie Novosti*, no. 7990 (December 12, 1909): 4.

———. *Slovo o Polku: Istoriia Evreiskogo Legiona po vospominaniiam ego initsiatora*. Paris: Imprimerie d'art Voltaire, 1928.

———. *Story of the Jewish Legion*. Translated by Samuel Katz. New York: Bernard Ackerman, 1945.

———. "Urok iubileia Shevchenki." *Odesskie Novosti*, no. 8355 (February 23, 1911): 3.

———. "Urok iubileia Shevchenki." In *Fel'etony*, 231–41. Berlin, 1922.

———. "Vne ocheredi." *Odesskie Novosti*, no. 8398 (April 21, 1911): 2.

———. "Vskol'z': piatero." In Jabotinsky Institute in Israel Archive: F-1910/902/RU.

Jabotinsky, Vladimir [Altalena, pseud.]. "*The Hebrew Accent*—Handwritten and Brochure." In Jabotinsky Institute in Israel, Ref. no. A1-7/82. http://www.infocenters.co.il/jabo/jabo_multimedia/Files/linked/א1%20-7_82.PDF.

———. "'Hesped' (Eulogy)—Poem." Translated by Joseph Leftwich. In Jabotinsky Institute in Israel Archive, Ref. Code A1-10/2, p. 3. http://en.jabotinsky.org/archive/search-archive/item/?itemId=115645.

———. *Judge and Fool: The Story of Samson and Delilah*. New York: Horace Liveright, 1930.

———. Letter to Ahad Ha'am, March 16, 1905. In Jabotinsky Institute in Israel, Archive. Letter # 98, Ref. no. A1-2/1.

———. *Nation and Society: Selected Articles*. Edited by Elazar (Gad) Pedhazur. Tel Aviv: Shilton Betar, Department of Education, 1961. Jabotinsky Institute in Israel, J-190. http://en.jabotinsky.org/archive/search-archive/item/?itemId=115795.
———. *Prelude to Delilah*. New York: Bernard Ackerman Inc., 1945.
———. "'Race and Nationality' Handwritten Article (in English; 1939)." In Jabotinsky Institute in Israel, A1–7/2. http://en.jabotinsky.org/archive/search-archive/item/?itemId=114713.
———. *Samson*. Translated from German by Cyrus Brooks. New York/Miami: Judaea Publishing Company, 1986.
———. *Samson Nazorei: Roman*. Berlin: Slovo, 1927.
———. "Slovo o Polku." In *Povest' moikh dnei*, 103–292. Jerusalem: Biblioteka Alia, 1989. Reprint of the 1985 edition.
Jahoda, Gustav. "Intra-European Racism in Nineteenth-Century Anthropology." *History & Anthropology* 20, no. 1 (2009): 37–56.
Judt, Ignacy Mauricy. "Evrei kak fizicheskaia rasa (Antropologicheskoe issledovanie)." *Evreiskaia Zhizn'* 1 (1904a): 125–49.
———. "Evrei kak fizicheskaia rasa (Antropologicheskoe issledovanie)." *Evreiskaia Zhizn'* 2 (1904b): 120–45.
———. "Evrei kak fizicheskaia rasa (Antropologicheskoe issledovanie)." *Evreiskaia Zhizn'* 3 (1904c): 95–128.
———. "Evrei kak fizicheskaia rasa (Antropologicheskoe issledovanie)." *Evreiskaia Zhizn'* 4 (1904d): 151–77.
———. "Evrei kak fizicheskaia rasa (Antropologicheskoe issledovanie)." *Evreiskaia Zhizn'* 5 (1904e): 132–50.
———. *Die Juden als Rasse*. Berlin: Jüdischer, 1903.
———. *Żydzi jako rasa fizyczna: Analiza z dziedziny antropologii. Z 24 rysunkami, mapa i tablicami w tekscie*. Warsaw: Wydawn. kasy im. Mianowskiego, 1902.
Kan, Sergei. *Lev Shternberg, Anthropologist, Russian Socialist, Jewish Activist*. Lincoln: University of Nebraska Press, 2009.
Kaplan, Eran. *The Jewish Radical Right: Revisionist Zionism and Its Ideological Legacy*. Madison: University of Wisconsin Press, 2005.
Kareev, Nikolai I. *Rasy i natsional'nosti s psikhologicheskoi tochki zrenia*. Voronezh, Russia: Filologicheskie zapiski, 1876.
Kasten, Erich, ed. *Jochelson, Bogoras and Shternberg: A Scientific Exploration of Northeastern Siberia and the Shaping of Soviet Ethnography*. Fürstenberg/Havel, Germany: Der Kulturstiftung Sibirien, 2018.
Katsis, Leonid. "Vladimir (Zeev) Jabotinsky and His Recently Discovered Works: Problems of Attribution and Analysis." In *IJS Studies in Judaica*, vol. 13, *The Russian Jewish Diaspora and European Culture, 1917–37*, edited

by Jörg Schulte, Olga Tabachnikova, and Peter Wagstaff, 417–36. Leiden, Netherlands: Brill, 2012.

Katz, Ethan, Lisa Moses Leff, and Maud Mandel, eds. *Colonialism and the Jews*. Bloomington: Indiana University Press, 2017.

Katz, Shmuel. *Lone Wolf: A Biography of Vladimir (Ze'ev) Jabotinsky*. 2 vols. New York: Barricade Books, 1996.

Kautsky, Karl. *Are the Jews a Race?* London: International Publishers, 1926.

King, Charles. *Odessa: Genius and Death in the City of Dreams*. New York: Norton, 2011.

Kleebatt, Norman L. ed. *Too Jewish? Challenging Traditional Identities*. New York: Jewish Museum, 1996.

Kleiner, Izrail. *Vladimir (Zeev) Jabotinsky i ukrains'ke pytannia: vseliudskist' u shatakh natsionalizmu*. Kyiv: Kanads'kyi Instytut Ukrains'kikh Studii, 1995.

Knight, Nathaniel. "Ethnicity, Nationality and the Masses: *Narodnost'* and Modernity in Imperial Russia." In Hoffmann and Kotsonis, *Russian Modernity*, 41–64. New York, 2000.

———. "Vocabularies of Difference: Ethnicity and Race in Late Imperial and Early Soviet Russia." *Kritika: Explorations in Russian and Eurasian History* 13, no. 3 (2012): 667–83.

Kotsonis, Yanni. *States of Obligation: Taxes and Citizenship in the Russian Empire and Early Soviet Republic*. Toronto: University of Toronto Press, 2014.

Krutikov, Mikhail. *Yiddish Fiction and the Crisis of Modernity, 1905–1914*. Stanford, CA: Stanford University Press, 2001.

Lagneau, Gustav. "Sur la race juive et sa pathologie." *Bulletin de la Société d'Anthropologie de Paris* 2 (1891): 539–57.

Lemon, Alaina. "'What Are They Writing about Us Blacks?' Roma and 'Race' in Russia." *Anthropology of East Europe Review* 13, no. 2 (1995): 34–40.

Levin, Vladimir. "Jewish Politics in the Russian Empire during the Period of Reaction, 1907–1914." [In Hebrew]. PhD diss., Hebrew University of Jerusalem, 2007.

Linskii, V. [V. A. Vakulin]. "Novyi teatr." *Teatr i Iskusstvo* 48 (1905): 740.

"Literaturnye nabroski." *Altheuland* 9 (1906): 166–75.

Liubimova, M. Iu. "Dramaturgiia Evgeniia Chirikova i russkaia stsena 900-kh gg." In *Russkii teatr i dramatrugiia epokhi revolutsii 1905–1907 godov*, edited by A. Ia. Al'tshuller et al., 34–57. Leningrad: LGITMIK, 1987.

Lohr, Eric, Vera Tolz, Alexander Semyonov, and Mark von Hagen, eds. *The Empire and Nationalism at War*. Russia's Great War Series. Bloomington: Indiana University Press [Slavica Publishers], 2014.

———. *Nationalizing the Russian Empire: The Campaign against Enemy Aliens during World War I*. Cambridge, MA: Harvard University Press, 2003.

———. *Russian Citizenship: From Empire to Soviet Union*. Cambridge, MA: Harvard University Press, 2012.

Low, Alfred D. *Jews in the Eyes of the Germans: From the Enlightenment to Imperial Germany*. Philadelphia: Institute for the Study of Human Issues, 1979.

Madison, Charles. *Yiddish Literature: Its Scope and Major Writers*. New York: F. Ungar, 1968.

Maiorova, Olga. *From the Shadow of Empire: Defining the Russian Nation through Cultural Mythology, 1855–1870*. Madison: University of Wisconsin Press, 2010.

Makolkin, Anna. *History of Odessa, the Last Italian Black Sea Colony*. Lewiston, NY: Edwin Mellen Press, 2004.

Mandelstamm, Max. *How Jews Live: A Report on the Physical Conditions of Jews, a Sidelight upon Alien Immigration*. London: Greenberg, 1900.

Maor, Yitzhak. *The Zionist Movement in Russia*. [In Hebrew]. Jerusalem: Y. L. Magnes, 1986.

Massad, Joseph. *The Persistence of the Palestinian Question: Essays on Zionism and the Palestinians*. London: Routledge, 2006.

McMahon, Richard, ed. *National Races: Transnational Power Struggles in the Sciences and Politics of Human Diversity, 1840–1945*. Lincoln: University of Nebraska Press, 2019.

———. *The Races of Europe: Construction of National Identities in the Social Sciences 1839–1939*. London: Palgrave Macmillan, 2016.

McReynolds, Louis. "P. I. Kovalevskii: Criminal Anthropology and Great Russian Nationalism." In *Born to Be Criminal: The Discourse on Criminality and the Practice of Punishment in Late Imperial Russia and Early Soviet Union: Interdisciplinary Approaches*, edited by Riccardo Nicolosi and Anne Hartmann, 63–84. Bielefeld, Germany: Transcript, 2017.

Menzhulin, Vadim. *Drugoi Sikorsky: Neudobnye stranitsy istorii psikhiatrii*. Kyiv: Sfera, 2004.

Miklashevskaia, Liudmila, and Nina Katerli. *Chemu svideteli my byli: zhenskie sud'by, XX vek*. St. Petersburg: Zhurnal "Zvezda," 2007.

Miliukov, P. "Natsionalizm protiv natsionalizma." *Rech'* 68 (March 11, 1909): 2.
Miller, Alexei. *The Romanov Empire and Nationalism. Essays in Methodology of Historical Research*. New York: CEU Press, 2008.
———. *The Ukrainian Question: The Russian Empire and Nationalism in the Nineteenth Century*. New York: CEU Press, 2003.
Mintz, Matityahu. "Jewish Nationalism in the Context of Multi-National States." [In Hebrew]. In *Jewish Nationalism and Politics: New Perspective*, edited by Jehuda Reinharz et al., 201–24. Jerusalem: Zalman Shatzar Center for Jewish History, 1996.
Mogilner, Marina. "Between Scientific and Political: Jewish Scholars and Russian-Jewish Physical Anthropology in the Fin-de-Siècle Russian Empire." In *Going to the People: Jews and the Ethnographic Impulse*, edited by Jeff Veidlinger, 45–63. Bloomington: Indiana University Press, 2016.
———. "Classifying Imperial Russianness: Race and Hybridity in the Nineteenth–Early Twentieth Century Russian Imperial Anthropology." In *National Races*, edited by Richard McMahon, 205–40. Lincoln, 2019.
———. *Homo Imperii: A History of Physical Anthropology in Russia*. Critical Studies in the History of Anthropology. Lincoln: University of Nebraska Press, 2013.
———. *Mifologiia "podpol'nogo cheloveka": Radikal'nyi mikrokosm v Rossii nachala XX veka kak predmet semioticheskogo analiza*. Moscow: NLO, 1999.
———. *A Race for the Future: Scientific Visions of Modern Russian Jewishness, 1860s–1930s*. Cambridge, MA: Harvard University Press, 2022.
———. "Racial Psychiatry and the Russian Imperial Dilemma of the 'Savage Within.'" *East Central Europe* 43 (2016): 99–133.
———. "Racial Purity vs. Imperial Hybridity: The Case of Vladimir Jabotinsky against the Russian Empire." In *Ideologies of Race: Imperial Russia and the Soviet Union in Global Context*, 103–31. Montreal: McGill-Queen's University Press, 2019.
———. "Toward a History of Russian-Jewish 'Medical Materialism': Russian-Jewish Physicians and the Politics of Jewish Biological Normalization." *Jewish Social Studies* 19, no. 1 (2012): 70–106.
Morris-Reich, Amos. "Arthur Ruppin's Concept of Race." *Israel Studies* 11, no. 3 (2006): 1–30.
Myers, David. *Between Jew and Arab: The Last Voice of Simon Rawidowicz*. Waltham, MA: Brandeis University Press, 2008.

Naor, Arye, and Abigail Jacobson. *Oriental Neighbors: Middle Eastern Jews and Arabs in Mandatory Palestine*. Waltham, MA: Brandeis University Press, 2016.

Natkovich, Svetlana. *Among Radiant Clouds: The Literature of Vladimir (Ze'ev) Jabotinsky in Its Social Context*. [In Hebrew]. Jerusalem: Magnes Press, 2015.

———. "A Land of Harsh Ways: 'Trista da Runha' as Jabotinsky's Social Fantasy." *Jewish Social Studies* 19, no. 2 (2013): 24–49.

———. "The Rise and Downfall of Cassandra: World War I and Vladimir (Zeev) Jabotinsky's Self-Perception." *Medaon–Magazin für jüdisches Leben in Forschung und Bildung* 10 (2016): 1–11.

Natkovich, Svetlana, and Cedric Cohen Skalli. "Vladimir Jabotinsky's Perception of Mediterranean Culture and Italian *Mediterranismo*." Unpublished conference paper. I am grateful to the authors for allowing me to read this manuscript.

N-m. "Evreiskaia pechat'." *Evreiskaia Zhizn'* 12 (March 22, 1909): 23–26.

———. "Everiskaia pechat'." *Razsvet* 15 (April 12, 1909): 11–14.

Noemi, A. "Chuzhbina." *Razsvet* 13 (March 28, 1910): 34–37.

Nordau, Max "V. Kongressrede." In *Zionistische Schriften*, 112–39. 1909. Reprint, Cologne: Zionistischen Aktionskommittee, 1923.

Novershtern, Avraham. *Der Fraynd*. https://web.nli.org.il/sites/jpress/english/pages/dfr.aspx.

O'Keeffe, Brigid. *Esperanto and Languages of Internationalism in Revolutionary Russia*. London: Bloomsbury Academic, 2021.

Orbach, Alexander. "Zionism and the Russian Revolution of 1905: The Commitment to Participate in Domestic Political Life." *Bar-Ilan* 24–25 (1989): 7–23.

Ostrogorsky, Moisei. *Democracy and the Organization of Political Parties*. 2 vols. Translated from French by F. Clarke. New York: Macmillan, 1902.

———. *La démocratie et l'organisation des partis politiques*. Paris: Calmann-Lévy, 1903.

Pasmanik, Daniel. "Natsiia li evrei?" In *Natsional'nyi Vopros: Stat'i Maksa Nordau, A. Idel'sona and D. Pasmanika*, 26–49. St. Petersburg: Vostok, 1913.

———. "Rasovyi antisemitism." *Razsvet* 41 (October 9, 1911): 6–10.

Penslar, Derek J. "The Foundations of the Twentieth Century: Herzlian Zionism in Yoram Hazony 'The Jewish State.'" *Israel Studies* 6, no. 2 (2001): 118–28.

———. "Is Zionism a Colonial Movement?" In *Colonialism and the Jews*, edited by Ethan Katz, Lisa Moses Leff, and Maud Mandel, 275–300. Bloomington: Indiana University Press, 2017.

———. *Zionism and Technocracy: The Engineering of Jewish Settlement in Palestine, 1870–1918*. Bloomington: Indiana University Press, 1991.

Perez Sheldon, Mirna. "Race and Sexuality: A Secular Theory of Race." In *A Cultural History of Race in the Age of Empire and the Nation State*, edited by Marina Mogilner, 149–64. Vol. 5 of *A Cultural History of Race*, edited by Marius Turda. London: Bloomsbury Academic, 2021.

Petliura, Symon. "Uvagy pro zavdannia ukrains'kogo teatru: Peredmova." In *Evrei: P'esa na 4 dii; pereklad Leonid Pakharevs'kii*, edited by E. M. Chirikov, iv–xviii. Kyiv: Druk S. A. Borysova 1907.

Pianko, Noam. *Zionism and the Roads Not Taken: Rawidowicz, Kaplan, Kohn*. Bloomington: Indiana University Press, 2010.

Pil'skii, Petr. "Jabotinsky." *Sibir'–Palestina* 48 (December 16, 1921), 7–8.

Pipes, Richard. *Struve: Liberal on the Left, 1870–1905*. Cambridge, MA: Harvard University Press, 1970.

———. *Struve: Liberal on the Right, 1905–1944*. Cambridge, MA: Harvard University Press, 1980.

"Pis'mo Sh. Ascha." *Razsvet* 10 (March 8, 1909), 11.

Podbolotov, Sergei. "Tsar' i narod: Populistskii natsionalizm Nikolaia II." *Ab Imperio* 3, no. 3 (2003): 199–223.

Poliaki i evrei: Materialy o pol'sko-evreiskom spore po povodu zakono-proetka o gorodskom samoupravlenii v Pol'she. Iz statei i zaiavlenii Grabskogo, R. Dmovskogo, N. Dubrovskogo, V. Zhabotinskogo, dep. I. Petrunkevicha i A. Sventokhovskogo. Odessa: Tipo-lit. knigoizd-va M. S. Kozmana, 1911.

Poliakov, Leon. *The Arian Myth: A History of Racist and Nationalist Ideas in Europe*. London: Cambridge University Press, 1974.

Poliakov, S. "Ariiskie Rytsari." *Razsvet* 41 (October 9, 1911): 5–6.

Prakash, Gyan. "Edward Said in Bombay." *Critical Inquiry* 31, no. 2 (2005): 498–504.

"Programma po izucheniiu natsional'nogo voprosa." *Evreiskaia Zhizn'* 3 (1905): 126–47.

Quine, Maria Sophia. "Making Italians: Aryanism and Anthropology in Italy during the Risorgimento." In *Crafting Humans: From Genesis to Eugenics and Beyond*, edited by Marius Turda, 127–52. Goettingen: V&R Unipress, 2013.

Rabinovich, Girsh M. "Fel'eton." *Russkii Evrei*, no. 27 (July 15, 1883): 30–37.

Rabinovitch, Simon. *Jewish Rights, National Rights. Nationalism and Autonomy in Late Imperial and Revolutionary Russia*. Stanford, CA: Stanford University Press, 2014.

Rainbow, David, ed. *Ideologies of Race: Imperial Russia and the Soviet Union in Global Context*. Montreal: McGill University Press, 2019.

Ratner, Mark B. "Sovremennaia postanovka evreiskogo voprosa." In *Nakanune probuzhdeniia: Sbornik statei po evreiskomu voprosu*, edited by I. V. Gessen, M. B. Ratner, and L. Ia. Shternberg, 99–148. St. Petersburg: Izd-vo A. G. Rozen, 1906.

Remnev, Anatoly, and Natalia Suvorova. "'The Russian Cause' on the Asiatic Borderlands: The 'Russianness' under Threat and 'Questionable Kulturträgers.'" *Ab Imperio* 9, no. 2 (2008): 157–222.

Rhode, Maria. "A Matter of Place, Space, and People: Cracow Anthropology, 1870–1920." In *National Races*, edited by Richard McMahon, 105–40. Lincoln: University of Nebraska Press, 2019.

Richardson, Tanya. *Kaleidoscopic Odessa: History and Place in Contemporary Ukraine*. Anthropological Horizons. Toronto: University of Toronto Press, 2008.

Ripley, William Z. *The Races of Europe: A Sociological Study*. New York: D. Appleton, 1899.

———. *The Races of Europe: A Sociological Study*. London: Kegan Paul, Trench, Trübner, 1900.

———. "The Racial Cartography of Europe: A Sociological Study. Supplement: The Jews." *Appleton's Popular Science Monthly* 54, no. 2 (1898): 163–75.

———. "The Racial Cartography of Europe: A Sociological Study. Supplement: The Jews." *Appleton's Popular Science Monthly* 54, no. 3 (1899): 338–51.

Ronen, Omri. "Chuzheliubie." *Zvezda* 3 (2007). https://magazines.gorky.media/zvezda/2007/3/chuzhelyubie.html.

Safran, Gabriella. "Jews as Siberian Natives: Primitivism and S. An-sky's *Dybbuk*." *Modernizm/Modernity* 13, no. 4 (2006): 635–55.

Said, Edward. "Cairo Recalled: Growing Up in the Cultural Crosscurrents of 1940s Egypt." In *"Reflections on Exile" and Other Essays*, 268–75. Cambridge, MA: Harvard University Press, 2000.

Sanborn, Joshua A. *Drafting the Russian Nation: Military Conscription, Total War, and Mass Politics, 1905–1925*. DeKalb: Northern Illinois University Press, 2003.

Savino, Giovanni. "A Reactionary Utopia: Russian Black Hundreds from Autocracy to Fascism." In *Entangled Far Rights: A Russian-European*

Intellectual Romance in the Twentieth Century, edited by Marlene Laruelle, 31–46. Pittsburgh: University of Pittsburgh Press, 2018.

Schechtman, Joseph B. *Fighter and Prophet: The Last Years*. New York: Yoseloff, 1961.

———. *Rebel and Statesman: The Vladimir Jabotinsky Story*. New York: Yoseloff, 1956.

Scherr, Barry P. "An Odessa Odyssey: Vladimir Jabotinsky's *The Five*." *Slavic Review* 70, no. 1 (2011): 94–115.

Selzer, Michael. *The Aryanization of the Jewish State*. New York: A Black Star Book, 1967.

Semyonov, Alexander. "Imperial Parliament for a Hybrid Empire: Representative Experiments in Early 20th-Century Russian Empire." *Journal of Eurasian Studies* 11, no. 1 (2020): 1–10.

———. "Russian Liberalism and the Problem of Imperial Diversity." In *Liberal Imperialism in Europe*, edited by Matthew P. Fitzpatrick, 67–90. New York: Palgrave Macmillan, 2012.

Sergi, Giuseppe. *The Mediterranean Race: A Study of the Origin of European Peoples*. Oosterhout, N. B., Netherlands: Anthropological Publications, 1961. Originally published in English, London, 1901.

———. *Origine e diffusione della stirpe mediterranea: Induzioni antropologiche*. Rome: Società Editrice Dante Alighieri, 1895.

———. *Specie e Varietà Umane: Saggio di una sistematica antropologica*. Turin, Italy: Fratelli Bocca, 1900.

Shanes, Joshua. *Diaspora Nationalism and Jewish Identity in Habsburg Galicia*. Cambridge: Cambridge University Press, 2012.

Shevelenko, Irina. *Modernism kak arkhaizm: Natsionalizm and poiski modernistskoi estetiki v Rossii*. Moscow: NLO, 2017.

Sh-g, L. [Lev Shternberg]. "Besedy s chitateliami." *Novyi Voskhod* 10 (Thursday, March 10, 1911a): 6–10.

———. "Besedy s chitateliami." *Novyi Voskhod* 31 (Thursday, August 4, 1911b), 5–7.

Shindler, Colin. *The Triumph of Military Zionism: Nationalism and the Origins of the Israeli Right*. London: I. B. Tauris, 2010.

Shumsky, Dmitry. *Beyond the Nation-State: The Zionist Political Imagination from Pinsker to Ben-Gurion*. New Haven, CT: Yale University Press, 2018.

———. "Stalin's Nationalities Policies and Jewish Assimilation: A Reappraisal." Paper presented at the conference Thinking Race in the Russian and Soviet Empires, University of Illinois at Chicago and University of Chicago, March 5–7, 2020.

Sig. "Okolo zhizni." *Odesskie Novosti*, no. 5859 (January 15, 1903): 3.
Sikorsky, Ivan. *Antropologicheskaia i psikhologicheskaia genealogia Pushkina*. Kyiv: Tipografiia S. V. Kul'zhenko, 1912.
———. *Chto takoe natsiia i drugie formy etnicheskoi zhizni?* Kyiv: Litotipografiia S. V. Kul'zhenko, 1915.
Slavinsky, M. "Russkie, velikorossy i rossiiane." *Slovo* 736 (March 14, 1909): 2.
Slezkine, Yuri. *The Jewish Century*. Princeton, NJ: Princeton University Press, 2004.
Slutsky, Yehuda. *The Russian-Jewish Press in the Twentieth Century, 1900–1918*. [In Hebrew]. Tel Aviv: ha-Agudah le-Heker Toldot ha-Yehudim, ha-Makhon le-Heker ha-Tefutsot, 1978.
Stahl, Nanette, ed. *Sholem Asch Reconsidered*. New Haven, CT: Beinecke, 2004.
Stalin, J. V. "Marxism and the National Question." In *Works*, vol. 2 (1907–1913), 300–381. Moscow: Foreign Languages Publishing House, 1953.
Staliūnas, Darius. *Making Russians: Meaning and Practice of Russification in Lithuania and Belarus after 1863*. Amsterdam: Rodopi, 2007.
Stanislawski, Michael. *Autobiographical Jews: Essays in Jewish Self-Fashioning*. Seattle: University of Washington Press, 2004.
———. *Zionism and the Fin de Siècle: Cosmopolitanism and Nationalism from Nordau to Jabotinsky*. Berkeley: University of California Press, 2001.
Stenographisches Protokoll der Verhandlungen des IV Zionisten-Congresses, August 15, 1900. Vol. 4. Vienna: Erez Israel, 1900.
Stoler, Ann Laura. *Race and the Education of Desire: Foucault's History of Sexuality and the Colonial Order of Things*. Durham, NC: Duke University Press, 1995.
———. "Racial Regimes of Truth." In *Duress: Imperial Durabilities in Our Times*, 237–68. Durham, NC: Duke University Press, 2016.
Struve, Peter. "Intelligentsiia i natsional'noe litso." *Slovo* (March 10, 1909): 3.
———. "Na raznye temy." *Russkaia Mysl'* 1 (1911): 175–87.
———. "'Sovremennost'' i 'elementarnost'' russkoi revolutsii." In *Patriotika: Politika, kul'tura, religiia, sotsializm*, 22–28. Moscow: Respublika, 1997.
Sum, Gomo. *See* Zamenhof, Lejzer Ludwik
Sunderland, Willard. "The Greatest Emancipator: Abolition and Empire in Tsarist Russia." *The Journal of Modern History* 93, no. 3 (September 2021): 566–98.
Tan, V. G. "Evrei i literatura." *Svobodnye Mysli* (February 18, 1908): 3.
———. "K voprosu o natsionalizme." *Svobodnye Mysli* (April 7, 1908): 3.

Tan, V. G. [V. G. Bogoraz]. "Posle pogroma (iz gomelskikh vpechatlenii)." *Russkie Vedomosti* 352 (December 19, 1904a): 4–5.

———. "Posle pogroma (iz gomelskikh vpechatlenii)." *Russkie Vedomosti* 356 (December 24, 1904b): 3.

———. *Sobranie sochinenii V. G. Tana*. Vol. 5, *Amerikanskie Rasskazy. Ocherki i rasskazy*, 293–452 ("Gomel'skie siluety"). St. Petersburg: Prosveshchenie, 1911.

Tarnovskaia, Praskov'ia N. "Antropometricheskie issledovaniia prostitutok, vorovok i zdorovykh krest'ianok-polevykh rabotnits (zasedanie 21 noiabria 1887 g.)." In *Protokoly zasedanii obshchestva psikhiatrov v S.-Peterburge za 1887 god*, 189–208. St. Petersburg: n.p., 1888.

———. *Vorovki (antropologicheskoe issledovanie)*. St. Petersburg: Tipografia doma prezreniia maloletnikh bednykh, 1891.

———. *Zhenshchiny-ubiitsy: Antropologicheskoe issledovanie s 163 risunkami i 8 antropometricheskimi tablitsami*. St. Petersburg: T-vo khudozhestvennoi pechati, 1902.

Tarnowsky, Pauline. *Étude anthropométrique sur les prostituées et les voleuses*. Paris: Progrés mèdicale, 1889.

Taylor, Paul Michael. "Anthropology and the 'Racial Doctrine' in Italy before 1940." *Antropologia Contemporanea* 1, no. 2(1988): 45–58.

Teffi, Nadezhda. "Evrei i russkaia literatura." *Zritel'* (February 10, 1908): 10.

Tolstaya, Elena. *Mir posle kontsa: raboty o russkoi literature XX veka*. Moscow: RGGU, 2002.

Tolz, Vera. "Discourses of Race in Imperial Russia, 1830–1914." In *The Invention of Race: Scientific and Popular Representations*, edited by Nicolas Bancel et al., 133–44. London: Routledge, 2014.

———. *Inventing the Nation: Russia*. London: Arnold Press, 2001.

———. "Re-negotiating Cultural Diversity: The Rise and Endurance of Nationality, National Religion and Race in Modern Russia and Its Empire." Paper presented at the conference Thinking 'Race' in the Russian and Soviet Empire, University of Illinois at Chicago and University of Chicago, March 5–7, 2020.

———. *Russia's Own Orient: The Politics of Identity and Oriental Studies in the Late Imperial and Early Soviet Periods*. Oxford: Oxford University Press, 2011.

Tsurumi, Taro. "An Imagined Context of a Nation: The Russian Zionist Version of the Austro-Marxist Theory of Nationality." In *Bounded Mind and Soul: Russia and Israel, 1880–2010*, edited by Brian Horowitz and Shai Ginsburg, 77–96. Bloomington, IN: Slavica, 2013.

———. "'Neither Angels, nor Demons, but Humans': Anti-Essentialism and Its Ideological Moments among the Russian Zionist Intelligentsia." *Nationalities Papers* 38, no. 4 (2010): 531–50.

———. "Was the East Less Rational Than the West? The Meaning of 'Nation' for Russian Zionism and Its Imagined Context." *Nationalism and Ethnic Politics* 14 (2008): 361–394.

Turda, Marius, and Paul Weindling, eds. *Blood and Homeland: Eugenics and Racial Nationalism in Central and Southeast Europe, 1900–1940*. Herndon, VA: Central European University Press, 2006.

Uri, Scott. *Barricades and Banners: The Revolution of 1905 and the Transformation of Warsaw Jewry*. Stanford, CA: Stanford University Press, 2012.

Vdovin, Alexey. "'Dmitry Tolstoy's Classicism' and the Formation of the Russian Literary Canon in the High School Curriculum." *Ab Imperio* 18, no. 4 (2017): 108–37.

Veidlinger, Jeffrey. "'Emancipation: See Anti-Semitism'—the *Evreiskaia entsiklopediia* and the Jewish Public Culture." *Simon Dubnow Institute Yearbook* 9 (2010): 405–26.

———. *Jewish Public Culture in the Late Russian Empire*. Bloomington: Indiana University Press, 2009.

Vinaver, Maxim. "Otkrytoe pis'mo Struve." *Rech'* 70 (March 13, 1909): 4.

Vital, David. *Zionism, The Crucial Phase*. Oxford: Clarendon, 1987.

"V. Jabotinsky: Pis'ma russkim pisateliam." *Vestnik Evreiskogo Universiteta v Moskve* 1 (1992): 200–21.

von Hagen, Mark. *War in a European Borderland: Occupations and Occupation Plans in Galicia*. Seattle: University of Washington Press, 2007.

von Humboldt, Alexander. *Cosmos: A Sketch of the Physical Description of the Universe*. 2 vols. Translated by Elise C. Otté. New York: Harper, 1850–1858.

———. *Personal Narrative of a Journey to the Equinoctial Regions of the New Continent*. Translated by Jason Wilson. London: Penguin, 1996.

Vsia Odessa 1902–3 gody: Adresnaia i spravochnaia kniga. Odessa: A. Shultse, 1902.

Vucinich, Alexander. *Darwin in Russian Thought*. Berkeley: University of California Press, 1988.

Weinberg, Robert. *Blood Libel in Late Imperial Russia: The Ritual Murder Trial of Mendel Beilis*. Bloomington: Indiana University Press, 2014.

———. *Stalin's Forgotten Zion: Birobidzhan and the Making of a Soviet Jewish Homeland*. Berkeley: University of California Press, 1998.

Weindling, Paul. *Health, Race and German Politics between National Unification and Nazism, 1870–1945*. Cambridge: Cambridge University Press, 1989.
Weiskopf, Michael. "Mezhdu Bibliei i avangardon: fabula Jabotinskogo." *Novoe Literaturnoe Obozrenie* 80, no. 4 (2006): 131–44.
———. "Predislovie." In *Chuzhbina: P'esa, komediia v piati deistviiakh*, edited by Vladimir Jabotinsky, 14. Jerusalem: Gesharim, 2000.
Wortman, Richard. *Myth and Ceremony in Russian Monarchy from Peter the Great to the Abdication of Nicholas II*. Princeton, NJ: Princeton University Press, 2006.
———. *Scenarios of Power*. Vol. 2, *From Alexander II to the Abdication of Nicholas II*. Princeton, NJ: Princeton University Press, 2000.
Zamenhof, Lejzer Ludwik [Gomo Sum, pseud.]. *Gillelizm: Proekt Resheniia Evreiskogo Voprosa*. Warsaw: Tip. M. Veidenfel'd i Ig. Khel'ter, 1901.
Zangwill, Israel. "The Jewish Race." In *Papers on Inter-Racial Problems, Communicated to the First Universal Races Congress, Held at the University of London, July 26–29, 1911*, edited by Gustav Spiller, 268–79. London: P. S. King and Son, 1911.
Zhitomirskii, K. "Prakticheskie tseli evreiskoi shkoly." *Evreiskaia Shkola* 12 (December) 1904: 3–16.
Zimmermann, Andrew. *Anthropology and Antihumanism in Germany*. Chicago: University of Chicago Press, 2001.
Zipperstein, Steven. *Elusive Prophet: Ahad Ha'am and the Origins of Zionism*. Berkeley: University of California Press, 1993.
———. *The Jews of Odessa: A Cultural History*. Stanford, CA: Stanford University Press, 1986.
"'Znachenie Gimnastiki dlia Evreev' Maksa Nordau." *Budushchnost'* 4 (January 30 1904): 77–81.
Zollschan, Ignaz. *Jewish Questions: Three Lectures*. New York: Bloch, 1914.
Zorin, Andrei. *By Fables Alone: Literature and State Ideology in Late-Eighteenth–Early-Nineteenth-Century Russia*. Boston: Academic Studies Press, 2014.

INDEX

Acculturation, 2, 5, 28
Adler, Victor, 36
Africa, 17, 59, 60, 62, 64, 66, 93; Northern, 55, 56
Altalena. *See* Jabotinsky, Vladimir (Zeev)
America(ns), 61, 64, 79, 112, 136, 138, 148, 169n28; *See also* United States (of America)
Amorites, 56, 68, 70, 116
An-sky, S. (Shloyme Zanvl Rappoport), 110
Anthropology, 2; criminal, 22, 71, 171n60; physical, 4, 5, 6, 7, 10, 38, 46, 47, 54, 58, 67, 110, 120, 151, 168n2; Russian liberal, 93; Zionist, 66, 72
Antisemite/ism, 7, 12, 14, 33, 34, 42, 86, 91, 94, 96, 105, 112, 113, 117, 118, 120, 128, 129, 130, 132, 133, 134, 135, 139, 154, 172n67; racial, 1, 13, 117, 118, 121, 130, 154
Anuchin, Dmitry, 93, 94
Armenians, 34
Aryans, 60, 63, 64, 107, 109, 114, 116, 117, 169n23, 173n67
Asia(n), 17, 53, 58, 60, 93; Middle, 56; Central, 56

Asch, Sholem, 128, 129, 130, 181nn13–14
Assimilation, 14, 19, 27, 36, 100, 101, 120, 139, 141, 145, 147, 148
Austria(n), 36, 80; Empire: *See* Habsburg Empire; Marxism, 36, 80
Authenticity, national, 19, 21, 25, 27, 28, 75, 87, 92, 99, 151, 155; of identity, 26; cultural, 69, 105, 111, 181n14
Autonomism, 7, 28, 32, 34, 35, 36, 76, 77, 102, 103
Azef, Evno, 145

Basel, 38, 84, 90, 92, 93, 98, 142
Bauer, Otto, 35, 36, 164n25
Beddoe, John, 49
Bedouins, 53, 116
Beilis, Mendel, 113
Belarus(ians), 120, 137, 138, 139
Berlin, 37, 38, 67
Betar, 3
Bialik, Chaim Nachman, 28
Biopolitics, 17, 23, 27, 39, 106, 109, 151, 152
Blechmann, Bernhard, 48, 49

Blood: as in "blood and soil," 2, 26, 27, 29, 45, 66, 67, 68, 70, 92, 102, 127, 128, 137, 146; group, 60; Jewish, 24, 28, 67, 83, 91, 101, 105, 153; libel, 113; mixing of, 102, 103, 105; purity, 14, 100, 101, 102, 103, 105, 107, 117, 129, 152, 153
Bogoraz (Tan), Vladimir, 110, 120, 121, 122, 180n38
Borokhov, Dov, Ber, 41, 98, 166–67n52
Broca, Paul, 60
Brutzkus, Ber, 136
Brutzkus, Julius, 33, 39
Buber, Martin, 28, 153, 154
Bund, 33, 34
Bureau for Jewish Statistics, 37, 38

Canaan, 56, 58, 63, 65, 67, 68, 70, 108, 168n13
Canudo, Ricciotto, 71
Chamberlain, Houston Stewart, 111
Chirikov, Evgenii, 128, 129, 130, 131, 132, 133, 136; *"Evrei,"* 130, 131, 132, 133, 182n21
Chlenov, Yehiel, 39
Christians, 112, 120, 121, 122, 144, 146; Orthodox, 11
Chukchees, 110
Chukovsky, Korney, 43, 44, 45, 118, 119, 122
Chwolson, Daniel, 47
Citizen[ship], 12, 33, 64, 65, 77, 92, 102, 112, 122, 138, 164n25
Colonial/ism, 13, 35, 62, 63, 75, 149, 154, 156; city, 148; condition, 100, 105, 123, 125, 140, 148, 152; culture, 130, 149; discourse, 30, 119, 124; domination, 27, 73, 75, 78, 87, 92, 109, 151; movement, 156; periphery, 23, 109; politics, 149; resistance, 25, 39; subjects, 76, 100; world, 121
Constantinople, 127

Cosmopolitan[ism], 16, 60, 82, 84, 85, 100, 118, 148
Croce, Benedetto, 71

Darwinism, 4, 14, 38, 165n35; social, 39, 71
Degeneration, 38, 41, 141
Deniker, Josef, 48, 60
Diaspora, 30, 31, 45, 55, 58, 98, 115, 139; autonomism, 28; cultural politics, 33
Du Bois, W. E. B., 63–64, 65, 66, 67, 73
Dubnov, Simon, 28, 35, 47

El'kind, Arkadii Danilovich, 5–7, 10, 28, 54, 55, 93
Endogamy, 14, 17
Esperanto, 16
Eugenics, 28, 37, 60, 72
Eurasia[n]: empire, 21; history, 22; studies, 21, 23
Eurocentrism, 48, 53, 54, 60, 61, 64, 72, 172ft67
Europe[an], 59, 60, 61, 62, 63, 64, 65, 66, 69, 70, 72, 73, 85, 90, 91, 94, 102, 119, 127, 128, 148, 155; Central, 38, 76; culture, 84, 100, 126, 137, 148; Eastern, 34, 38, 76; environment, 10; geography, 25, 127; science, 7, 22, 48, 61; Western, 18, 25, 37, 55, 56, 172n67; *See also* Jews: Eastern European; Nationalism: European; Race: European; Zionism: European
Evreiskaia shkola, 44
Evreiskaia Zhizn', 15, 39, 40, 42, 43, 44, 46, 47, 48, 50–52, 53, 57, 58, 67, 68, 95–97, 98, 130, 132

Ferri, Enrico, 71, 171n60
Finland (Finns), 32, 108, 138
Folkspartei, 33, 35
France (French), 25, 55, 59, 60, 62, 71, 80, 100, 102, 127, 148
Fraynd, Der, 128, 129, 181n7

Georgia[ns], 8, 9, 34, 35, 119
Germany (Germans), 7, 10, 38, 49, 55, 59, 60, 63, 80, 91, 100, 115, 117, 119, 126, 142
Ghetto, 13, 90
Graetz, Heinrich, 111, 117
Gruzenberg, Oskar Osipovich, 113, 149

Ha'am, Ahad, 31, 47, 77, 98, 109
Habsburg (Austro-Hungarian) Empire, 4, 12, 20, 26, 77, 85, 149, 153, 155
Hamites, 70
Helsingfors Program, 32
Herzl, Theodor, 54, 76, 93, 94, 95, 98, 99, 100, 117, 140, 163n6
Hess, Moses, 47
Hittites, 56, 68, 70, 116
Hrushevskii, Mikhail (Mykhailo), 80
Humboldt, Alexander von, 61, 169n28
Hybridity, 60, 62, 114, 119, 139, 145, 148, 149, 153; cultural, 25, 63, 101, 153; imperial, 11, 21, 72, 73, 74, 75, 86, 87, 105, 108, 121, 141, 154; racial, 66, 101

Idelson, Abraham (Avram), 39, 98
Ikow, Constantine, 48, 55
Ilovaiskii, Dmitry, 117
Inorodtsy, 42, 43, 110, 134
Italy/Italian[s], 55, 59, 60, 61, 62, 63, 65, 70, 71, 72, 73, 80, 84, 90, 91, 92, 102, 148, 169n23, 171n63

Jabotinsky, Vladimir (Zeev), 1, 2, 3, 4, 13, 16, 17, 18, 21, 23, 25, 26, 27, 31, 32, 38, 39, 40, 42, 43, 66, 67, 68, 69, 70, 71, 72, 73, 74–106, 112, 116, 117, 145, 149, 150, 151, 152, 153, 154, 155, 156, 163, 170n48, 171n60, 173n9, 174n29; Altalena, 142, 143, 144, 171n63; [and the] "Chirikov incident," 129–130, 132, 134, 135, 136; "Chuzhbina," 143, 177n83; "Edmee," 126–128, 137; "Five, The," 98, 141–149; "Hebrew Accent, [The]," 70; "Hesped," 93, 96, 97, 176n57; and postcolonial language politics, 118–125; "Samson the Nazarite," 67, 68, 69, 70, 169–170n41, 170n47; and Sikorsky, 107–115 "Story of the Jewish Legion [The]," 70, 83; "Story of My Life," 78, 83, 85, 87, 98, 99, 123, 126, 141, 175n31; and Struve, 137–140
Jellinek, George, 81
Jewish People's Group (ENG), 17, 18
"Jewish question" ("problem"), 13, 30, 17, 90, 139
Jews, 1, 5, 6, 13, 14, 16, 17, 20, 23, 30, 33, 35, 36, 37, 38, 41, 44, 47, 48–53, 57, 58, 59, 62, 78, 80, 83, 88, 94, 98, 99, 100–103, 107, 110, 112–115, 116, 117, 120, 123, 128, 137, 139, 151, 156; [of] Algeria, 55; American, 35; Ashkenazi, 53; Asian, 37; Assyrian, 17, 93; [of] Balkans, 55; [of the] Caucasus, 8, 10, 54; [of] Crimea, 10; Daghestanian, 35, 45; Eastern European, 37, 38, 55; [of] Egypt, 10, 17, 93, 148; European, 10, 25, 54, 55, 58, 61, 63, 65, 66, 70, 94, 155; Falashas, 59; Galician, 37; Georgian, 8, 9, 35; German, 117, 126; [of the] Habsburg Empire, 27, 85; Italian, 55, 90–92; Lithuanian, 91; [of the] Mediterranean, 55, 58, 60, 63, 70, 155; modern, 2, 12, 13, 17, 20, 21, 56, 85, 105, 120, 131, 148; Moroccan, 37; [of] Moscow, 5; [of] New York, 14; nonterritorial, 36; [of] Northern Africa, 55; [of] Palestine, 10, 17, 56, 67–68, 69, 108, 149; Polish, 5, 47, 148; Romanian, 37; Russian, 1, 4, 5, 10, 19, 21, 27, 28, 29, 31, 33, 34, 35, 37, 42, 46, 55, 64, 72, 78, 79, 82, 85, 86–87, 89, 92, 93, 104–5, 109–113, 115, 116, 118–19, 120–22, 126, 128–33, 134–37, 139, 141, 142, 144, 145, 147, 148, 149, 151, 154; Sephardi, 49; [of] Southern Russia, 10; [of] Spain, 55; [of] Syria, 10, 17; [of] Turkestan, 10; Turkish, 37, 55;

[of] Warsaw, 7; Western, 5, 7, 10, 37, 54, 55, 70, 116. See also Race: Mediterranean; Race: Semitic
Judaism, 16, 44, 69, 102
Judt, Ignacy Maurycy, 47–57, 58, 59, 60, 61, 63, 65, 66, 67, 68, 69, 70, 72, 80, 167n67

Kareev, Nikolai, 46
Kautsky, Karl, 36
Katzenelson, Yehude Leyb, 39
Khazars, 59
Khodotov, Nikolai, 128, 129
Kohn, Hans, 26, 27, 28, 85
Kopernicki, Izydor, 49, 168ft2
Korolenko, Vladimir, 84
Korneichukov, Nikolai. See Chukovsky, Korney
Kostomarov, Nikolai, 80
Kotliarevskii, Ivan, 120, 121
Kushites, 56
Kyiv/Kiev, 23, 38, 108, 113, 132, 178n2, 182n21

Lagneau, Gustav, 55
Lamarckism, 4, 28
Le Bon, Gustav, 46
Lenin, Vladimir, 34, 36
Lithuania, 91; as Polish-Lithuanian Commonwealth, 31
Lombroso, Cesare, 71, 171n60
London, 13, 38
Luschan, Felix von, 38

Maklakov, Vasily, 135
Majer, Józef, 49, 168n2
Mandelstamm, Max, 38
Marx(ism/sist), 18, 34, 35, 81, 98, 105, 122, 133, 165n35; Austrian, 36, 80
Men'shikov, Mikhail, 116
Milgrom: family, 141, 142, 143, 145, 147; Lika, 141, 143, 144, 148; Marko, 141, 143, 144; Marusia, 141, 143, 144; Serezha, 141, 142, 143, 144, 145, 147, 184n66; Torik, 141, 144, 147
Miliukov, Paul, 134, 135, 136
Minority (national), 25, 36, 68, 89, 102, 155, 156
Moscow, 5, 6, 7, 10, 38, 42, 46, 54, 93, 128, 140

Nationalism: academic/scientific, 26, 42, 47, 151; anti-imperial, 3, 12, 13, 21, 25, 33, 43, 58, 75, 76, 87, 88, 108, 124, 132, 133, 135, 149, 152, 153, 156; Arab, 149; European, 63; Great Russian, 135; imperial, 12, 42; Italian, 60, 62, 63, 65, 72; modern, 11, 19, 30, 34, 48, 66, 72, 73, 74, 88, 111, 113, 122, 124, 133, 135, 136, 150, 152, 154, 166n47; modern Jewish, 11, 13, 14, 25, 26, 27, 28, 29, 32, 35, 36, 40, 42, 45, 47, 63, 68, 70, 72, 76, 88, 102, 103, 105, 110, 117, 123, 132, 140, 145, 148, 149, 152, 154, 163n8; modern Russian, 11, 18, 23, 107, 108, 110, 113, 114, 116, 117, 133, 137, 139, 140, 152; Polish, 139, 140; postcolonial/postimperial, 30, 148, 149; Russian, 12, 110, 112, 113, 121, 130, 133, 140; territorial, 66; Ukrainian, 34, 132, 136, 137, 139, 140
Nationalitätenstaat / state-of-nations, 75, 76, 77, 78, 89, 102, 108, 135, 137, 150
Nation-state, 4, 20, 21, 23, 29, 33, 38, 63, 65, 73, 76, 77, 108, 109, 138, 139, 152, 156, 167n62
Niceforo, Alfredo, 61, 169n23
Nordau, Max, 37, 38, 94, 98, 165n37
Novoe Vremia, 116

Odessa, 2, 43, 71, 82, 83, 84, 86, 88, 89, 90, 91, 92, 118, 121, 132, 140, 141, 142, 143, 147, 148, 149, 171n60, 183n52
Odesskie Novosti, 71, 84, 90, 92, 126, 142, 143, 170n48, 183n56

Ostrogorsky, Moisei, 79, 80
Ottoman Empire, 4, 77, 83, 102, 149, 155, 173n8

Pale of Jewish Settlement, 7, 88, 89, 101, 115, 139, 145
Palestine, 10, 33, 55, 56, 69, 73, 77, 83, 89, 127, 149, 155, 172n67, 173n9
Party of Constitutional Democrats (Kadets), 17, 79, 134, 135
Party of Socialist Revolutionaries, 39, 145
Pasmanik, Daniel, 39, 40, 115, 116
Petliura, Symon, 132
Philistines, 67, 70
Pil'sky, Petr, 84
Pinsker, Leon, 76, 163n6
Poale Zion, 19, 98, 163n10
Pogrom, 30, 104, 105, 112, 131, 132, 133, 135, 136, 139, 145, 182n21; in Gomel (1903), 120, 180n38; in Kishinev (1903), 90
Poland (Poles/Polish), 5, 12, 31, 34, 46, 47, 54, 132, 137, 138, 139, 140, 148, 149
Politics: anti-imperial, 21, 25, 34, 102, 150, 151; cultural, 33; imperial, 12, 21, 24, 25, 111, 126, 145, 149, 155; [of] language, 14, 19, 25; liberal, 18, 31, 80, 133, 135, 153; liberal Jewish, 13, 17, 28, 31, 78, 79, 110, 136, 139; mass, 1, 2, 25, 28, 30, 33, 72, 78, 80, 86, 123; modern, 21, 22, 47, 62, 106, 107, 133, 135, 137; modern Jewish, 17, 20, 27, 29, 30, 32, 37, 61, 73, 76, 80, 85, 90, 92, 93, 94, 105, 108, 121, 123, 136, 140, 150, 155; parliamentary, 78, 79, 80; [of] population, 23, 155; populist Russian, 13, 110, 120, 121, 122; [of] race, 2, 4, 11, 22, 25, 42, 61, 74, 75, 81, 111, 150, 151, 154, 157; Russian Jewish, 1, 16, 24, 27, 33, 36, 145, 150, 155, 156; scientific, 5, 10, 11, 12, 37, 38, 44, 72, 80, 92, 108, 113, 121, 122, 124, 151, 154; socialist, 104, 121, 123; socialist Jewish, 78, 103, 104, 105; subaltern, 3; Zionist, 30, 39, 48; *See also* biopolitics
Popovici, Aurel, 81
Prinkipo, 127, 128
Psyche, 44; national, 82, 111; racial, 74, 81, 100, 103, 111, 113, 137, 151

Race: African, 17, 62, 64, 66; Alpine-Himalayan branch of the Asiatic-European family, 58, 59; Aryan, 60, 63, 64, 108, 109, 114, 116, 117, 169n23; black, 112; classification of, 59, 60, 62; [as a] concept, 1, 2, 3, 4, 16, 18, 19, 20, 24, 26, 27–28, 35, 37, 40, 43, 49, 74, 75, 81, 82, 87, 102, 103, 108, 110, 111, 114, 121, 122, 133, 149, 151, 153, 155, 156, 160, 170n47, 184n75; Dinaric (or Eastern European), 60; Eurafrican, 62; European, 53, 54, 55, 58, 59, 60, 65, 70, 127; Finnish, 108; [in] historiography (of the Russian Empire), 21–24, 160n13; Jewish, 1, 5, 10, 13, 14, 20, 33, 37, 48, 49, 50–52, 53, 54, 55, 57, 58, 59, 61, 65, 67, 68, 70, 87, 91, 92, 93, 94, 100, 105, 107, 109, 111, 112, 113, 114, 115, 116, 117, 118, 127, 139, 151, 154, 155, 171n60; [as a] language (in an imperial situation), 1, 3, 4, 11, 16, 17, 25, 29, 125, 150, 152, 156; Mediterranean, 55, 58, 59, 60, 61, 62, 63, 64, 65, 66, 70, 71, 72, 73, 155, 169n23, 172n67; mixed, 55, 66, 67, 108, 115; Nordic, 59, 62; pure, 10, 27, 48, 49, 55, 66, 74, 81, 105, 140, 151; Russian, 98, 105, 107, 108, 109, 114, 116, 117, 124; science of, 4, 5, 7, 10, 13, 21, 37, 38, 41, 46, 47, 53, 60, 63, 67, 80, 93, 151; Semitic, 17, 49, 53, 55, 56, 58, 62, 109, 116; Slavic, 108; [in] Zionism, 2, 24, 25, 26, 29, 30, 39, 48, 82, 83, 85, 92, 98, 101, 106, 115, 153, 165n33; *See also* Politics [of] race; Universal Races Congress

Racism, 2, 13, 39, 112, 113, 115, 122, 136, 155, 160n13
Razsvet, 67, 98, 113, 115, 116, 119, 129, 130, 146, 164n14, 181n13, 183n47
Rech', 135, 136
Renan, Ernest, 80, 114, 120
Renner, Karl (Springer), 75, 80
Revolution of 1905–1907 (First Russian Revolution), 17, 18, 19, 20, 25, 30, 31, 34, 35, 38, 41, 46, 75, 121, 123, 131, 132, 136, 143
Ripley, William, 59, 60
Rome, 64, 70, 71, 90, 92, 119, 143
Ruppin, Arthur, 37, 38, 39, 165n33
Russian(s), 23, 42, 43, 67, 70, 71, 82, 86, 88, 91, 93, 98, 104, 105, 107, 108, 109, 110–14, 115, 117, 119, 120, 121, 124, 125, 128, 129, 130, 132, 135, 137, 138, 139, 140, 141, 145, 154; anthropology, 7, 8, 10, 46, 54, 93; culture, 2, 45, 84, 85, 87, 100, 118, 119, 122, 124, 126, 128, 129, 130, 134, 138, 140, 142; Esperantists, 16; Great, 22, 118, 124, 135, 139; history, 2, 21, 22, 23; intelligentsia, 33, 42, 75, 84, 122, 123, 133, 134, 135, 152, 153; liberalism, 18, 84, 133, 135; Little, 138, 139; modernity, 22, 24; parliament, 76; Southern, 124; *See also* Jews: Russian; Nationalism: modern Russian; Nationalism: Russian; Politics: populist Russian; politics: Russian Jewish; Race: Russian; Revolution of 1905–1907 (First Russian Revolution); Russian Empire; Zionists: Russian
Russian Empire, 1, 2, 3, 4, 7, 10, 12, 20, 21, 22, 24, 25, 29, 30, 32, 34, 39, 46, 72, 74, 75, 78, 80, 82, 85, 86, 91, 102, 107, 109, 112, 119, 122, 124, 126, 130, 137, 138, 141, 145, 149, 150, 154, 156
Russkie Vedomosti, 120
Russkii Antropologicheskii Zhurnal, 7, 8–9, 54

Russkii Evrei, 5
Russkoe Slovo, 128, 129

Said, Edward, 127, 148, 149
Sergi, Giuseppe, 60, 61, 62, 63, 64, 65, 66, 73, 169n23
Shevchenko, Taras, 140
Shternberg, Lev, 13–14, 16–17, 28, 110, 111
Siberian, ethnography, 110; natives, 110, 111
Sikorsky, Ivan, 23, 107, 108–10, 112, 113, 114, 115, 117, 124, 137, 178n2
Slavinsky, Maksim, 136
Slavs, 11, 46, 55, 59, 108, 109, 110, 116, 137, 138; *See also* Race: Slavic
Society for the Attainment of Full Civil Rights for the Jewish People in Russia, 31, 79
Stalin, Joseph, 34, 35, 36, 164n26
State Duma, 30, 31, 76, 78, 79, 80, 134, 136, 143, 152
statistics: economic, 38; intellectual, 38; Jewish, 37, 38; medical, 45, 151; racial (anthropometric), 2, 37, 38, 45, 48, 49; social, 11, 45, 71, 155
Stolypin, Petr, 116
St. Petersburg, 39, 79, 104, 128, 131
Struve, Peter, 18, 133, 134, 135, 136, 137, 138
Sum, Gomo. See Zamenhof, Lejzer Ludwik.

Tatars, 34, 42
territorialism, 13, 14, 29, 34, 36, 66, 68, 69, 76, 141, 151, 155
Topinard, Paul, 46
Trivus, Solomon, 47
Trotsky, Leon, 82, 83

Ukraine (-ian[s]), 34, 42, 80, 88, 104, 119, 124, 125, 132, 136, 137, 138, 139, 140, 182n21
Ukrainskaia Zhizn', 42, 132

United States (of America), 14, 79, 111, 112; *See also* America
Universal Races Congress, 13, 14
Ussishkin, Menachem, 39
Utro Rossii, 129

Vermel, Solomon, 38
Vinaver, Maxim, 136
Vogt, Carl, 48
Voskhod, 47

Warsaw, 7, 19, 130, 131
Weininger, Otto, 38, 111
Weissenberg, Samuel, 7–10, 28, 38, 49, 59

Zamenhof, Lazar' Markovich, 16
Zangwill, Israel, 13, 14, 15
Zionism/Zionist(s), 25, 26, 30, 34, 37, 38, 42, 77, 78, 83, 84, 87, 92, 106, 119, 120, 134, 150, 156, 172n67; aesthetics, 94; Eastern European, 30, 163; Eurocentric, 48, 54; European, 29, 48, 54, 92; [in the] Habsburg Empire, 28, 85, 153, 154, 163n8; history of, 2, 3, 163n6; labor, 41; Mediterranean, 66; novel, 67, 89; Polish, 47; political, 2, 20, 29, 30, 31, 47, 74, 82, 87, 91, 92, 93, 99; racialized, 37, 39, 40, 71, 75, 83, 85, 92, 98, 106, 151, 152; revisionist, 3, 83, 99, 142; Russian, 1, 3, 15, 24, 26, 29, 30, 31, 32, 33, 37, 39, 43, 45, 54, 66, 72, 82, 95, 98, 115, 118, 130, 131, 142, 163n10, 166n45, 166–67n52; scientific, 24, 25, 26, 28, 29, 37, 44, 45, 46, 55, 58, 66, 72, 80; spiritual, 31; [in the] State Duma, 78; Western, 3, 54, 58; *See also* Anthropology: Zionist; Zionist Congress
Zionist Congress: Fourth, 38; Fifth, 38; Six, 83, 84, 92, 142
Zollschan, Ignaz, 37, 72, 111, 168n13

MARINA MOGILNER holds the Edward and Marianna Thaden Chair in Russian and East European Intellectual History at the University of Illinois at Chicago. She is cofounder and coeditor of the international journal *Ab Imperio* and author of *Homo Imperii: A History of Physical Anthropology in Russia* and *A Race for the Future: Scientific Visions of Modern Russian Jewishness, 1860s–1930s*.

For Indiana University Press

Tony Brewer, Artist and Book Designer
Brian Carroll, Rights Manager
Gary Dunham, Acquisitions Editor and Director
Anna Francis, Assistant Acquisitions Editor
Brenna Hosman, Production Coordinator
Katie Huggins, Production Manager
Dan Pyle, Online Publishing Manager
Jennifer Witzke, Senior Artist and Book Designer
Stephen Williams, Marketing and Publicity Manager

www.ingramcontent.com/pod-product-compliance
Lightning Source LLC
Chambersburg PA
CBHW030648230426
43665CB00011B/1004